INNOCENCE UNDER THE ELMS

Louise Dickinson Rich has also written:

WE TOOK TO THE WOODS

HAPPY THE LAND

START OF THE TRAIL

MY NECK OF THE WOODS

TRAIL TO THE NORTH

ONLY PARENT

INNOCENCE
UNDER THE ELMS

Louise Dickinson Rich

Parnassus Imprints
Orleans, Massachusetts

To My Sister

ALICE DICKINSON HOKE

WHO WILL BE THE ONLY COMPETENT JUDGE
OF THIS BOOK

PREFACE TO THE 1983 EDITION

Almost thirty years have passed since the publication of INNOCENCE UNDER THE ELMS; and well over twice that long since my sister Alice and I went our innocent ways beneath the elms of Bridgewater, Massachusetts. Now I am in my eighties and Alice is right behind me. Is it possible that we who were so short a time ago so very, very young are now old ladies? Old Ladies! We, who used to classify any woman over thirty-five as "Old Lady So-and-so" and consign her to her dotage!

The physical world that we inhabited so fecklessly exists no longer. All the elms are gone, victims of the Dutch elm disease. Carvers Pond, once deep in what seemed to us the forest primeval, is now overlooked by a neat housing development. Ice hasn't been cut there for decades and the old icehouse was torn down long ago. The narrow country roads leading out of town are now four-lane highways, and the meadows where we gathered flowers for Decoration Day are black-topped parking lots and shopping malls. In a very real sense, the world we little girls knew is as long-gone as our childhood.

And, along with the elms and the daisy fields and my old cat Smut, innocence too has faded away: - both our personal innocence, which perhaps we should have guarded more fiercely against Life's depredations; and the world's innocence, eroded by increasing sophistication in technology and education and politics; by the atom bomb and Freud and acid rain; by space travel which tore the veils of mystery and beauty from the moon; by DDT and air pollution and toxic waste and the loss of faith in Virtue.

Preface

Alice and I were born just in time. We came in under the wire, before pesticides killed off all the bluebirds and hop-toads and while little girls could roam unmolested wherever their young feet could carry them. We were born in the right place for growing up, in a small New England village where everyone was known and therefore to be trusted. We never had to be afraid, a benison in itself.

The world we took for granted has gone forever and its like will never be known again. Its passing makes me sad. But even in my sadness I can also give thanks that we were so very lucky as to have known that world at all.

Mattapoisett, MA
May 1983

Louise Dickinson Rich

CONTENTS

INTRODUCTION

When I returned with my children after an absence of twenty years to the town that saw me grow up, it was like taking a long step back into the past. Perhaps because I had been away for so long without revisiting the scenes of my childhood, it was as if the years between had never existed. I was amazed not by the superficial changes that had taken place—houses remodeled, fences replaced by hedges—but by the lack of change. A root of the big maple halfway along Spring Hill Avenue still humped up in the middle of the sidewalk, just as it had done when I tripped over it periodically and skinned my knee. Carver's Pond was still the place to go for pussy willows, and the stone wall along Winter Street, neither more nor less tumble-down than it had always been, the place for bittersweet. People still sat on the benches on the Common and talked; the halls of the Academy building smelled the same, of chalk and varnish and rubber; and children with the same names as the children I had played with coasted on Campus Hill. The same air of unhurried calm pervaded the tree-arched tunnels of the wide streets. The spiritual climate of the town—or so it seemed to me at first—was the same as it had always been, and I would have suffered neither surprise nor alarm to meet, on turning a corner, men and women whom I knew to be long dead. I found myself experiencing the emotions and reactions, not of the mature woman I am, but of the little girl I used to be. I was literally transplanted into another time.

Of course, it didn't last. The town had changed, as all things must. Part of the change was physical—a tree cut down

9

here to make room for a filling station, a country road widened and resurfaced there into a four-lane highway; but the physical changes were not important. The important change was more fundamental, a change in a whole way of living and in values and attitudes. It is a change not peculiar to this little Massachusetts town, but a phenomenon of the times. Had I not gone away and returned, I probably would not have been so impressed by it. But I did go away and I did return; and now I have been here long enough so that my clear awareness of things past is fading, its outlines overlaid and blurred by events of the present. So I would like, before the memory returns to limbo, to make a record of how things were when I was a child.

INNOCENCE UNDER THE ELMS

I

Home Town

BRIDGEWATER IS NEITHER HAY NOR GRASS. IT'S NEITHER A
suburb, being too far south of Boston for the influences of
the city to have permeated to any marked degree, nor a rural
four-corners. It has some of the characteristics of both suburb and crossroads. A scattering of citizens commute daily to
Boston and more shop there occasionally; and a large part of
the traffic which flows through the center consists of people
who are on their way somewhere else—mostly Cape Cod—
and who seldom know or care what the name of this particular settlement may be. Bridgewater is not a resort town. It
has nothing to offer the vacationist—neither ocean nor mountain nor health-giving spring. It's not primarily an industrial
town, either, although it does boast a small shoe factory or
two, a foundry, a wire and nail plant, and a leatherboard
mill. But these enterprises are conducted quietly and with
strict decorum—no smog, no rioting strikers, no ear-splitting
factory whistles—and cause no wrinkle on the face of the
village.

Bridgewater is, in short, just a typical New England small
town, and its history, geography and place names could serve
almost without correction as a pattern for one of those sur-
veys so dear to the hearts of statisticians and economists. You
know the sort of thing I mean. Some earnest soul concocts

from his collected data a village which he names Middletown or Normville, U.S.A., population 9,683, since figures that end in an odd number rather than a multiple of ten are illogically convincing. He calls the center of Normville, Central Square, for obvious reasons, and the streets running from it, Main, Broad, South and School Streets, because one is the principal artery, one is demonstrably broader than the others, one leads south, and the school is located on the last. The loose system of thoroughfares which connect these routes into—or out of, depending on your point of view—the center, like a careless spiderweb, are known variously as Pleasant Street (and it is pleasant, too), Summer Street (and of course Winter and Spring Streets, although not, ordinarly, Autumn Street), High Street (up on the rise by the standpipe), Oak Street, Maple Street, Grove Street, and Park Avenue; yes, and Laurel Street, too, and sometimes Elm, and if there is a lake in the vicinity, the Professor comes up with a Lakeside Drive. The ground-work thus laid, he goes on with his thesis, which is that the Average American eats more meat than anybody else, smokes too much, owns a car and a half, thinks Wally Cox is funny, or what have you.

That's the kind of town Bridgewater is, except that we have a Bedford Street leading out of Central Square toward New Bedford, and a Plymouth Street; and three guesses where you'll land if you follow that far enough. All these streets are wide and tree-shaded, and along them stand the homes of the residents. Some are larger than others, but there aren't any that approach the class of estates or show places. Almost everybody has a lawn and trees and a garden, but until very recently nobody had a swimming pool; and we have one now only because the young homeowner built it himself. So great a stir did that project cause that pictures of it appeared in the papers, and the traffic on Union Street is swollen beyond belief by the curious. You won't find the estates of Bridgewater and the great houses with pools by going to the outskirts of town, either. Beyond the limits of the village proper, you'll find what you ought to find in the country: farms.

That's the way Bridgewater is now, and that's the way it was when I was a child: just another New England town.

When I was a child, though, it didn't seem like that. It didn't seem *like* anything. It was where my sister Alice and I lived with our mother and father, and that was all there was to it. There wasn't any other place, any other trees and streets and houses and people and dogs and horses and cats, anywhere in our experience. Bridgewater wasn't subject to any opinion or judgment. It wasn't a pretty town or an ugly town or a wonderful or deadly town. It just *was*, to be seen, heard, smelled, touched and tasted, but never questioned. We knew what water was, naturally, and what a bridge was. And yet we didn't wonder why a village nowhere near a body of water and certainly not conspicuously overstocked with bridges should be called Bridgewater.

When I was four, my Great-aunt Julia Dickinson started me on a simple patchwork quilt, because it was unthinkable that a young woman should approach her marriage without an ample supply of bedding; and in the fashioning of the same, if she started young enough and four was none too young, she would inevitably develop skill with the needle. As important as small, even stitches was careful cutting of the pieces. They must be square—not nearly square or square enough. The four sides must be *exactly* even, and the corners just *so*. Therefore I knew a square when I saw one. I loved squares, with a passionate, personal love. They were mine, my own special, private property, one thing in which my sister, who was only two and couldn't be expected to understand, had no share. I searched for and found with a secret, joyful recognition squares everywhere—in the plaids of dresses, in wallpaper patterns, in the stained-glass windows in church, in architecture or a scored pan of fudge; but never in growing things, although I dreamed of a square daisy or leaf, or a chipmunk marked like a checkerboard. There was something so right and satisfying about squares, so balanced and proper. They made me feel good.

Nevertheless, the fact that Central Square was really not a square but a long, slightly elliptic rectangle didn't disturb me at all, so complete was my acceptance of the established world. It couldn't very well be square, because then there wouldn't be room for the Academy building, the Town Hall, and the Swedenborgian and Congregational churches at the south end; or else the Bridgewater Inn, A. I. Simmons' Market, Casey's Ice Cream Parlor, and the watering trough at the foot of the Common would have to be lopped off the north. Central Square obviously had to be the way it was.

Most of the stores of the town, except for a slight overflow down Broad Street, were situated around the Square, facing each other across sidewalks, streets, and the stone-posted two-railed iron fence of the Common. I'd heard a lot about common sense, common pins, and common people, as well as about wearing my best shoes for common when I started to outgrow them, in my few years; but there was never any confusing that kind of common with the Common. If anyone had called it a park, I wouldn't have known what they were talking about. It was a very pleasant place, carpeted with grass, roofed with tall trees, crisscrossed by concrete paths for easy passage from one side of the Square to the other, and equipped with wrought-iron benches in a leafy vine design for the recuperation and relaxation of shoppers and those at loose ends.

A lot of people used to sit on those not especially comfortable benches when I was a child. Housewives sat on them while they checked their shopping lists or rested before starting the trip home with their bundles. Chance-met acquaintances sat on them to exchange gossip. Men out of work through Fate or congenital inclination, or on vacation, or waiting for the trolley car sat on them and talked with their cronies or with the policeman, if he happened to be around. Children, flushed and breathless from forbidden climbing over the bandstand that occupied the mathematical center of the Common, or drying off from the water-fight at the trough and drinking fountain before facing their mothers, sat on them. Lonely people and busy people and aimless people and even some people who simply wanted a good place in which to think, all sat on the benches in the Common.

Yet it never seemed overcrowded or noisy. The iron fence, with the long, patient faces of the tied-up horses of the farmers drooping over it, encircled a space of sun-dappled quiet and peace, where there was all the leisure and all the time in the world.

Outside the fence, life went on. The trolley cars from Brockton on the north and Taunton on the south came clanging in every hour, and there was a brief heightening of activity around the Square. Merchants moved to the front windows of their stores to check on who was taking his business to Brockton, where there were admittedly bigger and better stores. (We Dickinsons almost never went to Brockton, since my father was the owner and editor of the weekly Bridgewater *Independent,* and he felt, probably rightly, that those who largely supported us by advertising in that publication would resent our taking their money out of town; and so insistent was he upon this point that for years the word Advertiser was synonymous with Bogeyman in my mind, and it wasn't until I'd grown up and lived away from home for a long time that I could wear a garment bought Out-of-town without having to combat a craven desire to whip around a corner and safely out of sight whenever I met an Advertiser on the street.) Those who had been waiting, hatted and gloved, on the Common for the arrival of the trolley moved over to the loading point in front of Churchill's store; and the worn travelers who had returned safely from the eight-mile trip dispersed in the several directions of their homes, scattering bits of information about the big sale at Edgar's in Brockton and trailing almost visible auras of worldliness. The motorman leaped down, seized the wire controlling the trolley proper, and ran it around to the opposite end of the car in preparation for the return safari, because Bridgewater was the end of the line from both directions. The conductor, who had been furiously slamming the backs of the seats over to face in the reverse direction, shouted, " 'Board!" and the trolley took off with a great banging of gongs, flying of sparks, and screaming of metal on the curve into Main Street around Simmons' Market.

That was the Brockton trolley. The Taunton trolley was a cat of another color, although it looked the same as the Brockton trolley, traveled about the same distance, charged the same fare, and went through much prettier countryside. But to be seen taking the Taunton trolley was to be suspect. Respectable and prudent persons made a point of stating not once, but several times while they waited, that they were going only as far as Scotland on church affairs, or to the Nip, fishing. Nobody would admit Taunton as a destination. Taunton was doubly damned. It was the seat of an Asylum for the Insane, and it was Wet.

When I was young, insanity in the family was disgraceful, and one who Drank—and Drinking with a capital meant imbibing anything at all containing alcohol, and carried inexorably in its wake delirium tremens, unspeakable vices, the squandering of hard-earned wages, the pitiful cries of hungry children and brutalized wives, filth, squalor, poverty, and anything else reprehensible that happens to occur to you—one who Drank, then, was *ipso facto* an unnatural monster. I don't think I ever had all this explained to me in words of one syllable. It wasn't necessary. The tone in which my teetotaling family and their equally abstemious circle of associates spoke of Rum and Whiskey—when they could bring themselves to enunciate the awful words at all—told more than a dozen treatises plus a tour of an alcoholic ward could have done. Much more, since no horror known to experience can possibly match the horrors of the unknown as imagined by the innocent. Drink! The very word made me sick and cold and frightened; and Taunton was Wet. They sold Drink there. I saw it as a place where red-eyed, slavering beasts in Man's image roamed the streets, while the air quivered constantly with the inhuman shrieks of madmen, foaming at their barred windows in a huge, dreary building on a hill.

That is why the Taunton trolley always seemed shabby and sly and disreputable—that and the leering way in which the upright were apt to say, "Hmm. I see So-and-so's off to Taunton again!" with a shake of the head and a censorious tightening of lips. Or my mother would say on a rainy day when

Alice and I were confined to the house and were acting unusually fiendish, "If you children don't stop that bickering,
you'll have me in Taunton; that's what." We knew she
didn't mean in a barroom. She meant in the Insane Asylum,
which again would involve—or so we believed—taking the
Taunton trolley. No wonder we viewed askance anyone who
boarded that hellish transport, which sneaked quietly down
South Street—a straight route out of town, as it happened,
with no need for clanging gongs and the application of un-
lubricated brakes—and bore its doomed cargo away from
Bridgewater. Bridgewater, as you may have gathered, was as
dry as an enlightened electorate could make it, voting faithfully against the powers of evil in accordance with the law of
the Commonwealth of Massachusetts, which allowed each
town to determine its own policy in regard to the sale of
liquor within its confines.

I never went to Taunton until I was nearly grown, and it
was with a sense of betrayal that I discovered it to be an extremely pretty and prosperous little city, with a Common as
peaceful and quiet as our own, and never a drunkard or
maniac to be seen. I felt a little foolish. But it was too late
then. There was no retrieving the lost opportunities of
youth, when an empty whiskey bottle was worth anywhere
from two cents to a nickel at one of the local drug stores.
The small boys of my circle and even some of the more in-
trepid and abandoned little girls made a good thing out of
that. If they could escape parental observation on Sunday, a
day devoted to church and Sunday School, big dinners, and
sedate afternoon walks, they'd make the rounds of the recognized drinking spots—drinking was largely a Saturday night
affair, since Saturday was the universal payday—and collect
the dead soldiers. The Unitarian cemetery—so-called because
it was near the Unitarian Church, although not necessarily
sacred to Unitarians—was usually a rewarding field, being
close to the center, unfrequented, and dark. So was the alley
near the Chinaman's, or the rear of any of the stores around
the Square. Probably there were drinking men who carried
their bottles home and swigged in peace and comfort, but it

is undoubtedly a fact that there were also many who apparently couldn't wait to tip the vile brew to their trembling lips, and so staggered off the trolley to the nearest semi-private refuge. That's the way those far gone in Drink were supposed to act, and the evidence in the form of empties indicated that that was the way some of them at least did in truth act. So a really hardened, agile, and alert operator could confront the druggist the first thing Monday morning with fifteen or twenty cents' worth of redeemable glassware, enough to keep him in funds throughout the week.

Not the little Dickinson girls, though. It wasn't that we were above such traffic in the trappings of dissipation. We were just plain scared. If, even a year after the stricken one had read it, you could catch measles from handling a Library book that hadn't been fumigated—and it was commonly accepted that you could—who knew what we'd catch by handling a bottle hot from the hand of a drunkard? Besides, if our mother ever saw us or heard of us walking brazenly through Central Square carrying a whiskey bottle— Well, the rewards just weren't worth the risk! We'd satisfy our perpetual craving for candy by some less dangerous means, such as catching our father at an auspicious moment and holding him up for the penny apiece that would get us out of his hair.

You could do a lot with a penny in those days, and a penny was neither lightly bestowed nor carelessly spent. Our family never had much money, but even so, I don't imagine that the handing out of a few cents a week would have crippled domestic finance. The idea was, I guess, to teach us the value of money by making it hard to acquire. We heard a lot about easy come, easy go, but it didn't make much impression on us. We never got our hands on any easy money, in the first place. If some relative or well-wisher honored our birthdays by a sizable donation, such as a quarter, that was pronounced too much money to spend all at once, and we had to put it into our banks, small replicas of iron safes, where it was as lost to us as if we'd thrown it into the sea. There was no taking money out of those banks, once it had disappeared into their maws. Money in expendable amounts was definitely not easy money. We had to convince our parents that we needed it, and this was almost impossible to do, since the stated desire to buy candy was not allowed as a legitimate argument. Just because you wanted something was no reason why you should have it; quite the contrary. To get a penny to spend foolishly and self-indulgently, we had to resort to guile, or to employ softening-up and wearing-down tactics. Our parents didn't soften up easily or wear down at all. When they said *no*, they meant *no*, and considered a change of mind a sign of a weakening of the moral fiber and the setting of a dangerous precedent.

Alice and I found that our best bet was to approach our father at his place of business, preferably when he was talking with one of the endless stream of people who drifted in and out all day long with or without an excuse, and make our modest request. Very often he was too much interested in his conversation to inquire too closely into the matter. It was worth a try, anyhow. If there happened to be no one in the office, we took the local temperature and tested the local wind carefully before proceeding. If our father was at his desk writing his weekly editorial, chances were apt to be pretty good. In his soul searchings for the precise word he wanted to convey a shade of meaning, he might easily give us a handout without even registering our presence. If he was distributing type from the previous week's issue of the *Independent*, it was a toss-up how we'd make out. Type distribution is an automatic job, which an experienced printer can do in his sleep, and we'd have no clue as to whether his private and independent train of thought augured well for us or not. If he was setting up an ad, we just forgot all about the whole thing and pretended we'd come in to get a drink of water. The setting of advertisements required the use of both hands and the whole of a man's attention, so that the white spaces would be effective and the prices quoted by the advertiser correct. We knew better than to expect him to lay down his stick, lose his place on the copy, wipe his hands, and take off his apron for access to his pants pocket, just so we could have a penny apiece to squander at Alden's.

All the grocery stores sold penny candy, but we favored Alden's for reasons that were sound and compelling to us, irrelevant as they might appear to adult logic. None of these reasons had to do with the quality or assortment of the candy, which varied not at all from store to store. Alden's was not the largest grocery store, or the most convenient, but the horse that hauled their delivery wagon all over town was a personal friend of ours, a big, amiable gray with a mind of his own, so that if he thought the delivery man was spending too much time in the kitchen of a customer, he'd unassumingly take matters unto his own cognizance and amble along to the next regular stop. We felt that it would be disloyal to him to patronize any other store. In addition, Alden's displayed a life-size Fairy Soap poster, showing the picture of a little girl with long curls, and demanding searchingly, "Have you a little fairy in *your* home?" This was at once our joy and our despair. We'd stand there in our homemade, plain and practical dresses with our straight hair skinned back in tight, neat braids—by no stretch of the imagination could the most astigmatic mistake us for little fairies out of anybody's home—and wish that we looked exactly like that little girl, and that we had fur-trimmed coats and bonnets just like hers.

Then too, Alden's had a peanut butter machine, a marvel of modernity. At the other stores, peanut butter was dipped in the required amounts out of tubs into cardboard containers. If you were smart, you transferred it to a glass jar as soon as you got it home, because the oil separated from the solid peanut particles and oozed through the cardboard all over the place; and you stored the jar upside down to encourage a more even texture to the spread, although this gambit was never entirely successful. Even Alden's marvelous machine didn't have the answer to this technical difficulty, which today's manufacturers seem to have overcome; but the gourmets of the peanut butter world maintained that there was no comparison possible between the ordinary tub butter and that which came fresh out of Alden's revolutionary machine, a simple red-and-gold-painted grinder into the top of which went whole peanuts and salt, and out of the bottom of which, when the clerk turned the hand crank, came the peanut butter in a rather revolting manner. We didn't think so then, though. We thought the whole thing was fascinating; and moreover, once in a while we were allowed to help ourselves to a cracker out of the barrel, scrape the residue of peanut butter from the machine's vent, and eat it. It tasted ambrosial, much better than the same thing did at home.

The barrel of common crackers—common crackers were the large, rather hard kind that you could split in two through the middle—stood on the public's side of the counter, in the aisle, uncovered and exposed to every dust-ladened draft that blew in from the street; and it's my opinion that the power and virulence of germs have been grossly exaggerated. Those crackers must have been teeming with the things, and by any modern prognosis my sister and I should have filled early graves. Far from it; we throve. Whenever one of my mother's friends was moved to butter her up and make her feel good but couldn't in honesty say we were pretty little girls, she'd exclaim, "Aren't they the picture of perfect health!" We were, to our disgust. We favored an appearance of fragility and interesting invalidism.

The last reason we cheered and honored Alden's with our patronage was the clerk, a young man named Tom Alden, the son of the house. Now there was a man who was lousy with glamour! To start with, he was ill, and he looked it. He had terrible asthma, coughed rackingly, and had to smoke herbal cigarettes, which we liked to think of as the dangerous drug that kept his body and soul precariously together. In a day when you were disparagingly labeled a fresh air fiend if you opened your bedroom window more than an inch in winter, Tom Alden slept with his whole head and shoulders outdoors all year round. We knew, because we could see the back of the Alden house from the back of our house, across the abutting vegetable gardens. There was an awning summer and winter over one of the windows, and Tom's narrow bed was balanced on the sill, half under the awning, the other half presumably in his room. On blizzardy February nights, our tender young feminine hearts would be wrung with pleasurable pain at the thought of the rigors he was undergoing out there in the night and the storm, poor thing, and we'd hope that at least his dog, sleeping faithfully—we liked to think, although very possibly the Aldens put the dog down cellar of nights—at his feet, was warm enough.

That dog was another of Tom Alden's romantic appurtenances. It was a small, dark brown and white Boston bull. Every morning it would go alone down to Casey's, which was the paper store as well as an ice cream and candy parlor, accept the paper being held for him, and carry it home in his mouth. During the rest of the day he was a friendly enough dog, but he had no time for anybody while he was fetching the paper. A good way to lose an arm was to try to interfere with him in the performance of his duty. He smoked a curve-stemmed briar pipe, too; or at least he ran around with one in his mouth, looking rakish and devil-may-care and putting it down carefully in the shelter of a bush if he saw a cat that needed chasing. He was just the kind of dog that best became Tom Alden, Alice and I agreed.

And last, Tom Alden always had all the time in the world for us. He must have known perfectly well that our top spending power never exceeded four cents, and yet no matter who was waiting to be served, he'd stand relaxed and patient and courteous while we made our difficult choices, coping with the complicated mathematics involved with no sign of any other emotion than sympathetic helpfulness. There were no candy bars in those days. Adults bought boxes of chocolates sometimes, on very special occasions. Children bought penny candy: "liquorish" shoe strings, candy cigarettes, little "nigger babies," large semi-translucent pink or white peppermints, candy pipes, candy pebbles that looked real, candy corn that did not, and little foil pie-plates full of sweet goo and accompanied by Lilliputian spoons, fine for doll's teas. Then there were bright red cinnamon drops that bit the tongue, and lollypops with poisonous-looking green or red bull's-eyes in the centers, and big sticks of OK gum in red wrappers, and hoarhound lozenges, and striped pepper-

mint sticks, and candy ice-cream cones, and a dozen other
strange and wonderful confections.

Some things were a cent apiece, but only the foolish and
improvident invested in those, or in soft candies that were
gone in a gulp. Alice and I worked too hard for our money
to fritter it away like that. We chose the more-for-a-penny
kinds, and Tom Alden let us split up our purchase: one of
these at ten for a penny leaves nine tenths of a cent, minus
two of these at five for a penny leaves you half a cent. These
are two for a penny; you could have one of these; or five of
any of this kind here; or two of these *and* one of these. He'd
count them carefully into the small paper bag, gay with
green and pink and purple pin-stripes against its unbleached
beige surface. I don't know why he bothered. Perhaps he
was just too worn out with his coughing to care what he did
with his time. Perhaps he was simply representative of a
more leisurely era. At any rate, he certainly was nice to all
children.

Since my mother was not a particular crony of Alden's
horse or especially under the spell of Tom Alden, she dis-
tributed her trade among all the grocery stores, the choice
being determined by two considerations: which merchant
had advertised in the *Independent* that week, and which was
giving the best allowance for eggs. Families of all social
brackets kept a few hens in the back yard, and it was common
practice to take care of any surplus of eggs, first, by putting
them down in waterglass against the rainy winter day when
the flock wouldn't be laying so well. We had a large stone
crock down under the cellar stairs filled with a mixture of
waterglass and water, and every day my sister or I ran down
with the three or four eggs over and above our current needs
and dropped them in carefully. The density of the milky
solution was sufficient so that they sank slowly and gently to
the bottom of the crock without our getting our hands wet.
We didn't mind putting down the eggs at all. The rub came
when my mother ran short of cooking eggs and someone had
to go down and fish a few out of the crock. We hated to put
our hands into the emulsion. We knew that it was perfectly

clean and harmless, but it felt horrible—slimy and nasty and as though it were full of fur-bearing snakes. We had terrible fights about whose turn it was to get the eggs.

If, when the crock was full to the top, the hens continued to lay prodigally, the spare eggs were exchanged at any store for those staples such as sugar, flour and tea, not indigenous to the New England soil and climate. The storekeeper allowed you a few cents less than the retail price, whatever he considered fair; and the price varied from store to store, depending on how many eggs were in stock at the time in any given store. So we'd shop around, checking market trends.

The stores were wonderful places, rich and bountiful. Cream of Wheat came in packages, and so did Quaker Oats and confectioner's sugar, but almost nothing else did. Brown sugar, full of delicious lumps that melted exquisitely on the tongue, and flour and crackers and dill pickles and walnuts stood about in barrels. Huge whole cheeses, from which the clerk would cut a sliver so you could try before buying, and wicker baskets of eggs rested on the counters. There were two tubs of butter, creamery and dairy, from which a really good clerk could cut a pound block to the fraction of an ounce on the first try. Cookies didn't come pre-packaged, but were weighed out of glass-fronted boxes into the brass scoop of a balance scale. I can see the hand of the grocer yet, poised, full of gingersnaps, over the scales as he debated with himself the dropping of the one more that would bring it a hair over the pound or just letting it ride as it was. And there was a type of Nabisco colored and shaped like a paper-shelled almond and filled with a firm, pale fondant. My idea of the ultimate bliss was that one day I would be able to buy absolutely all of those that I could eat. But of course I never had enough money for that; and now that I could possibly, if pressed, scrape up the cash, I never see them any more. That's Life; and no doubt it's better so. Without doubt they'd have lost the heavenly flavor they used to have.

Coffee beans roasted to deepening shades of brown stood in galvanized buckets on the floor along the counter in those days, and you selected the roast you preferred, either to be ground on the spot in the hand-operated grinder, or taken home to be ground as you used it in your own square little wooden grinder with the drawer that pulled out at the bottom. All the stores always smelled of fresh-ground coffee and of the kerosene which spilled, in spite of the potato that the clerk took out of the barrel and stuck firmly onto the spout of the gallon can you'd brought to be filled. Bananas hung in heavy strings from the ceiling, the fruit pointing oddly and to our ignorant eyes unnaturally upward from the stem. You always walked warily in the vicinity of the bananas, because once, so it was rumored, down in Balboni's Fruit Store on Broad Street, they'd found a tarantula in a bunch of bananas and it was a wonder Caesar Balboni was still alive. We *loved* to do errands for our mother. You never knew what adventure might befall.

One thing wasn't going to happen to us, that was for sure. We weren't going to lose the money. My mother would write on a slip of paper, "½ lb. fat salt pork" and pin into the pocket of one of us the note and the approximate sum of money required, since charge accounts were frowned on in our family, leading as they surely would to extravagance and the danger of not knowing where you were at on the first of the month. Dungarees were unheard of and unimaginable, and dresses were not designed with pockets, the assumption being that little ladies had no need for such things. The criterion of dress and deportment was the little lady. Every little lady, of course, went equipped with a handkerchief— white, always, to start with at least, since colored handkerchiefs were vulgar. I don't believe we ever, once, left the house between the time we could walk and our respective wedding days without our mother's calling after us, "Have you got a clean handkerchief?" Some little girls carried them tucked chastely up their sleeves, some thrust them demurely down the necks of their dresses to rest in what would someday be their bosoms, and some had them pinned conveniently to their fronts.

None of these systems seemed to work very well with the little Dickinson girls. We shed handkerchiefs from sleeve and bosom as daisies shed petals. (There must be a better comparison than that; we were in no other respect particularly flowerlike.) The front-pinning device wasn't too successful, either. We always started out with impressively snowy scraps of lawn fastened to our chests with the pins Aunt Linnie had sent from the World's Fair, little enameled flowers, blue for Alice and pink for Louise. Before noon these immaculate accessories had deteriorated into filthy rags which any self-respecting chimney sweep would have shuddered to touch. Before the day was over, they'd have been tied into knots, some holding lucky pebbles, some holding grimy pieces of partly sucked hard candy, some holding caterpillars, and one just a knot to remind us of something important.

So my mother resigned herself to Fate or to the hopeless and heretical natures of her daughters, and put unorthodox pockets into the dresses she made us. These could not be obvious patch pockets for all to see, since only boys had pockets and she was loath to advertise our unwomanly tendencies. Instead, they were hidden pockets, let into the side seams of our skirts, like pants pockets, and they were a great comfort to us.

Everybody wore homemade clothes then, and it was a big day, along come the end of August, when we accompanied our mother to either Churchill's or Scotton's to pick out the material for new dresses to wear on the first day of school. Other mothers might get their yard goods in Brockton or even Boston, but not ours. Miss Churchill and Mr. Scotton were Advertisers. Therefore we showed up at school dressed in material identical with that clothing half the other kids in town as well as the minister's wife, who also had a duty to her public, and Miss Churchill's clerk, who got it wholesale. The charming fiction was that we could each, without let or hindrance, pick out the gingham that we liked best for ourselves, but it never worked out that way. Too many factors were working against it.

First of all, there was the ever ominous question of cost. This was a bit more complicated than it sounds, since we did not, as others did, deal in the coin of the realm. No, we operated on a barter system, taking out in trade the current indebtedness of the Advertiser to my father for touting his wares in the *Independent.* If my mother had bought our long black cotton stockings, our maidenly Ferris waists, and some dish toweling at Scotton's, the chances were that the credit had been used up, and even if Scotton's had material of such beauty that it made our mouths water, nevertheless we cut across the Common to Churchill's and climbed the four shallow steps leading from the novelty department to the yard goods section.

Even there, the lovely and expensive imported Anderson ginghams were not for us. Local advertising rates were far from exorbitant. So we had to be satisfied with lesser fabrics which were probably going to shrink and fade even in a tubful of mild Castile soap and lukewarm water, let alone in the more rugged brew that our unlady-like indifference to proper care of our clothes necessitated in laundering. Light greens, some blues, and all lavenders were especially treacherous, so we could have no part of them or anything that looked like them. They had a way of completely changing color on the first washday, which might not have been so bad if they'd done it evenly instead of in streaks and blotches. Solid colors showed wrinkles and light prints showed the dirt too easily. By the time all these initial ground rules had been observed, our choice was boiled down to about five bolts of material, and the war hadn't even started yet.

What it amounted to was that Alice and I had to agree on a material of the few survivors that my mother approved. Far from picking out our own individual materials, all we had to do was arrive at a meeting of minds as to which of her choices was least objectionable. We had to have dresses alike, not because any of the three of us entertained sloppy sister-act sentiments, but because by making two dresses out of the same length of goods, our mother could save a yard or more in the cutting. This wasn't quite as tough on me as it was on Alice. I had to wear the darn thing only two years. (Our mother believed in deep hems, generous seams, and other aids to letting down and out to accommodate growth.) **Poor** Alice was stuck with the deal for three or possibly four **years,** under the hand-down policy, whereby she inherited **my** clothes after they became indecent on me; unless, of **course,** I'd worn them out, which was less likely than it sounds. **Our** mother performed miracles comparable to that of the **loaves** and the fishes when it came to eking out, using parts **of** Alice's discarded identical dress to supply the deficiencies **of** my passed on number. Alice couldn't win.

So with Alice's plight in mind, my mother thumbed down any really striking design, such as scarlet plaid or Roman stripes. Folks, she said, would get sick of it. "There goes Alice Dickinson," she warned us they'd say, "in that same old bright red dress." By this time I had usually seen the writing on the wall, which read plainly that this year was no differ-ent from last, and again we'd be saddled with a navy-and-dark-green Black Watch plaid, or something equally humdrum. I learned early to know when I was licked.

Fall was the time of year when Central Square came to life. The horses who had been content all summer to fall asleep on their feet when tied to the rail of the Common felt the nip in the air and showed the whites of their eyes at blowing paper bags and yapping dogs. Once in a while one broke halter and went careening along the street with an iron clatter of hooves and a scattering in all directions of any groceries that had been stashed in the body of the wagon. Women shrieked and seized their young and fled to the safety of store entrances. Dogs barked, and the spine-chilling cry of "Runaway horse!" leaped like wildfire around the Square. Brave men rushed out into the streets waving their arms and frightening the poor animal into greater bursts of speed. Finally some hero managed to grasp the beast by the bridle and bring him to a heaving halt, about when he was ready to quit anyhow. The drummers who'd sprung up from their normal positions of sitting with their feet on the railing of the porch of the Bridgewater Inn—they'd returned after the summer's slow spell to show their Christmas lines—sank back and started telling each other the proper approach to a runaway horse: Never run out in front of it, waving and shouting; run alongside with a hand on the shaft to prevent falling under the lethal hooves, work your way forward, speaking soothingly— Everyone knew that much. It was elementary. Nothing to stopping a runaway horse, they'd agree, and go back to ogling the passing girls.

There were a lot of passing girls in the fall, when the State Normal School at the corner of School and Summer Streets reopened and the huge dormitories began to fill. The streets were full of them, walking six abreast and crowding resentful taxpayers into the gutters. They were known as Normals, and nobody seemed to find that a funny term or to make the more obvious cracks. If you went to a Normal School, naturally you were a Normal; and most Normals were girls, since all teachers except principals and high school math and science instructors were women. The town was of two minds about the Normals. They did bring trade, such as it was; but the consensus was that that didn't give them the license to act as if they owned the place. Just because they bought a few peanuts at Hayes' or a banana split at Casey's—

Hayes' salted peanuts were a fall and winter feature. Mr. Hayes, who ran one of the ice cream parlors, roasted and salted them himself every day, taking them out of the oven in the late forenoon. There were never any peanuts like them anywhere, and people made a point of stopping in to get them while they were still hot. He kept them in an enormous age-crazed cream-and-rose china bowl, bigger than the biggest punch bowl, on the front corner of the soda fountain, with a teacup alongside; and for a nickel you could buy a cup full to overflowing. Nobody'd dream of buying peanuts anywhere except at Hayes'.

Casey's was the place to go for a sundae in the afternoon, although you might go to Hayes' at any other time of day. Hayes' had round tables with wire legs, and wire chairs, and they served saltines with their ice cream. But Casey's was really elegant. They had square tables with attached stools which swung out on arms to accommodate the sitter, and the parlor was separated from the less genteel transactions of the store proper by a bead curtain, which struck my sister and me, on the rare occasions when some well-heeled relative treated us there, dumb with admiration, so that we found it difficult—but not impossible—to indicate our choice of sustenance. We always had the same thing, the nut-fudge-marshmallow special, covered with chocolate shot and topped by a maraschino cherry. Casey's fudge sauce—well, we swooned at the thought of it. It was hot and darkly thick, and congealed to a gummy consistency around the cone of vanilla ice cream. An effete detail of Casey's service was the silver (simulated, I'm sure) dish with paper liner in which the sundae was presented. We discovered early that we could take the liner out, flatten it to a disc on the table top, and scrape off the last, lingering, delicious trace of the sauce, which otherwise might have been criminally wasted. We didn't get behind Casey's bead curtain often, but when we did, we made the most of it.

There was more to the town than just the Square and the stores around it, though; much, much more. There was the street on which we lived and the immediately adjacent streets to which our mother limited our unsupervised roamings—or thought that she did. We should have felt restricted, but ordinarily we didn't. The world has never seemed as big and various since as it did then, when it was bounded by a few blocks—only we didn't call them blocks, but simply streets. (A block was a toy or a business building.) Because our range was geographically narrow, we learned its minutest detail, knew each stone, each hollow in the sidewalks, each wall and ornamental shrub and vine. Every dog and cat was a friend, and every tree an intimate, its personal characteristics familiar and loved. Max Sturtevant was a good dog, except that he chased cats; Jack Boyden didn't like to be rubbed about the ears; and Fluff Gow was everybody's friend, always, not barking even at tramps and peddlers. The purple beech back of the Hunts' garden was the best for climbing, the elm opposite the Severances had wonderful holes about its roots for the hiding of treasures, and our own

maple dropped the prettiest leaves in the fall. Miss Lily
Worcester was nice about coasting down the bank that
sloped from her porch to her orchard, but you'd better not
cut across Mrs. Gurney's lawn. At best she'd rap sharply on
her windowpane with a thimbled finger—a strangely admon-
itory sound, like the stab of Conscience—and she might even,
if you persisted, don her sealskin coat, the hat with the velvet
pansies, and white gloves, and pay a call of complaint on
your mother.

Beyond the neighborhood, there were traditional places to
go on the Sunday afternoon walk *en famille,* formal outings
upon which my father carried the cane which stood during
the rest of the week in the corner of the front hall, along
with the umbrellas. Sometimes we went into the woods
around Carver's Pond, a shallow body of water that seemed
at the ends of the known world—and was, as far as we were
concerned—although a ten-minute stroll took you there easily.
Sometimes we went up Great Hill, a modest elevation which
nevertheless dominated the level terrain. Sometimes we went
up Sprague's Hill—another hummock—to the standpipe
which held the town's supply of water. Or we walked around
any of the streets away from our own reservation and with
a sense of tremendous discovery found out where some of the
other children in our grades in school lived. Seen away from
the familiar context of blackboards and teachers, dressed in
unfamiliar Sunday or play clothes, absorbed in games of their
own that we didn't know, they seemed like strangers. We
found it hard to speak to them, almost as if we weren't sure
they didn't have another language which they used in their
own surroundings; and we never mentioned these chance encounters to them when we saw them again at school on Monday. That was one of the never expressed but always
understood tabus.

Those were the limits of our experience and our rovings,
and they were wide enough. Everything that could have
happened to us anywhere—joy and grief, gain and loss, contentment and furious revolt, all of the things we were to
encounter in greater or lesser degree up to the days of our
deaths—happened to us within these boundaries.

2

Uncatalogued Family

OUR FAMILY OCCUPIED A RATHER EQUIVOCAL POSITION IN
Bridgewater, which, like all New England towns of the day,
had a fairly rigid social structure. There were the Old Families, whose ancestors were original settlers, or nearly enough
as didn't matter, and who lived in the houses that had been
handed down to them through several generations. They
were as well established for good or ill as the rocks in the
fields about the village; and if one of their sons turned out
badly or one of their daughters went queer, it was a matter
to be regretted and hushed up, as the saying went, as quickly
and completely as possible.

At the other extreme were the Foreigners, the immigrants
who in those days before the Immigration Act of 1921, with
its establishment of quotas, poured into this country. Bridgewater, situated as it was in a coastal industrial area although
not an industrial center itself, received a great many immigrants. These were lumped together under the heading of
Foreigners. Most of them were Italians, Portuguese, Arme-
nians and Poles—known as Polanders, and the term Polander
included Lithuanians, Latvians, and Estonians—with a few
Greeks, Russians and Spaniards thrown in. The Irish didn't
count as Foreigners, probably because they spoke English, or
perhaps because they so quickly made themselves so thor-

oughly at home. The real Foreigners often couldn't speak any English at all when they arrived, and they lived down across the railroad tracks, keeping themselves pretty much to themselves. If anything untoward happened to their sons and daughters, nobody cared because nobody knew about it.

In between these two extremes were several classifications. There was the Normal Click. At least that's the way it was pronounced and the way I thought it was spelled, although it must have been the local version of *clique*. This consisted of the teachers at the Normal School and their families. They rated high on the social scale, combining as they did respectability with the intellectual. So did the ministers of the six Protestant churches. All these people came from elsewhere, as we had, but they had behind them the prestige of the institutions with which they were identified. Then there were some who were identified with an established industry—the paymaster or chief chemist or owner-manager of one of the factories—and they too had predetermined ties and a place into which they fitted neatly. One or two families moved to Bridgewater because of close friends or relatives living here, and whether they worked in town or commuted to Brockton or Boston, they also settled comfortably into established niches, and who they were and what they stood for was never for a moment in doubt. They bought or built homes and were assimilated fairly quickly, if you can call the customary New England five-or-ten-year probation period quickly.

We Dickinsons didn't fall into any of these categories. We came from Huntington, two hundred miles away at the other end of the state, a long way in the days when the automobile was only a fad of the wealthy and doomed to short favor. It's true, we rated as Old Settlers back there. One ancestor founded South Hadley and another not only founded but was scalped by the Indians at Northfield; a collateral relation, Emily, was the talk of Amherst and the literary world with her eccentric behavior and her poetry; another of the Dickinson girls married Cyrus Field, who astonished his in-laws by becoming responsible for the laying of the Atlantic cable; my own grandfather was a Congregational minister known and loved throughout the Berkshires; and the city of Springfield was full of Dickinson Streets and Dickinson Squares. But all this cut no ice in Bridgewater, where we were just fly-by-nights, or dark horses, or whatever else anybody wanted to call us, except Foreigners. We weren't Foreigners, that much at least was allowed.

But we weren't connected with the Normal School or any of the churches or industries. We weren't connected with anything, since the *Independent* was strictly a one-man enterprise, involving no social, business, or fraternal bonds. All our relations we'd left back around Huntington, and we didn't know a soul in or near Bridgewater to sponsor us. It wasn't friendship that had put my father on the track of the *Independent*. He'd been working on the Westfield *Valley Echo* and fostering the newspaperman's dream of owning his own little weekly. So when he saw one advertised for sale, he bought it from a man named Pliny Jewell, a total stranger. I never laid eyes on him in my life. His name is all I know about him, although I called my best doll, with gold curls and eyes that really closed, after him. I thought it was a wonderful name, full of glitter and grace and mystery, and I'd go about saying it under my breath, "Plinyjewell, Plinyjewell." But that didn't help place us in the Bridgewater scheme.

I don't know, because I was just a little over two when the transaction took place, what the financial arrangement was; but I'm sure my father was operating on a shoestring, and this radical move must have stretched the shoestring to the near-breaking point. That is undoubtedly why during all my childhood we always lived in rented houses, in a town where almost everybody owned his own home. Even the Foreigners managed by prodigious feats of industry and thrift to buy plots of land and put up shacks which were replaced in a surprisingly few years by presentable residences. But we never seemed to be able to manage it; partly, I guess, because our parents didn't bring to bear upon the problem the fanatical single-minded attention that the Foreigners did. Be that as it may, Alice and I have no Olde Family Homestead to look back on with nostalgia. We have a series of them.

You can dry your tears and put away your handkerchief. All this—the friendlessness, the homelessness, boo-hoo—was no great hardship to us. If our parents suffered at first, we were too young to realize or appreciate it. We were so young when we came to Bridgewater—Alice a suckling babe in arms— that our wants were fundamental: food, clothing, and shelter. These were provided, and if we had any deep-seated phychological needs beyond them, we were in happy ignorance of the fact. Nobody worried in those days about the child's psyche, or the shattering results of unfortunate prenatal memories, or even about the bad scars that unhappy early conscious experience might cause on his personality pattern. Nobody told my mother that moving all over town was going to give us a sense of insecurity; and I guess it wouldn't have made any difference if they had, except to provide her with one more thing to worry about. When we had to move, we had to move. By the time we were old enough to pay attention to what went on, moving was an old story to us.

In fact, we grew to like moving. It was exciting to go through a strange house, exploring it from cellar to attic, opening doors which might lead who knew where—on to a secret staircase, into a conservatory full of roses, or *the* perfect room where the doors were placed just right and there were seats in the windows. Of course they always did open into quite ordinary rooms or coat closets or preserve cupboards, but there was always that off chance that we would discover something that had been overlooked for years by previous tenants. One house had a little sliding panel between the pantry and the kitchen, so that the housewife could save herself steps by passing cooking materials back and forth. We thought that was the ultimate in ingenuity. Another had a closet within a closet under the front stairs, very inconvenient and therefore never used. Alice and I never mentioned it to anyone, not even to our mother, in hopes she'd forget about it. We were saving it for an emergency. Some day we might want to hide a runaway slave—this was during our *Uncle*

Tom's Cabin phase—or even use it ourselves to hide from burglars or murderers; or possibly—who knew?—a handsome young man, who looked like Wally Reid and was falsely (naturally) accused of some heinous crime, would accost us in the henhouse when we went to pick up the eggs and beg us to conceal him while he recovered the stolen papers that would establish his innocence. We'd smuggle him into the cupboard and bring him food in the dead of night, we planned, and we kept a supply of apples and peanut butter and graham cracker sandwiches ready in a shoe box under our bed, until our mother found it and threw it away.

One house had once had a buzzer for the maid in the middle of the dining room floor. Before our tenancy, some equally maidless occupant had removed the bell, leaving a hole about the size of a silver dollar right down through to the cellar. This was an inestimable boon to us. When we moved there, we were in the throes of organizing one of our silent rebellions, this time against eating bread crusts. Our mother had told us that bread crusts would in time bring about curly hair. So for what seemed to us a long, long time but was probably only about six months, we'd religiously and faithfully eaten our crusts at every meal; and every night we'd looked long and hard at our string-straight hair. Finally we had to face the fact that the charm wasn't working, and the even more disillusioning truth that either our mother was pretty gullible or else she was deliberately deceiving us.

In either case, we were not, repeat, not going to eat any more bread crusts, we agreed, and we also agreed that open revolt wasn't going to get us anywhere. It never did. So we concealed the crusts in our napkins and at the end of the meal, when our father had gone into the living room to read the paper, our mother had retired to the kitchen to stack the dishes, and we were supposed to be clearing the table, we fed them down the hole into the cellar. Out of sight, out of mind, we considered; and if we considered further, it was to assume that the cat would eat them for us. It was the least he could do in return for the love we lavished on him.

He didn't see it that way, the selfish ingrate. Come spring-

cleaning time, cellar turning-out time, all was discovered;
and for your information, it doesn't do a couple of pecks of
bread crusts any good to lie in a damp, dark cellar for a matter of months. It doesn't do your mother's temper any good
to find them there, either.

That same house (this was one of our more elegant perch-
ing places) had a butler's pantry with glass-doored china
closets lining the walls, which were much better than mirrors
because they reflected us dimly enough so that we could imagine any improvements in our appearances that our hearts
desired. In those glass doors, we had blue eyes and curly hair
and dimples, like Dorothy Dainty, or else very patrician features and short upper lips, like the Little Colonel. The two
charming girls in the reflection finally strained even our own
credulity, and so they became two other girls entirely, secret
friends of ours named Lloyd and Stanley. We'd just discovered that girls *could* have boys' names, and we were pretty
bitter about our parents' saddling us with insipid Alice El-
dora and Sarah Louise.

Lloyd and Stanley became more real to us than the little
girls with whom we went to school. We had long conversa-
tions with them, and told them everything, including a lot of
lies. It goes without saying that when they retired off to the
left-hand end of the cupboard doors, they were not simply
going out into the kitchen to wipe the dishes or empty the
garbage, as we were. The Lloyds and Stanleys of the world
had devoted retainers to attend to such matters. They were
going to change into their riding clothes and go for a swift
canter over their estate; or else they were going for a sail in
the yacht. Obviously we couldn't let them get away with
that, just because we were named Alice and Louise and had
straight hair and brown eyes. So we'd beg to be excused on
the grounds that we had to go pick out a St. Bernard pup that
our father was buying for us. Then we'd clear the table the
hard way, by going around through the living room and the
back entry instead of by the direct route through the butler's
pantry, so that they wouldn't catch us at this menial task.

All was not always sweetness and light between the little

Dickinson girls and Lloyd and Stanley Montmorency. We
had terrific quarrels with them, too, usually when the light
in the butler's pantry was poor and their already cloudy
images even more vague than ever. It was very easy then to
suspect Lloyd of taking a patronizing attitude toward my sister, or Stanley of looking down her aristocratic nose at me.
Alice and I would draw together, just as Stanley and Lloyd
were drawing together, and we'd face each other hostilely
through the dim glass barrier. "They think they're smart,"
Alice would say to me. "Let's not tell them what we're going
to do tomorrow."

"No, the stuck-up things," I'd agree. "I *was* going to give
Stanley a gold locket on a chain for her birthday, but now I
won't. I'd rather throw it down the cesspool than give it to
her!" And I'd stick out my tongue at the haughty Stanley.

Alice would listen intently, and an expression of outrage
would contort her normally sweet round face. "Sticks and
stones may break my bones, but names will never hurt me,"
she'd tell the offensive Montmorency's. "Come on, Louise;
let's not *demean* ourselves talking with them. Let's put on
our fur coats and walk down to feed the swans. Of course,
their mother won't let *them* near the pool, for fear they'll get
their feet wet." And we'd both laugh scornfully.

We didn't mind leaving that house much. Lloyd and Stanley were becoming a little boring, and we didn't quite know
just what to do about them. They were too real to be rele-
gated back to the status of shadows in a glass, and we could
neither kill them off nor forget them; not when we met them
face to face every time we went from the dining room into
the kitchen.

We loved exploring the yards of our new homes just as
much as we did the houses themselves. Whereas a series of
occupancies does not necessarily or even ordinarily improve a
house, it does improve a plot of land. Every house in Bridgewater had a yard, and everyone who had a yard, even if it was
only a rented one, apparently succumbed to the old itch to
dig in the dirt. I think it was partly because most people
then were only a generation removed from farm life, or had

actually been brought up on farms, and partly because growing things for the table in your own garden and raising your
own eggs and poultry was an integral part of domestic econ-
omy, and not merely a hobby. Only the very shiftless bought
green vegetables. Solid citizens raised them in the back yard,
and their wives canned the surpluses against the winter, when
all you could buy in the stores was potatoes, cabbages, turnips,
and a few other imperishables. So every yard had a vegetable
garden and henhouse out back, as well as flower gardens in
front. In addition, most people—even if they knew their stay
would not be permanent—from time to time planted a rose
bush someone had given them, or transplanted a bleeding
heart or Dutchman's britches vine from their old home place,
or started an asparagus bed. When they moved on for one
reason or another, they perforce left these things behind, a
legacy for the new tenant.

We inherited through this system some wonderful treasures: a Baldwin apple tree that was perfect for climbing; a
corner full of raspberry canes in the middle of which we
crushed down an area for a hiding place should we be beset by
enemies; a shady bed of deep purple, double, scented violets
which we picked and took to Teacher when we felt a little
fence-mending in that quarter was indicated. Nobody had a
landscaped garden in those days, but every yard was the result
and sum total of years of living and of loving care and labor,
rather hodgepodge and thrown together, but easy and charming all the same. One of the great pleasures of moving was
investigating the yard; and if the hegira happened to take
place in winter, we could hardly wait until spring to see what
the climbing sun and damp south wind would summon up
out of the frozen and sleeping earth: the green spears of
daffodils, the tender folded hearts of violet leaves, the tiny
red clenched fists that would grow into columbine or great
heavy-headed peonies.

The reasons for our being so often dispossessed were various. Sometimes the owner of the house died, or the house
was sold over our heads, and the new owner wanted to live
there himself. Once the house was given to the Methodists,

who decided to move it and build a new church on the site.
The only reasons not in effect were the classic ones. We were
never thrown out into the night and the storm (a) because we
didn't pay the rent, or (b) because the wicked landlord was
foiled in his designs on the beautiful daughter's virtue. Alice
and I were not of an age to rouse the beast in man, and our
beauty never became such as to goad the male temperament
to deeds of madness.

The reason that we were never in arrears with the rent was
not because the *Independent* was a little gold mine. Nothing
could be further from the truth. No, it was because our parents didn't believe in biting off more than they could chew.
They believed—to use another of the aphorisms on which we
were brought up—in cutting the coat according to the cloth.
We therefore lived in houses the rent for which there was a
good probability our father would be able to pay each month.
They varied considerably in style and layout, but some things
they all had in common. They were all old, un-modernized,
and in from poor to terrible repair. Otherwise we wouldn't
have been living in them. The question of good or poor
neighborhood never came up, because in Bridgewater at that
time almost all the neighborhoods were good.

It didn't make any difference to Alice and me what house
we happened to be living in. Our lives were just the same.
We never had a bathroom in any of them, nor electricity, and
we had a furnace in only one, the one with the Lloyd-and-
Stanley haunted butler's pantry. In the others, the downstairs
rooms were heated by stoves, and the upstairs rooms were
not heated at all. We slept and dressed in cold rooms, except
in the bitterest weather, when we raced along frigid halls and
stairways with our clothes over our arms to the comparative
warmth of downstairs. In winter our feet were almost always
cold and chilblained, and our hands red and rough. Our
chores included not only the maidenly doing of dishes and
dusting of bric-a-brac, but also the bringing in of the wood
and coal, cleaning of the woodshed and henhouse, and other
jobs that would normally have fallen to the boy of the family,
if there had been a boy. We read by the light of kerosene

lamps and bathed in a huge tin tub set in the middle of the kitchen floor, before the open oven door of the cooking range. We lived almost primitively in a time and place that was not primitive and not geared to primitive living.

It would have been fun to live like pioneers, if we'd been pioneers, if we'd lived on a frontier where everyone else was undergoing the same privations and where there was a generally accepted level of cleanliness, comfort and style dictated by conditions common to all. The compensation of being a pioneer is the conviction that what one is enduring is to some important purpose, that the foes with whom one joins battle are real and worthy, like the weather or hostile Indians, that the victories will be over a worthwhile adversary, like an untamed land, and worth fighting for. Particularly must it be of immeasurable satisfaction to the pioneer, so that no hardship is disproportionate to the reward, to know that he is the adventurer, the daring one, the *first*. Real pioneering is a constructive and creative thing, and while it is possibly not as romantic as it has sometimes been made to sound, it has a certain grandeur, the realization of which is inescapable. The Foreigners who lived down across the tracks were in a sense true pioneers. They were establishing a new way of life in a strange land among the equivalent of hostile Indians, making a safe place for those of their kind who were to follow after; and their sacrifices of comforts and luxuries were communal and brought an easily visualized goal perceptibly nearer. There was some point in the way they lived.

We weren't pioneers in any sense. Of course, when Alice and I were very little, we didn't know or care what we were, or if we were anything. The world was as we found it, a place where you ate and worked and played—just as, presumably, everyone else did—in your own house and yard which was just like everyone else's, with your own sister. When you grew a little bigger, you went to school with boys and girls just like you, and you learned a lot and had a wonderful time. That's what we'd been told, and that's what we believed. We found out, though. Far from facing an inspiring new challenge with each new day, as the pioneers did, or a sympathetic society of our peers, as we'd been led to expect, we had to face a world peopled with little girls whose dresses were always a little nicer than ours, who had dressed in lovely warm rooms after dawdling around bathrooms for half an hour, and who spoke of breakfasting in the dining room as though it were the most natural thing in the world. We'd eaten our breakfasts in the kitchen, because at that time of day the kitchen was the only warm place in the house.

In spite of the handicap imposed on us by the ramshackle and inconvenient houses in which we lived, we had to look and act and talk as though we were members in good standing of this privileged society. We had all the discomforts and none of the compensations of an adventurous life. All our victories were picayune, pointless, and unrewarding, mere matters of successful simulation, by which we gained nothing, but which had to be won, nevertheless, since to lose would be unthinkable. There'd be no place for us anywhere if we lost. We couldn't go over to the Foreigners, secure behind the wall of their own folkways and languages and religions and philosophies. They wouldn't have accepted us, either. We were Alices-in-Wonderland, tearing our legs and lungs out with running to stay where we were.

We should have suffered pneumonia and what was known as galloping consumption, to say nothing of nervous breakdowns brought on by the strain of living double lives; and if we survived at all, we should have been frail flowers of budding womanhood. We weren't. We had the stamina of stableboys. The Foreign kids often fell victim to the various epidemics that swept through the schools, undoubtedly because large families of them lived in cramped quarters for the sake of the warmth that was denied us. Our more delicately nurtured little friends from steam-heated, electrified, two-bath homes commonly missed day after day of school attendance with head colds, tonsillitis, or chills and fever, from inadvertently getting their feet wet or sitting in a draft. But not us. Sitting in drafts was the thing we did best. Those that didn't come in under the doors of the houses we lived in sneaked in around the windows. We felt lonesome without a good lively draft on the backs of our necks.

Perhaps we were born tough; perhaps the rigors—if you want to call them that—of this in-between world in which we lived made us tough; or perhaps it really is true that a great deal of illness is genuine enough, but nevertheless unnecessary and avoidable if you have the right mental attitude. Don't think that we had any conscious or carefully cultivated attitude toward illness. We didn't. We merely *knew* that we couldn't possibly be sick on Tuesday or Wednesday, most particularly on Thursday, which was the day the *Independent* went to press. There'd be nobody home to take care of us. It was as simple as that.

In a day when it was neither fashionable nor common for wives and mothers in good standing to work outside the home, our mother worked. Nobody else's mother did, and we tried hard to convince ourselves that what our mother did was not really working, but just helping our father. For some reason, that made it seem a little less peculiar, and us a little less unlike other children. Our mother worked, all right, no matter how we chose to regard it. She worked hard, selling advertising space, setting type, correcting proof, and collecting local news items, all day Wednesday and Thursday and a large part of Tuesday. Nobody had to tell us, because it was in the very air we breathed, that nothing could interfere with getting out the paper. The sun rose in the morning, water ran down hill, and the *Independent* was printed late on Thursday, for sale Friday morning.

I don't know what would have happened if one of us had been stricken with acute appendicitis on publication day, except that I'm sure that somehow the paper would have been printed. But that isn't the point. The point is that we never were so stricken. It was out of the question that we should be; the idea was never entertained for a split second by anyone concerned; therefore we were not. Nobody told us we'd be committing the unpardonable sin if we developed symptoms between Monday and Friday, but we knew it. We concealed stomach-aches, headaches, sinking feelings, and spots before the eyes, as though they were shameful and guilty secrets, or deliberate acts of naughtiness conceived for the unspeakable and blasphemous purpose of fouling up publication day; or further fouling it up, since it was always hectic enough without any additional monkey wrenches from us. And after a while our symptoms would go away of their own accord. It would have had to be a more rugged symptom than any then known to medical science to have stood up against the steam roller inexorability of Thursday. I don't suppose that we really believed that our mother would punish us severely if we collapsed of a dread disease on one of the crucial days, but she certainly wasn't going to congratulate us or be very pleased about it, and we weren't taking any foolish chances. We'd wait until the pressure was off and someone had time to bother with us before we started complaining.

And of course by that time it was Friday, and the next day was Saturday, the only decent day in the week. We certainly weren't going to spend Saturday in bed; not if we could avoid it simply by keeping our mouths shut about a minor ache or pain, if it was still with us. It usually was not. On Friday the tension that had been growing and growing ever since Monday was miraculously dissipated. Another edition was safely off the press, Ma didn't have to go to work today, and tomorrow was Saturday! The knots in our stomachs unkinked. We felt marvelous.

There were other constants in our lives besides the brooding shadow of publication day, which made all this flittering about from one house that had seen better days to another of the same ilk less unsettling than it might have been. We never had to change schools, for one thing, or Sunday Schools. You could move from one side of the town to the diametrically opposite side and still be within easy walking distance of Central Square and the church and school. We didn't have to break into a new gang, either. No matter where we moved, we already knew the children who lived in that neighborhood, from school association. At first, of course, we didn't know them as well as the ones we'd left behind, but very soon the emphasis shifted, so that the boon companions of yesteryear became this year's recess-time-only cronies. We didn't have secrets with them any more, but we still liked them. Our secrets we reserved for those with whom we spent our Saturdays, those who now lived closest; all except for the top secrets. Those were between Alice and me, serving as fixed points in each others' shifting frames of reference. We took the same beat-up old furniture along with us wherever we went, too, and the same pets, and the same family institutions. We learned early that short of death, possibly, there is no escape. Wherever you may run, certain things go along with you.

One of the things we'd have been very happy to leave behind us was an institution called The Black Stick. I don't know where it came from, since I don't remember a time when it didn't rest balefully across two wires by which the mirror in the kitchen was suspended. It was black and it was a stick, a thin bamboo cane with a curved end, such as are sold, complete with pennants, at football games and county fairs. I could be, and probably am, wrong about this, but I certainly got the impression that the last thing to be moved from the old house and the first to be installed in the new was the kitchen mirror, not because anyone was vain or idle enough to be looking into it, but solely to accommodate The Black Stick. I'd sidle into the strange new kitchen, determined not to look, because maybe by not seeing it I could put it out of existence; but before I was halfway across the floor my eyes would be drawn in helpless and horrid fascination to the mirror over the sink; and sure enough, there it would be, The Black Stick, possessed of a positive and malevolent sentience of its own. It *wanted* me to be bad. It could be patient. It could afford to wait, because it knew that eventually—maybe not today or this week, but surely by next—either Alice or I would drive our mother to saying the terrible words, "I'm going to have to get down The Black Stick!"

I'm not sure why this was such a terrible threat. It wasn't because applications of The Black Stick hurt so much. All our mother ever did with it was switch our legs a few times, which stung like blazes but didn't compare with some of the

self-inflicted pains we bore in silence when we were practicing up to emulate the Spartan boy or in training to acquit
ourselves like men in case anybody should try to torture important information out of us. An encounter with The Black
Stick wasn't a patch, really, to a good toothache or what happened when you were so foolish as to put your tongue, some
frosty morning, on the iron rail at school, at the behest of an
older, wiser upper-grader. And yet just the threat of The
Black Stick reduced us to abject whimpers. I guess it was a
case of good old applied psychology, in a day when even the
term was not known. Recourse to The Black Stick was The
End. When we'd been that bad, we'd put ourselves outside
the pale, and what was more, we knew it. I guess that knowledge was the real burden of the penalty. Our own black
hearts were punishing us.

Another institution that was peculiar to our household
was reading the Bible and repeating the Lord's Prayer at
breakfast every day of the year. This was not common practice then, no matter what it may have been at an earlier
period. (After all, I'm not all *that* ancient, that I remember
the signing of the Mayflower Pact, or even Cotton Mather!)
It was, rather, a hangover from the pious rearings of our parents. My grandfather Dickinson, as I said, was a minister
(and a bee-keeper, and an observer of the stars, and a student
of Greek, and many other things that were simple and child-
like and unworldly), and in his home it was as natural as
breathing to start each day in communion with God.

My grandfather Stewart was a deacon of the church, when
being a deacon was an important seven-day-a-week job, and
not just something you worked at on Sundays. He was also
a wheelwright, a politician, and a martinet, and it is my
possibly mistaken conviction that one of the reasons his
church appointed him to the position was that they knew that
if he couldn't be a deacon, he wouldn't play at all. Be that
as it may, he brought the full weight of his not inconsider-
able personality and powers to bear upon the problem, ran
the church (always for its own good as he saw it, be sure) with
an iron hand, and decreed family prayers in his own baili-

wick, because as senior deacon he had an example to set.
With the same idea in mind, he banned all Sunday papers
from his house and would allow only absolutely imperative
work to be done on the Sabbath. Feeding the hens and the
children, smoothing up the beds, giving the kitchen floor a
lick and a promise with a broom in case of scattered crumbs,
yes. But sewing on a button, pressing a wrinkled skirt, or
rinsing out a pair of stockings—a thousand times no. In his
house, you couldn't even read for pleasure on Sunday—just
the Bible, or *Pilgrim's Progress,* or a church magazine called
The Congregationalist.

So our parents came honestly by their attitude. Alice and
I chafed considerably because we had to sit through all the
begats (our father read the Bible from start to finish, and
then started in all over again), when the other kids just ate
their cereal and ran outdoors to play; but I guess we were
lucky at that. It could have been worse. Of course, five days
a week—the school days—we got a double dose, since by law
the school day opened with a reading from the Old Testament, the Lord's Prayer, and a salute to the flag; and on
Sunday we got two extra rations, one at church and one at
Sunday School. But in some other things our parents were,
according to their bringings-up, downright lax.

We always had a Sunday paper, for example, because my
father claimed he needed it in his business; and anyhow, most
of the work involved in its publication had been done on
Saturday. If you had to skip a paper on grounds of Sabbath-
breaking, he said, the one to skip was the Monday morning
edition. So Alice and I were very familiar with the doings of
Billy the Boy Artist, the Katzenjammer Kids, and Hair
breadth Harry and the Beautiful Belinda. We weren't allowed to lift a needle or a hammer or a paint brush,
naturally, or to play any noisy games that involved whooping
and hollering or running; and we couldn't indulge in par-
chesi or checkers or lotto or any game involving cards; and
we weren't supposed to read any except improving books.
But we did play with our dolls and with paper dolls, rather
frivolous occupations. I don't know how we got away with

that, come to think of it, except that at least we were quiet about it, and probably our mother was letting sleeping dogs lie, as she did about our Sunday reading.

The houses we lived in were almost invariably equipped not only with living rooms (called sitting rooms), but also with parlors, stiff rooms which were shut up most of the time in reserve for special formal occasions like weddings, funerals, and Sunday. (It must be obvious that the reason these barracks were for rent at a price within the Dickinson range was that the movement toward smaller, more convenient, modern homes was well under way.) In our various parlors were kept books suitable for Sunday reading: Lamb's *Tales from Shakespeare,* a simplified version of Bulfinch's *Age of Fable,* and something called *Bible Stories Retold for Children.* This was a perfectly enormous book, weighing probably about twenty pounds, much too heavy to hold. We put it on the floor and lay on our stomachs to study it. We didn't bother with the text, an emasculated rehashing of the meaty stories we already knew backward and forward, with all the really good parts left out and namby-pamby morals appended. We concentrated on the illustrations, full page reproductions of Doré engravings. I can't imagine the type of mind that considered those pictures either appropriate or desirable for a book designed for the young. Either the editor was a sadist, or he hated children as a class, or else his primary objective was to keep the little dears quiet on Sunday afternoon by the simple method of scaring them stiff. Doré didn't miss a trick when it came to picturing the awful plight of the damned. Fortunately Alice and I were made of pretty stern stuff. We enjoyed them thoroughly.

Then, after we'd glutted ourselves with horror, it was a fairly easy matter to switch quietly over to the secular books we'd obtained from the Public Library: the Frank Merriwells and Mark Tidds and the Andrew Lang fairy books, red and green and blue. If our mother noticed, she let it go as the better part of valor.

There were other things besides church attendance and a day otherwise devoted to the cultivating of a state of suspended animation that set Sunday apart. The food was one of them. Since our mother worked, the meals on weekdays were sometimes a little sketchy—perfectly adequate, but designed primarily for nourishment and not to be savored and lingered over. On Sunday they were more elaborate. During the months with an R in them, we always had oyster stew for breakfast. Why, I don't know. Other people had bacon and eggs, or the traditional Saturday night baked beans warmed over, or fish cakes, or oatmeal, or whatever else they fancied. We *always* had oyster stew as a matter of course, although it does seem now to be a rather improbable thing to eat in the morning. It was good. There was butter floating around on top, and little oyster crackers, and once in a while there'd be a tiny orange crab; but never a pearl, although we looked and hoped for one.

On Sunday, dinner was at one o'clock, when we'd got church and Sunday School off our chests, so to speak. I never did and still don't see the great allure offered by the slogan, "Chicken Every Sunday." We had it, almost every Sunday, in one form or another, and pretty darned sick of it we got, too. Remember, we kept a flock of hens. In the fall, when my father was weeding the roosters out of his flock, we had fried chicken for a while, and then when the victims grew a little bigger, we had roast chicken. Along in February we ran out of roasters, and my father started culling, picking out the tough old hens who no longer paid their keep in eggs. So then we had chicken fricassee or chicken stew or chicken pie—all very well and good, except that we were tired of chicken. We wanted something different.

Once we got it. One spring one of the mysterious ailments to which chickens are heir struck a hatching of day-old chicks and killed off all except one. This one was in a bad way, lying on its side with its beak open, gasping, its black and yellow down—our father favored barred Plymouth Rocks—all draggly and limp. It seemed to be only a matter of hours, so our father returned the mother to the henyard and, because he couldn't just leave the poor little chick to die all alone, brought it into the house.

Alice and I were enchanted. We lined a strawberry box
with soft outing flannel, put the chick into it, and tended it
by inches. Against all normal probability—if for no other
cause, he should have died of an overdose of kindness—he
survived and became our special property and joy. We named
him Harry, and we doted on him. We lugged him around
with us everywhere, first in a shoe box, then under our arms
or on our shoulders, swung him in the swing under the maple
tree until he was dizzy and sick to his stomach, fed him
exotic tidbits like raisins and cooking chocolate, and quite
literally made a fool of him. Our mother insisted that he
was feeble-minded, and I guess perhaps he was. When he was
half-grown, all leggy and half-feathered and generally far
from prepossessing—although he was beautiful to us—, an
attempt was made to rehabilitate him in the flock; but it
didn't work. The others all picked on him, and when he
heard Alice's or my voice, he would run like mad toward us,
almost knocking his poor silly brains out on the henyard
fence, falling over his own big feet, and squawking pitifully.
So finally he was let out to roam, partly for his own protection and partly because Alice and I put up such a holler. He
followed us around like a dog, came when we called, and
submitted to being dressed up in dolls' clothes and wheeled
around in a doll carriage. He was sort of an idiot, at that,
but we'd have fixed anyone good who said so to us, pattern-
ing our methods on the works of Doré.

Then one Sunday, after we'd polished our plates and were
waiting to see what was for dessert, our mother said, "You've
just eaten Harry."

We looked at her, ready to string along with the joke; but
something in her face told us she wasn't joking. We looked
at each other, and then, in spite of all our self-imposed standards of conduct—and whatever else objectionable we were,
we were far from cry-babies; we *scorned* tears—our heads
went down plunk! into our dirty plates, and we gave way to
devastating grief. We cried until we were sick, and then we
cried some more. We hated the whole world in which there
was no more foolish Harry to run trustingly to our call, and

we hated ourselves for having eaten him, for not having been informed by some loving instinct what flesh was set before us.

In fairness to my mother, I'll have to say that I'm sure she didn't realize how we felt about Harry. We were close-mouthed little mutts when it came to expressing tender emotions, although we were voluble enough on other themes. I'm sure she didn't mean to be cruel in her bald and ill-timed anouncement, that she thought it best to face an unpleasant fact squarely, with no beating about bushes. And she did her best to make amends. Nothing would bring Harry back to life; but for several Sundays thereafter, until the first keen edge of sorrow had been dulled, we had something other than chicken for dinner. We'd thought—and said, over and over, at the tops of our lungs and in surly mumbles—that never-never-never as long as we lived would we ever eat another bite of chicken. We did, though; with enjoyment.

We enjoyed practically everything to eat, and if we didn't, we had to eat it anyhow. Our mother had no patience with what she called a finicky eater, and had anyone explained allergies to her, she'd have dismissed them with a sniff as being notional and just a bid for attention, a form of self-importance. She had no time to be fooling around with special dishes, although Alice was allowed to forego strawberries when it had been repeatedly and drastically demonstrated that they really did cause her to break out with hives. Otherwise we ate what was set before us, and what was set before us in those days before quick freezing and refrigerator cars was predictable. The only fresh fruits available in winter were oranges, apples, and bananas, and the only vegetables were the root crops. Nobody ever heard of lettuce in winter. You ate your year's quota of greens—known as garden sauce —in season, starting with dandelion and dock greens from the lawns and fields in early spring, before even the asparagus beds were up, running the gamut of lettuce, radishes, and Swiss chard through the summer, and ending with cucumbers, tomatoes, late lettuce, and spinach. Nobody had ever heard of broccoli, although it was rumored that the Foreigners raised some pretty queer truck in their lush and successful gardens down across the tracks.

We always had a barrel of apples stored in the cellar against the winter—Russets, Porters, Sheepnoses and Northern Spies, varieties now out of favor—and it was one of Alice's and my duties to keep the apple bowl on the dining room table filled. In the evening, our mother would sit with a pan of apples in her cleanly aproned lap and peel them with a silver, mother-of-pearl handled fruit knife, handing us the neat, moist quarters in turn on the tip to eat, because an apple a day kept the doctor away. Sometimes in the evening, too, we had popcorn, and that was a great treat. Oh, we had a pretty riotous night life, sitting around eating apples and popcorn over our books until half-past seven, which was our bedtime, come hell or high water. When, upon my being promoted from the eighth grade and on the brink of entering high school and woman's estate, our bedtime was ceremoniously and officially shoved along to eight o'clock, we felt that we were now really beginning to live.

We ate a lot of things that we weren't supposed to eat, too. We never sat down on the ground without pulling a grass stem from its smooth sheath and nibbling at the clean, pale end. We ate rose petals, and nasturtium stems and blossoms, and little raw carrots—nobody else did, then—and the aromatic bark of a nameless ornamental shrub with small, tight, black-red flowers that looked something like pineapples. We ate ground cherries and choke cherries and rose haws and all the red berries off our mother's Jerusalem cherry plant, so that she finally pitched it out, for fear we'd die of slow-working and cumulative poisoning. We were always chewing on twigs and branches and buds, and it's a wonder we didn't poison ourselves, at that. A modern dietitian or psychiatrist would probably diagnose us as cases of malnutrition or frustration of some sort, but I don't think that we were. We were just curious. We wanted to know what things tasted like. It was interesting to us; and besides, we felt vaguely that we were gaining some sort of undefined advantage by eating things that other people didn't eat.

Holidays to us were not really feast days, as they were to others, because we always had chicken again—the biggest and best of the flock, saved and fattened especially and augmented by cranberry sauce, extra vegetables, two kinds of pie, and mixed nuts, but still just the same old chicken. So Thanksgiving would have been simply another Sunday, except that it meant no school without the Sunday restrictions, and the putting off of the publication day jitters another twenty-four hours, a doubtful blessing. Christmas was The Day. Oh, we had chicken again, don't worry; but we had presents, and that made all the difference. Ours was not a family that showered gifts at the drop of a hat, partly because there was no money for prodigal giving, partly because our parents' rearing had formed a habit of austerity, and partly because it just wasn't the fashion to look for occasions for gift-giving. Nobody had heard of Mother's Day, for example, and penny valentines were considered ample recognition of that saint's day. We received presents on our birthday and on Christmas. That's what we expected and that's what we got. The birthday presents were minor—perfectly adequate but not overwhelming. Christmas was different.

The reason it was different was my father's Aunt Julia Dickinson, a little old maiden lady who was supposed to resemble her cousin Emily, although I guess the resemblance boils down to a shy and virginal air, a perfect contentment with her own company, a puzzling and unobtrusive self-sufficiency, and what was called a failure to marry. I doubt if failure is the correct term. She just didn't care to be bothered, in my mature opinion. In spite of her appearance of fragility, she was quite capable of looking after herself and her affairs, and did. I don't know where she acquired it or how she kept it out of the hands of the smooth operators who battened on the savings of widows, orphans, and defenseless old ladies in those days; but the fact remains that she was the only Dickinson in my experience who ever had any money to speak of.

Not that she ever did speak of it. She was a lady, and ladies didn't mention money out loud, except possibly to their bankers. Her actions spoke for her. We'd have had some fairly slim Christmases if it hadn't been for Great-aunt Julia. We didn't see her very often—after all, it was quite a trip for an old lady to take from the fastnesses of the Dickinson stronghold in the Berkshires to the flat and alien plains of the coast—but we loved her dearly. Cupboard love I'm afraid it was, but none the less genuine. We didn't know her well enough and in any case weren't old enough to realize and appreciate her quality; but Aunt Julia's Package was the highlight of Christmas and of the whole year.

Aunt Julia didn't confine herself to one nice present apiece, or any of that nonsense. She went hog-wild—a most inept expression to use in connection with a person so delicate in both body and spirit—when it came to buying Chrismas presents. She bought everything she saw, apparently, that she thought might appeal to two little girls. There were beautiful toys—gorgeous dolls and complete miniature teasets, with spouts on the pots that really poured, and games to play; there were rafts of books; and gay and impractical clothes that our mother wouldn't—because she couldn't—have considered buying for a moment, and that I'm sure Aunt Julia herself, with her black silk, real lace, and cameo brooch, wouldn't have been caught dead in at any age; and all kinds of fancy candy and glazed fruits in elaborate boxes which we cherished forever, or at least until they fell to pieces and the bright satin ribbons became frayed and bedraggled. Aunt Julia's Package furnished the one prodigal and superabundant note in a life that was of necessity careful and in some respects cramped. I don't anticipate any Utopia, and I'm not sure I'd like it much if by some miracle we were able to achieve it; but I do think it would be nice if every child of parents of restricted means could have just one generous and well-heeled relative, not to spoil him on three hundred and sixty-five days of the year, but merely to pamper him a little bit once in a while.

The other two really big occasions of our year were the day that the church Sewing Circle met at our house, and the day that Mrs. Cass came. About the first thing that our parents did after taking up residence in Bridgewater, as soon as the beds were set up, the stove pipe connected to the chimney, the carpets laid and the curtains hung, was to present their letters from the Huntington church to Central Square Congregational Church in Bridgewater, thus effecting a transference of membership. Events then took their course. Before you could say hemstitch, our mother was a member of the Sewing Circle, a group of ladies who devoted their united efforts to sewing for charity, raising money for the church, and other high-minded projects. They sometimes met in the church vestry for luncheon and work, and sometimes at the homes of the various members.

When it was my mother's turn to entertain them, the place was in an uproar for days in advance. Naturally, the whole house had to be cleaned. This didn't mean just the downstairs rooms and the one bedroom in which the ladies would leave their wraps. Oh my, no. It meant every corner of the house, including the back entry, the woodshed, and Alice's and my bureau drawers. I don't think that our mother really expected any of her guests to go snooping around, opening drawers and closet doors, but she played it safe, just in case. It meant washing all windows and curtains, and for all I remember, all blankets as well, in the improbable event that one or more of the ladies should be overtaken by illness and have to be put to bed. These luncheons were of the covered dish variety, to which each person brought some predesignated comestible, such as a casserole of scalloped potatoes, a bowl of coleslaw, or some baked ham; so the food was no problem to the hostess. However, she did have to provide china, silver, and napery. Therefore we washed not only the best wedding present Limoges and polished the good spoons until we were black in the face, but also the everyday cereal bowls and the Chicago souvenir spoons that our mother got on her honeymoon, and that nobody imagined for a moment were going to be used. When everything was ready, a day or two in advance, we tiptoed about the house, being careful not to muss up sofa pillows, and we ate out of an assortment of odd, unmatched dishes that had come in boxes of rolled oats, so that none of the preparations would be disarranged.

When the great day arrived, Alice and I were hustled off to school with our ears ringing with instructions: Come straight home this noon, and don't dawdle on the way. Don't get your dresses dirty, I want you to look like little ladies. (That was a waste of our mother's breath; we and dirt had a great affinity.) Come in the back door and eat your lunches in the kitchen *quietly*, without fighting. And this afternoon come straight home from school and change your clothes without my telling you. Then go out and play in the yard, and keep away from under the living room windows, and don't start fighting. (A stranger would certainly have retained the impression that Alice and I were constantly at each other's throat. which really wasn't the case. We fought only as much as most siblings do, or less.)

We'd go solemnly off to school, suffering as badly as our mother obviously was from the pre-party jitters.

And as unnecessarily. When we crept in at the back door at noon, the house would be humming with talk and laughter. Women would be bustling busily between the kitchen and the dining room, and someone would be sure to look at the plates our mother set before us on the kitchen table and exclaim, "Oh, they can eat more than that! I know growing girls. Here, take a handful of these nut cookies I made specially. I brought plenty." Our mother would be too busy herself to notice that we hadn't eaten all our potato and were filling up on Bavarian cream and chocolate cake, against all rules and regulations.

After school we had a regular binge. The ladies would still be there, but in the living room now, their fingers flying as they tied a quilt or hemmed dish towels and their tongues going ninety to the dozen as they got to the bottom of what really was the trouble between Mrs. Smith and Mrs. Jones who used to be so constantly living in each other's apron pockets. We didn't care what the trouble was. Nothing could have interested us less. Our entire attention was concentrated on the plates of leftovers on the kitchen sideboard— our own mother's familiar plates, so it was plain that what we were doing was legitimate, we hoped. We'd snitch a cinnamon roll here and a brownie there for the trip, and go upstairs by the back way, as quiet as mice. We'd change into our old dresses, hanging up our school clothes with uncharacteristic tidiness and a great smug sense of being good girls. The essence of being good children was being seen as little as possible and heard not at all, wasn't it? Well, then! And we'd fill our pockets with tidbits on our unobtrusive way out the back door. We just loved Sewing Circle day.

The advent of Mrs. Cass was something else again. Mrs. Cass was a woman who went out sewing by the day. Some people had her twice a year or more, for days at a time, while they whipped their spring and fall wardrobes into shape. We had her just once a year, for one day, to break the back of the sewing, as it were. Our mother was no slouch of a sempstress herself, but she simply didn't have the time, what with the *Independent* and all, to make the necessary clothes for my sister and herself and me. Besides, Mrs. Cass was unusually good at making over. She had both style sense and experience. She could take an old winter coat of my mother's and turn it into a good school jumper for me—and eventually Alice. She wasn't afraid of turning things upside down and wrong-side out to achieve her effects, nor of slashing boldly into a piece of new material in accordance with ideas of her own and regardless of the dictates of the tissue paper pattern. She got things cut out and pinned or basted together during her one frantic day with us, and our mother went on from there as she found time in the future.

Visitations by Mrs. Cass were not unmixed blessings or unalloyed joys. We'd come home from school to find the floor knee deep in a litter of patterns and scraps of cloth, and our mother harassed and irritable under the pressure of having to keep pace with Mrs. Cass and prepare an extra-special meal at the same time. It was a matter not only of pride but of defense policy as well to feed Mrs. Cass with epicurean liberality. You couldn't have her reporting to her next client that she'd received anything but the best, and plenty of it, at your house. Before we were well inside the door, we'd be commanded to take off our dresses and "just slip this on over your head."

"Hmm," Mrs. Cass would pronounce, standing back for a good look. "Just as I thought. Skimpy in the bust."

Skimpiness in the bust was the worst fault a garment could have, since it labeled the wearer as being immodest to the point of brazen shamelessness, a full-fledged woman of Babylon. We didn't have any busts, but that didn't matter. When people looked at our fronts, they weren't supposed to think in terms of anatomy or lack of it at all. They were supposed to be thinking only of what neat pintucks or gathers the material held, and skimpiness in the bust might topple their reveries from this high plane. We'd have to stand there like a couple of dummies—"Stand *still,* for Heaven's sake! Do you want to get stuck with a pin? Stand up *straight!* You've got one shoulder way up under your ear. Don't you *want* to look nice?"—while Mrs. Cass and our mother pulled and hauled us about, easing side seams to give a little more full-ness you-know-where and mumbling to each other through mouthfuls of pins. We didn't give a hoot whether we looked nice or not, or indeed whether we ever had any new clothes at all. We were hungry. We wanted to eat.

Finally the garment would be skinned gingerly off over our heads—"Careful now! Look out for those pins!"—and Mrs. Cass would remove the tape measure from around her neck and the row of pins from her shirtwaist front for the noon break. She'd wash her hands, sit down, cast an all-seeing eye over the groaning board, and the fun would begin. All the things our mother had been wanting to find out about since the last session, she'd ask; and Mrs. Cass always knew all the answers.

That woman got around. She knew who was related to whom, no matter how deviously, and who was mean to his wife. She knew whose hair was touched up a little, and who owed money all over town in spite of—or because of—the big front they put on. ("It's all *Her.* He's a good man, common as an old shoe, if She'd let him alone. But She's got these ideas, can't forget She was a Morey and don't want anybody else should forget it, either—") Mrs. Cass knew why the Baptist minister was leaving, and, no matter who told my mother what, it wasn't simply because he'd had a better job offered him. That's what they were telling around, but the truth of the matter was— There were currents and cross-currents to that affair, and Mrs. Cass had every one of them well charted, and a comprehensive compendium of opinion on the subject, both *pro* and *con*. She also had a large fund of esoteric knowledge to which Alice and I never became privy, since upon various occasions she'd look slant-eyed at us, purse her lips, and say, "Remind me to tell you about that later. Little Pitchers, you know."

She wasn't fooling Alice and me a bit. We knew all about Little Pitchers and their big ears. There had been a time back in the dim ages of a year or two gone by when any reference to Little Pitchers—and people seemed always to be referring to them—had forced us to waste a lot of time lying doggo behind furniture and around dark corners, eavesdropping. It was a waste of time, too. Instead of the murder, arson and mayhem we hoped for, people who spoke of Little Pitchers always discussed the stupidest and most boring things, like some girl going away to get a baby, or some woman whose husband traveled a lot being seen in Boston with A Man. We couldn't have been less interested. Eavesdropping was hard and dangerous work, and we decided by tacit consent to save our strength and cunning for occasions when the reward promised to be a little greater than a bit of tiresome information about someone's tiresome baby. We knew all about babies anyhow. The stork brought girls, and boys were found under cabbage plants, and what was so exciting about that?

Once Mrs. Cass had gone on to the next bivouac on her tour of the sewing rooms of town, we settled back into our accustomed routine. Perhaps people all lived less eventful, more ordered, lives then; or perhaps it was only we, in our peculiar circumstances, who were quiet and regimented. Our week was pinned firmly down at two corners by the demands of Sunday and Thursday, of course, which left little leeway for fancy flights. Saturday flapped gaily in the breeze, a fine, feckless tag-end-of-the-week day, on which we could do whatever we wanted to—within limits—after we'd finished helping our mother with the housework and cooking. She got us all baked up for the coming week on Saturday morning, since her time was pretty well limited by the demands of the *Independent* during the other days. We were supposed to hang around and help on Saturday morning, and for once doing what we were supposed to do wasn't a cross to bear. We were allowed to lick all the cooking dishes. Nothing in my experience since has ever tasted as good as raw cake batter, scraped painstakingly from the mixing bowl with a kitchen spoon and rolled on the tongue. Once, operating on the theory that if a little vanilla in cake batter was so good, a lot of vanilla drunk straight out of the bottle would be that much better, we swiped the vanilla bottle out of the pantry and smuggled it to our hidey-hole of the moment, a cave behind the stacked wood in the shed. We were going to fill it up with colored water, using our paintbox sepia for the purpose, and return it before our mother missed it.

There was a flaw in the theory somewhere. It tasted perfectly awful, and made us sick, besides. Our mother looked at our green faces, smelled our breaths, and reached for The Black Stick. On top of that, she gave us a Talking To about theft, deception, and what happened to little girls who poisoned their parents by introducing foreign matter like paint-colored water into the vanilla bottle. All in all, it was not a very successful experiment.

Monday, come what might, was washday. If it was raining or snowing too hard to allow outdoor drying, the clothes were strung up in the woodshed or attic or cellar. It was Monday or nothing, as far as the laundry went, because on Tuesday the Independent started yammering for attention again. The ironing was done at odd moments throughout the week as someone needed a clean garment, and the pieces left over were finished up on Friday, our mother's other day at home which she reserved for what she called catching up with herself.

We lived, as you see, a very tightly organized life, dominated by a strict sense of schedule, and it wasn't until we were grown up that we learned that a schedule could be broken. Not go to church on Sunday? Do the washing on Wednesday? That would have been pure iconoclasm!

3

The Little Dickinson Girls

WHEN I WAS VERY YOUNG INDEED, I THOUGHT THAT EVERYBODY
had a sister like mine, a second self, who thought and felt
and acted in complete accord and sympathy with one. Later,
naturally, when school attendance exposed me to the facts of
life, I found that such was not the case. I learned that lots of
girls had sisters so much older or younger than themselves
that they might as well not have been sisters at all; or that
they had so many sisters that their allegiance was dissipated
in forty—well, not quite—different directions. Some girls had
sisters whom they didn't even like very much; and some poor
girls didn't have any sisters. All this I knew, because I saw
it with my own eyes; but I couldn't imagine its being my lot,
and I still can't.

There is—or there can be—a very special relationship between near and dear and only sisters that is like no other
relationship on earth. I know. I don't say that it is better
than the bond between brother and sister, or mother and
child, or husband and wife. There just isn't any comparison
possible. It's entirely different, closer in some respects, but
less demanding. It is, if I may be forgiven the use of a cor-
rupted and commercialized word in its Victorian sense of free
from jealousy and possessiveness and baseness, as nearly *pure*
a relationship as you are likely to find in this world. With

your sister, if she is of about your own age, you share everything. You're of the same sex, with its emotional and physiological idiosyncrasies; you have the same parents and uncles and aunts and cousins, the same home background, the same training and cumulative daily experience, the same heredity. You eat the same food, wash with the same brand of soap, read the same books, breathe the same air. You suffer the same apprehensions (The Black Stick), uphold the same standards ("*We* don't cry"), cherish the same dreams (Wally Reid under the stairs), and giggle at the same jokes which nobody else finds funny, since they have been developed bit by microscopic bit over years that no one else has shared in such intimate and complete detail. You have private catchwords by which you can convey volumes to your sister, but which to anybody else sound like incomprehensible doubletalk. How can you help being close to a person like that?

In our case, this sameness was carried to extreme lengths. Short of bearing identical twins, I don't see how our mother could have done more. Not only did we both have straight brown hair, brown eyes, snub noses, and the kind of complexion described noncommittally on passports as medium, but our birthdays, although two years apart, fell on the same date, the fourteenth of June. For a long time we thought that all the children of any family had the same birthday, as we did, a sort of Divine mnemonic device designed to make birthday observance an easily remembered, mass production affair. We were the only two children, so this idea persisted for years, with no unorthodox mid-January birthday of a sibling to crop up and invalidate it. We also thought that the flags that flew all over town on June 14, in honor of Flag Day, were for our sole benefit, an illusion that gave us the quiet satisfaction of sterling worth generally recognized and acknowledged. For reasons that I have already explained, our mother dressed us alike most of the time; and in spite of my two-year seniority, she treated us alike all the time.

This was not as inequitable as it may seem on the surface. While I was older and bigger than Alice, she was the brighter of the two. It was first publicly demonstrated when, after two weeks in the second grade, Alice was shoved unceremoniously along to the third, putting her only one grade behind me.

In spite of this—and she now says that had she a child of her own, she'd break her leg and tie her home in bed before she'd let her skip a grade, such a scholastic and social strain did the leap subject her to—she managed to bring home report cards which made very monotonous reading, nothing but A, A, A, all the time. (I, skipping nothing, pulled down mostly B's, with a shameful C occasionally, and once in a great while a surprising A minus.)

Any possible argument about or discussion of our comparative intelligences was ended some years later when the Commonwealth of Massachusetts decided that it would be nice, not to say handy, to have on record the I.Q. of every child in the Commonwealth, as determined by means of Binet-type tests, given in all public schools. It turned out that I was fairly bright, presumably smart enough to know about coming in out of the rain, at least. But Alice—well, they made her take the test over, either because they couldn't believe their eyes, or because they thought she'd evolved some super-cribbing system, against which they wished to develop a defense. She did slightly better the second time, under the eagle eyes of a battery of proctors; and that settled that.

So the two years of time between us dwindled down to nothing, as far as companionship went. We were, for all practical purposes, the same age, although our mother dragged out that unfortunate two years once in a while, for her own ends. It speaks volumes for my sister's character and nature that I didn't hate her. I certainly was given reason to, often enough; and I probably would have, too, if she hadn't been so much fun and so apologetic about the intellectual prowess that she really couldn't help.

My mother would open our report cards on end-of-term day, tighten her lips, and look grim and disgusted. "I should think, Louise Dickinson, that you'd be ashamed of yourself! Your little sister, two years younger than you are and a whole grade ahead of herself, getting all A's, while *you* bring home a card like this! *C* in Arithmetic! I should think you'd have more *pride* than to let your little sister—" And so on and on and *on*.

I wasn't a bit ashamed of myself, I'm afraid. I was just dumb in Arithmetic, and I knew it. So I became surly and resentful and bored with the whole discussion. If she could just see some of the report cards taken home by kids in my grade—but I knew better than to bring forth that argument. What other little girls did or said or wore or thought was entirely immaterial and beside the point. The little Dickinson girls would act like ladies and scholars, speak only the truth, wear what their mother decreed, and think proper and conventional thoughts. Or so our mother hoped and intended.

The other perennial occasion upon which my two-years' handicap was brought forth unfailingly was the occasion of any fall from grace on our part, of whatever nature: getting our best dresses dirty, snowballing the neighbor's cat, eating up the cake that was being saved for supper, swiping apples from someone's tree, or not staying in the yard when we'd been told to. I could have sung the Bad Girl's Refrain in my sleep, and probably did. It went, "Alice should have known better, too, of course; but you're the elder, Louise, and it's up to you to set the Example."

Then I'd look at Alice, standing there so embarrassed and apologetic about her report card, or trying to get a word in edgewise to say that the apple-stealing had been as much her idea as mine, and my heart would soften. We were in this mess together, two against the unreasonable tyranny of all adults, and we'd fight it out along those lines if it took the rest of our lives.

Of course, the whole deal was even more unfair to her than it was to me. While I was constantly being blamed for shortcomings that I honestly couldn't remedy, or saddled with a responsibility that I was temperamentally unequipped to assume, because of an age difference that was none of my doing, she was being put in the impossible position of Little Angel, a position not conducive to popularity with one's peers. In addition, she was eternally engaged in a desperate effort to keep up with someone who was physically larger and stronger than she, and two years more mature and experienced—and two years, when you are under ten, is a lot, a sizable percentage of your present life span. She was the one who really got the dirty end of the stick.

Genes are truly wonderful things; and if you'd like to put that down as this week's trite and obvious remark, you certainly have my wholehearted permission. I know it is; but it's the only reason that Alice and I didn't turn out to be carbon copies of each other. We looked alike. We sounded alike. When we spoke to an unseen listener, he always had to ask who said that, Louise or Alice; and to this day friends of Alice, meeting me for the first time, exclaim, "Why, you sound exactly like your sister!" and people who don't know me from Adam's off ox tell Alice, "You talk just the way your sister writes." But there the resemblance stops.

In the first place, I'm noisy and she's quiet. I talk a lot, whether I have anything to say or not, and she listens until she has something worth saying. Then I'm impulsive and inclined to quick enthusiasms as quickly abandoned, while she thinks before she speaks or acts and then sticks to the course she has decided upon. She's painstaking and meticulous in everything she does, and I'm slap-dash and sloppy. She's conscientious in the true sense, and I'm careless. I'm sure that all these traits are inbred, outward manifestations of our born natures, since our heredity, environment, and training were identical and should normally have produced identical results. It *must* be the genes. That's the only way I can account for our differences in disposition.

Take the matter of the WCTU Pledge, for instance. When we were in the third and fourth grades, or somewhere around there, the school population was subjected to a lecture with lantern slides on the evils of alcohol. (Not that the little Dickinson girls needed it; we'd already been thoroughly indoctrinated.) A lady spoke feelingly of broken homes, hungry children, and weeping mothers both old and comparatively new. A gentleman, a Reformed Drunkard—looking in the clutches of this ordeal, I now realize, as though he'd give his left, or non-bending, elbow for a good stiff hooker to hoist—told about the ruin Drink had made of his life and begged us all to forgo it, putting special emphasis on the First Drink and pointing out logically that if there weren't a First, there couldn't ever very well be a Second. The slides were fascinating in a gruesome way. They showed what the insides of our stomachs would look like if we Drank, as well as two white mice, one of which was fat, healthy, and happy, while the other was a miserable, watery-eyed wretch of a thing, barely able to crawl around. Needless to say, the first had been brought up on a pure, if dull, diet of grain, cheese, fats and milk, while the other had been forcibly— "Because, children, animals *instinctively* refuse to touch alcohol; and in that respect they show themselves to be so *much* wiser than some humans, don't they?"—fed whiskey. Then the lady and the gentleman sang a duet, her shrill soprano mingling oddly and unnervingly with his drink-roughened tenor. It started out, "Johnson the Drunkard is dying to-night/ With tears of remorse on his face/ And something or other and hey-nonny-no/ Have *you* a boy for his place?" This multiple attack on our susceptibilities left us grade-schoolers considerably shaken and nicely softened up for the final step, the Signing of the Pledge.

I signed. It was the thing to do. All the other kids were signing, the teacher and the lady were waiting for me to do so, and it never occurred to me that there was any alternative. That was my attitude, and the attitude of everyone else from the kindergarten to, if not the grave, at least through the ninth grade. Besides, I had no desire to become a drunkard anyhow.

Neither had Alice, but she refused to sign. I'm still amazed that a child of her age could be capable of such long-range and mature thinking. At first she said she wouldn't sign because some day she might want to sample alcohol. No, very likely she wouldn't; but she didn't know. She might, to see what it was like, or for any one of several reasons, including fun, so she wasn't going to sign away her right to do so. Then she said that she didn't think it was anyone's business except her own what she ate and drank, and she hadn't made up her mind yet about alcohol. She could be a teetotaller all her life, she thought, if she finally decided that that was what she wanted to be, under her own steam and without the need or help of any written pledge. So there was no real need of her signing at all. Then she stopped saying anything at all, because the whole crew ganged up and went to work on her, using appeals, threats, and dire prophecy.

That's why she stopped talking. If she'd opened her mouth at all, sobs would have been torn from her, and that would have been too humiliating to be borne. Perhaps one of the reasons she and I made such a Thing of never crying was that normally we cried very easily. We had tender hearts where others were concerned and were self-conscious enough to be easily hurt on our own accounts. We acted as barometers for our school classes, I later learned. Each teacher passed on word to the next that the Dickinson face was the face to watch. If it began looking long, it was time to change the subject to something more cheerful. So if we hadn't really worked on never crying, we'd have been dripping all over the place about half the time.

On this occasion Alice didn't cry. She just sat in dumb, hopeless misery. The finger of scorn was pointed, and the rest of us were encouraged to treat her as a moral leper: Bad Alice Dickinson, the Wicked Girl who refused to sign the Pledge! Our parents were brought into the affray, so that the pressure went on for twenty-four hours a day, at home and at school, and her life must have been one unrelieved Hades. The whole thing was a stupid and barbaric performance, out of which only shamed, discredited Alice emerged with dignity and integrity intact.

My position was typical of the positions in which I often found—and find—myself. I suffered with her, but I'd tied my own hands. I wished passionately that I too had had the sense and guts to hold out, so there'd be one person in all the world on her side. But without thought, like a silly sheep, I'd trailed impulsively along with the flock, leaving my poor

little sister to fight the pack alone. I longed to cut off the
offending hand that had traitorously signed the Pledge.

Alice never did sign.

Without creating any difference between us, our mother
did attempt a distinction. She decided at an early stage of the
game, arbitrarily and without consulting us—we were too
young at that point to have an opinion, anyhow—that pink
was Louise's Color and blue was Alice's Color: pale pink
and baby blue. We wore, respectively, pink and blue bows
in our hair, had pink and blue ribbon run in the tops of our
slips, and sported pink or blue printed cotton or flannelette
nightgowns, depending on the season of the year. (Little
ladies wouldn't be caught at a dogfight in pajamas, once
they'd outgrown the Dr. Denton Sleeper stage. Unwomanly!)
My handkerchiefs sometimes had chaste little pink rosebuds
embroidered on them—nothing flamboyant, you understand—
and Alice's had forget-me-nots. My celluloid comb and brush
were pink and Alice's were blue; my bread-and-milk set (a
plate, bowl, and small pitcher) was pink-flowered and hers was
blue-flowered; I had some pink beads and she had some blue
beads; I had a pink sash on my best white Children's Sunday
dress, and she had a blue one; my facecloth was pink and hers
was blue. All our relatives had long since been given the
Word and had fallen docilely into line, so that Aunt Linnie
gave us the pink and blue enameled pins, Aunt Maud gave us
pink and blue felt slippers, Aunt Carrie gave us pink and
blue sachet bags to put among our underwear, and Aunt
Alice, who had married well and taken the Grand Tour,
brought us real French dolls from Paris with pink and blue
outfits, including pink (or blue) kid shoes and little straw
hats banded in pink (or blue).

If, when we went into a store with our mother, she saw
a baby blue silk dress on a form, she'd exclaim, "Oh, look!
Alice's Color! Some day when you're older—" Or if I showed
interest in a green or red kimono—this was before the day of
housecoats; this was the day when a lady confined the wearing of negligee (pronounced by us as nee-*gligg*-ee, with all the
g's hard) to her bed- and bathrooms, and didn't appear down-

stairs until she was fully clothed for the street, or else she was no lady— If, then, I showed interest in a green kimono, my mother would say in the final, flat tone of one stating a proved scientific fact, "But *pink* is Your Color." And if I got any kimono at all, it was a pink one, you can safely bet.

We *hated* pink and baby blue. We thought they were stupid, insipid, wishy-washy, spineless colors. We liked red and orange and clear yellow and all the deeper shades of green, and the blue-purple of wild grapes, all considered most unsuitable for little girls, who must wear darned old *dainty* colors. We liked colors to be bold and determined, and we also liked queer shades that we mixed up out of our water-color boxes, off-tones that would be called decorator colors nowadays, I suppose. We'd try to duplicate the green-gray of bayberries, or the fire-hearted black of a dahlia. Most of the time these experiments resulted in muddy splotches, but once in a great while we'd turn out a sample that was just exactly what we had in mind for the coats we were going to buy for ourselves the minute we were grown up. Pink and blue indeed! We were *never* going to wear them in our lives again, after we started buying our own clothes.

Why didn't we rebel? That's a good question, and easily answered. We didn't rebel because it wouldn't have done any good. Adults, especially parents and teachers, were absolutely powerful and always right. When a ukase went forth, there was no argument and no possible appeal. If we didn't see eye to eye with them on some of their pronouncements, that just proved that we were the victims of wrong thinking, or that we were deliberately being ornery, or that it was Our Age and we'd view things differently when we were Older. We doubted that, but we knew better than to say so. That would have been Saucy, and foremost on the list of crimes a child could commit came Sauciness or impertinence, and Answering Back. All we could do was to seem to agree, perform a token observance of whatever the dictate might be, and go about gaining our own ends by devious methods.

This sounds a lot more grim and discouraging than it was. Actually it was interesting and often exciting to put over a *coup* on the race of grown-ups—because they were a separate race. They certainly weren't friends. Parents and teachers didn't very often try to be pals with the young in those days, which was all to the good, since on the few occasions when one did, the result was painfully embarrassing all around. Our minds were incapable of functioning as theirs did, and if they'd ever had young ideas, it had been so long ago that they'd lost all recollection of them. We were polite about their misguided efforts, but we did wish they'd stop acting silly and go away. Adults weren't exactly enemies, either, although their aims and interests were often in direct opposition to ours—when our paths crossed, which was no oftener than we could help. They were a breed of people; that we would concede them; but people of such different standards and opinions and tastes and habits than ours that they might just as well have been a race from the Antipodes.

I remember well the first time we ever successfully, with deliberate intent, deceived our mother in a matter that we considered mutually important. It was such a world-shaking event that it's engraved forever on the tablets of my mind. The incident itself was trivial, but the implications were tremendous, indicating as they did that she was not after all infallible, and that therefore the other adults in our lives were probably equally liable to error. We must have been way up in the fifth and sixth grades, because our mother had left us alone at home, a thing she never did when we were small, while she worked at the *Independent* office. She had, however, left us a chore to be completed before she came home.

This chore consisted of the setting out of two dozen tomato plants from flats into the vegetable garden. We were old hands at setting out seedlings. Not only had we spent countless hours of our lives working in our father's various gardens, but we'd always, ever since we could remember, had small garden plots of our own, in which we could plant whatever we wanted to and use whatever methods of cultivation we fancied. We enjoyed gardening, and we were pretty good gardeners, since there is nothing like a garden of your very own to arouse interest and perfect technique. So we had the transplanting routine down pat. You dug the correct number of holes, correctly spaced and sized, in the designated section of the garden. You put fertilizer into the holes, filled them with water, let it sink into the earth a little, and then removed the plants individually from the flats, using an old kitchen knife and a small trowel and taking great care to disturb the root systems as little as possible and to keep as much soil as was feasible balled around them. This ball you placed tenderly in the hole, pressed the earth gently down all around the stem to eliminate the chance of air pockets in contact with the roots, filled the hole with dry earth, and then poured more water on to settle it. We could have done it blindfolded, working smoothly as a team—one of us digging and the other following after pouring water—in order to get the chore over quickly so we'd have that much more time for something that didn't come under the heading of work.

We had all the paraphernalia assembled—plants, knife, trowel, fertilizer, and bucket of water—except for a small receptacle for dipping the water from the bucket into the holes. I said I'd go get one, and did, plucking an aluminum cup off a shelf in the pantry instead of going down cellar and looking for a soup can, as I should have done. I was trying to save time and energy. We whipped through the transplanting in record time, and then we discovered the horrid truth. The cup I'd so light-heartedly snatched from the pantry was our mother's bacon fat cup, into which she poured the bacon drippings for storage against the time when she'd need them for frying potatoes or pancakes. Apparently she'd just started a new collection, so there was only about an inch in the bottom of the cup. That was why we hadn't noticed until it was too late and the hard surface of the solidified grease was thickly coated with rich, black sediment.

We looked at each other fearfully. "Ma's going to be mad," Alice announced unnecessarily. I knew Ma was going to be mad. She claimed she couldn't keep house without bacon fat and hoarded it, drop by drop. Probably right this minute her head was full of plans for this ruined third-of-a-cupful. Mad? She was going to be furious.

"Maybe we can scrape the mud off," I suggested without much hope. That sounded too easy to be workable.

However, we discovered that the deposit was only surface deep, so that it was a simple matter to remove it with a teaspoon. Our spirits perked up until we gave the result of our endeavours a really critical survey. Even the dimmest wit— and our mother's definitely was not that—would have grasped that something untoward had happened to the bacon fat. It looked as though a woodchuck had been burrowing in it.

Alice hit upon the solution. The fat had been hot when it was originally poured into the cup. Therefore if we dug it out, melted it, washed the cup, poured it back in, and chilled it in the icebox— Naturally the idea worked perfectly, as any fool should have known it would, even we, if we hadn't been so unnerved by the whole business. The only flaw was a slight lowering of the tide-mark, due to loss in scraping and transferring from dish to dish, which we hoped would escape our mother's notice. With scrupulous care, we scoured and put away all the implements used in the operation, returned the cup—surface of the fat now virgin and unsullied—to the exact spot on which I'd found it, and resigned ourselves to waiting for the ax to fall.

It never did fall. We couldn't believe our good luck and stole about with bated breath, carefully avoiding any reference to bacon, frying, or even pigs, for fear of nudging any dormant suspicion in our mother's mind into wakefulness. When the fact that we'd really got away with it finally penetrated, we held a meeting of mutual congratulation in the raspberry thicket outside the henyard. You'd have thought we'd discovered the secret of the Rosetta Stone, so great was our elation. And in a sense, I suppose we had. We'd discovered a truth that governed a certain percent of our future conduct: the amazing fact that adults could be gulled and misled. The discovery opened before us limitless and thrilling vistas.

Not that we used this piece of intelligence as a springboard from which to plunge into a life of crime. Far from it. I'm a little awed, looking back, to realize what really good, innocent little girls we were. This was partly because we were a product of the times. All children grew up more slowly then, and all harbored a healthy respect for authority which acted as a deterrent to true juvenile delinquency as the term is understood today. In my grade throughout the grammar school there were two Bad Boys, so-called, who were the bane of our successive teachers' lives. Breathless with delicious horror, we co-graders of Clarence and Sam would report at recess time to the kids of the other grades their most recent heinous offences. Once I held a circle spellbound with an account of an incident in which Clarence had outdone himself in iniquity. (I sat next to him, as we both, being large for our ages, occupied the larger back seats.) This time he'd really done it. When Miss Bennett told him to come to the front of the room, he'd risen with aggravating slowness and he'd muttered something under his breath. Even I couldn't hear what he said, and when Miss Bennett, her voice firm and chilling, asked him to repeat his remark, he'd refused to do so. That was the extent of his wrongdoing, but we felt toward him the revulsion of good citizens against a full-fledged Baby-face Nelson. *What* was going to happen to Clarence? we asked each other fearfully.

Plenty happened to him, and he emerged from the ordeal a subdued and much more courteous boy. Miss Bennett didn't waste any time trying to understand him and his problems. I don't know what she did to him, really; but whatever it was, it worked. This just gives you an idea of Crime and Punishment in the olden days. It's possible that fear is not the best agent of control, but it certainly was an effective one.

But other agents were at work upon my sister and me, to keep us within the limits of creditable and decorous behavior. For one thing, we were painfully shy. It was really agonizing for us to meet strangers, how agonizing only those who are victims of shyness can know. I have never fainted in my life, but the nearest I've ever come to it was when I was about five and unwittingly entered a room in which my mother was entertaining a member of the Sewing Circle whom I didn't know. She was a perfectly pleasant, nice woman, but upon seeing that strange face so unexpectedly, I felt the floor sway, the walls whirled around me, and my ears roared. It was a terrible feeling which I have not forgotten yet. Thereafter for a long time I hid if I thought there was any danger of encountering callers, climbing a tree or crawling under the porch and turning a deaf ear to all summons.

Alice was as shy as I, and this shyness extended to those of our own age. We made friends slowly, when we were very young, partly because we didn't need friends, having each other, and partly because we were convinced for some reason that everyone else knew a great deal more than we did about everything in the world, and that our simplicity and ignorance would be exposed almost immediately, and everyone would laugh at us. Like most primitives, including dogs, we didn't like to be laughed at, so we were chary of putting ourselves into a position where it might happen.

On top of that—as if that weren't enough—we were the worst cases of retarded development as far as maturing emotionally went that I have ever heard of. Talk about standing with reluctant feet where the brook and river meet! We didn't even know there was a river. Sex wasn't a closed book to us. It just wasn't, period. We'd never even glimpsed the cover of the book. Boys to us were simply more fortunate children who were allowed for some reason we couldn't fathom to wear sensible clothes which gave them an unfair advantage in climbing trees or leaping brooks. We envied boys like mad, but we didn't roll our eyes at them. They never got a giggle or a falsetto shriek out of *us,* no matter how the other little girls of our circle might respond to show-off performances on fence tops or to being honored by some youthful Lothario's threat to put angleworms down their necks or wash their faces with snow. We were pretty handy with angleworms and snow ourselves, if it came to that. Understandably, our unawakened—I believe that is the accepted polite word—attitude didn't make us the belles of any balls.

Once we were invited to a birthday party given by a little

girl in my grade, and our mother said we had to go. She said, quite rightly, that we'd got to learn to get along with people; that Mrs. Henry would be very much hurt and affronted if we refused to go to Lettie's party on the bald grounds that we plain didn't want to; that soon people would stop asking us to parties (which was all right with us); that then we'd be sorry (which we doubted); and that we'd have a good time after we got there, wait and see—which we were very sure would not be the case. We'd been to parties before.

We'd been to parties before, and we hadn't had a good time at all. There'd been a lot of noise and confusion, and everybody had acted unlike themselves, silly and unnatural. Almost all the girls had new, fussy dresses, while we were wearing our last year's Sunday Best, designed with an eye more on the practical future, when they would be demoted to Everyday, than on the festive present. Then there were games at which we were inept. When our numbers were called in Spin-the-Cover, we were so overcome with confusion at being cynosures that we always fumbled, we never were able to pin the tail anywhere near the right end of the donkey, and in Musical Chairs we were always the first to be eliminated, shoved roughly aside by more experienced and less diffident party-goers to stand awkwardly against the wall while the party eddied hilariously around us. And recently there had been a new development at parties which both puzzled and embarrassed us, something called Post Office, the object of which seemed to be to kiss or be kissed by—we weren't quite sure which—A Boy. The capitals are intentional. When Post Office was proposed, at a certain inevitable juncture of the party, the atmosphere immediately became coy, and boys automatically assumed upper-case status.

Ours was not a kissing family under any circumstances. We never kissed our relatives, even when we hadn't seen them for months; and while I had never participated in a deathbed scene, I'd imagined plenty of them in which I, the prospective corpse, Passed sweetly On, forgiving a grieving family and making them sorry they'd not been nicer to me. Tears and remorse figured prominently in these scenes, but never kisses. Therefore it didn't make sense to vie for the dubious privilege of exchanging kisses with some little boy, slicked up though he might be for the party, to whom we wouldn't give the time of day under ordinary conditions. We just couldn't understand some of the other little girls, girls whom we thought we knew well but who turned out to be changelings, whose laughter became shriller and shriller and whose cheeks became redder and redder as they were summoned again and again to the coat closet off the front hall to pay their forfeit to the stupid oaf—now transmogrified into A Boy—who was repeating the sixth grade and still getting the worst report cards in the room. It passed comprehension, and we had been known to wash our hands of the whole business, pick up any book that happened to be lying around loose, and retire to a quiet corner to read. I guess that it isn't surprising that we weren't greater successes at parties.

On this occasion our mother laid it down flatly that we had to go. Perhaps if we'd told her about Post Office, she'd have changed her mind; but Post Office didn't seem, somehow, to be a subject fit for her ears. The situation called for desperate measures, which we were prepared to employ, and for finesse, which we'd at least attempt. We talked it over in whispers after we'd gone to bed and agreed that we'd have to pretend to be willing and even anxious to attend the party. It was three days away, and two of them we'd spend praying for the Henry house to catch on fire—not a big fire, we carefully specified. We didn't want anyone burned to death, and we'd ask the Lord to hold property destruction down to a minimum: just enough smoke and water damage so that Mrs. Henry wouldn't feel up to a party on Saturday. If our prayers weren't answered by Friday noon, then we'd have to resort to Plan B.

Plan B wasn't, from our point of view, as satisfactory as Plan A, but we agreed that it would serve in a pinch. It simply required that we should become extremely, and genuinely, ill. Pretense wouldn't work. Our mother was uncanny when it came to detecting malingering. We knew, because we'd tried it. We'd have to produce real symptoms of a convincing and dramatic nature, such as throwing up, a widespread rash, blind staggers, diarrhea, and/or a temperature. It would be safest to have all these manifestations of lack of physical wellbeing, we decided, but we thought that probably a combination of any two or three might, with luck, turn the trick. The weakness of the plan lay in the fact that we'd be wasting a perfectly good Saturday, since if we were all that sick, our mother certainly wouldn't let us out of the house. But the day was destined to be a total loss anyhow, the way things stood, and staying home suffering was preferable to suffering publicly.

All that remained to be decided was ways and means, and this was no problem at all, since the season of the year was early fall and in our favor. Poison ivy, to which we were both highly allergic, flourished on the wall around the Unitarian cemetery, near enough the school building so that we might reasonably run afoul of it by accident. The Concord grapevine on our own back porch was loaded with grapes, purple enough to make eating them a conceivable—if not very probable after the first puckering taste—error. Scouting around the neighborhood, we found that the apples on Miss Bowman's tree, unlike our earlier variety, were good and hard and green, practical guarantees of *cholera morbus*, which was what our teachers called what my grandmother called the green apple quick-step. We were all set, in case our prayers went unanswered. We even had extra insurance in the form of a quart jar full of water super-saturated with salt. Alice had been reading about some men adrift in a boat, who had been forced to drink sea water, and in the story it made them very ill. Of course, it had also driven them mad, which we didn't consider necessary to our plot, really, although we were prepared to take that chance if all else failed. We figured that a pint apiece wouldn't make us very crazy, and a touch of light delirium might round out an otherwise imperfect picture of two pitiful invalids.

The town fire alarm hadn't sounded by noon on Friday, but we gave the Lord a good forty-five minutes to reconsider. He might be behindhand with His work, we thought, and

anyhow we couldn't conveniently get down to the Unitarian
wall until it was time to return to school from lunch. Since
our aim was an all-over rash, we put ivy leaves down our
necks as well as rubbing them on all exposed surfaces. After
school we hurried home and began systematically gorging
ourselves with green apples and green grapes. We must have
eaten a peck of the things. At least, between midnight and
dawn we'd regurgitated that amount or more. Plan B was a
honey, all right. We even ran real temperatures, and the
blind staggers, which we'd agreed we could safely fake if
necessary, were an actual fact. It's a little difficult, when you
are hollow and weak with the strain of throwing up your
boot heels and your eyes are swollen shut with ivy poisoning,
to walk a straight line firmly.

We didn't go to the party. We didn't go anywhere for a
week. We considered, even in our lowest moments when life
seemed to be ebbing fast away, that the reward was worth
the sacrifice. That's how unsociable we were.

Our ruling passion was books. I can remember well the
day I discovered that I could read. Up to that time, our
parents had read to us. It didn't make any difference what
they read. If our father was reading to himself, he just went
on from wherever he was, aloud. We probably didn't understand a tenth of what was read to us, but some of it stuck,
and we liked to be read to anyhow. We'd sit as still as mice
while the reader's voice went on and on, giving us glimpses
of a fabulous world outside our experience. What we didn't
understand we asked about, and if the explanation didn't
clear matters up, we pretended that it did, so that the reading would go on.

There was among the books in the parlor a paper-covered
pamphlet with a cover-picture of a man in old-fashioned
dress standing erect and brandishing a sword. The picture
intrigued us. The man was romantically handsome and dashing, and we wanted to know who he was and what he thought
he was doing. So we bedeviled our father to read us the story,
and finally, one Sunday evening, he found time to start it.
It was a brief history of the town of Hadley, Massachusetts,

up around where we came from, and after a little preliminary bandying about of names and dates, got to the heart of the matter, as far as we were concerned—the story of the man on the cover.

It seemed that two men, named Whalley and Goffe, had taken refuge in Hadley—this was way back before the Revolution—from the officers of the King of England, Charles the Second. Charles was after their hides because they'd been members of the court which sentenced his father, Charles the First, to death. They'd fled to Boston, then to Connecticut, and finally to Hadley, where a minister had hidden them in his cellar for fifteen years. (Here Alice's and my faces started lengthening. Those poor men, cooped up in a cellar all that time! Our father hastily assured us that probably they went out and walked around the countryside at night, looking at the stars and swimming in the river. We felt better, and he went on reading.) One day Indians attacked Hadley, and things looked pretty bad for the settlers, surprised and disorganized. But at the crucial point of the battle a strange man suddenly appeared from nowhere, rallied the white forces to beat off the Indians, and saved the day. It was—

At this point it was seven o'clock and our bedtime, so the book was closed with finality. Our father said he'd finish the story the next evening.

We went to bed and conferred in whispers about the identity of the hero. We were sure that it must be one of the men from the Reverend Russell's cellar, but we wanted the book to tell us so beyond doubt. We wouldn't be satisfied until we'd heard it hot from the printed page. The next day I took the pamphlet and turned the leaves, trying by sheer force of wanting to wring from them their secret. It was maddening. The information was there in my hands, but I couldn't get at it. The print on the paper told what I wanted to know, but I couldn't read it. I have never felt so frustrated since in my life.

Then suddenly a word leaped from the page and hit me between the eyes, a stunning blow. It was *regicide,* a word that our father had explained to us the night before. Don't ask me how I knew that those symbols spelled regicide. It sounds unlikely, but it's true. That's what they said, as plainly as though someone had shouted it in my ear. *I could read!* It was the most stirring and revolutionary thing that ever happened to me.

After that, I read all the time. Oh, probably it wasn't as quick as all that, but it seems so now. I was reading quite well when my classmates were still struggling with c-a-t cat, not because I was smarter than they, but simply because I was possessed to read, I guess, and found it the most fascinating occupation in the world. I still do.

Oh, yes. The man who saved Hadley did come out of the cellar, just as we'd suspected. It was the regicide Goffe, and he was known thereafter as The Angel of Hadley. Alice and I used to play Angel of Hadley a lot, taking turns being Goffe, and striding out of the cellar brandishing a wooden sword. Whichever one of us was not being Goffe played the role of Hadley citizens, and the flock of bewildered hens had to serve as extras representing an Indian war party. We considered this excellent casting, since they had feathers, made a lot of noise, and fled obligingly before the Angel-inspired counterattack.

We had a lot of games that we played together, and a great many of them were based on our reading. One of the best was Robinson Crusoe, but we couldn't play this very often, since we'd laid down some binding rules in connection with it. There was no reason why we had to abide by these rules or, if it comes to that, no particular sense to the rules in the first place. But the young have a deep seated craving for order, and the observance of rules provides it, especially if they are rules of your own making.

According to the rules, we could play Robinson Crusoe only on No-school days. A No-school day was not a Saturday or Sunday or vacation day, but a day upon which, because of inclement weather, regularly scheduled school didn't keep. This blessing occurred seldom, since the school authorities held that New England children were constructed to withstand New England weather, and any who hadn't learned to do so yet had better start learning at once. There were no school buses then to skid on icy roads, since the schools were not centralized, and a little walk in the rain or snow from home to the nearest schoolhouse certainly wasn't going to hurt anybody. So only in the very foulest and most brutal weather, when the thermometer stood well below freezing, the wind was blowing a cutting gale, and you couldn't see your hand before your face in the driven snow, did the village fire alarm sound the four groups of two signals each at eight A.M. sharp to indicate that, oh bliss unalloyed! nobody had to go to school.

Alice and I would cheer wildly upon these rare occasions, change quickly out of our good school clothes into our old play clothes, and set about planning what to do with the long, lovely unexpected day ahead of us. We'd read, we'd pop corn, we'd make entire new wardrobes for our paper dolls, we'd blow soap bubbles, we'd teach the cat to jump through a hoop, we'd paint pictures, we'd have a tea-party for our dolls, and, of course, we'd play Robinson Crusoe.

Our mother wasn't particularly enthusiastic about this game, and I don't blame her, since it left the house a shambles. Naturally we had to have a cave for Robinson to live in, and we constructed one by moving chairs from all over into proper juxtaposition with the dining-room table and draping this framework with blankets stripped from various beds. Then we crouched inside, in the roles of Robinson and Friday, sallying forth only to kill game for the pot or to repel cannibals. Our mother and the cat were elected to play these bit parts, and I must say that our mother was a great deal more co-operative than the cat was. Very soon he'd either hide somewhere in the house or start frantically wanting out. She bore up pretty well, although it must have been fairly disconcerting not to know when a pot shot was going to be taken at her as she tried to get through her housework, or when she was going to fall into one of the traps we'd rigged up.

We liked it in our little cave under the table. We felt secure there. And we felt fearfully gypped if it cleared off and the sun came out before bedtime. Here we were all set for an exciting day of storm and peril, and phhtt! things flattened out and we had to emerge from our private world into everyday life. It threw time out of joint. It was much better to go to sleep to the sound of the wind still throwing sleet against the windows as it had been doing when we awoke. It rounded the day off properly as an integrated unit. Then if it cleared in the night—well, that was all right. Tomorrow was another day, no matter how you looked at it, and could reasonably be expected to have a different kind of weather.

It wasn't in our own minds only that Alice and I were as inseparable as the two halves of an apple. Everybody always spoke of us, and probably thought of us, as linked—the Dickinson sisters, or Louisenalice Dickinson. This started when we were very young indeed, in the first and third grades, before Alice gained a year on me scholastically. There weren't any movies in Bridgewater at that time, or any other form of commercialized entertainment, except for a week in summer, when Chatauqua came. So it was the heyday of the amateur production, the home talent minstrel show, the stereopticon lecture, and selected readings from the Classics. Bridgewater was counted more fortunate than some of the surrounding towns, because we had the Normal School to spark us culturally and give us what were known as Opportunities. The year I was in the third grade, the head of the Normal School Art Department dreamed up a super-opportunity, a real treat, uplifting, educational, and artistic. She proposed to present to the public an evening of tableaux which would differ in more than name from the living pictures sometimes offered by other groups, such as churches and fraternal organizations. She was going to take her subjects from the Masters. None of this calendar-art or magazine-cover prettiness for her! She was going straight to the mouths of accredited and revered horses for her material.

Some of her models she drew from the student body of the Normal School itself. When she needed older subjects, she drafted them from among the faculty members and their families. But she got stuck on one of her proposed items, so she came talent-scouting down to the grade school that we attended, the so-called Model School run in conjunction with the Normal School for the training of would-be teachers.

Alice and I hadn't heard any rumor of what was afoot in the higher echelons, naturally, and the first inkling we had of the matter was when a lady in Grecian robes—the Art Supervisor at that time was an arty type—came into our respective classrooms, conferred with Miss Stuart and Miss Turner, and dragged us out into the primary grades' cloak-room. She stood us up against a background of winter wraps and stepped back to eye us in a thoughtful and what seemed to us sinister manner. We were scared stiff, a fact which helped us to maintain the rigid poses she seemed to desire. We couldn't think offhand of any recent crimes we'd committed, but with grown-ups you never could be sure. However, she finally smiled and nodded, handed us a bundle, a picture, and a note, and told us to take them home to our mother. We'd been tapped for the Tableaux.

I can't remember the name of the picture we were to portray, but it must have been a Gainsborough. I'm basing this conclusion on the style of the dresses our mother made for us out of the cloth in the bundle—white cheesecloth cut in long, flowing folds—and on the color of the wide sashes, a sort of deep robin's-egg blue characteristic of Gainsborough. Our mother made the dresses in faithful copy of the picture the lady had sent with the note, and rehearsed us in our poses. We were supposed to be Somebody-or-other's titled children, sitting quietly and nicely, and gazing into each other's eyes, although we learned to look at each other's foreheads instead, since eye-meeting brought on the giggles, to which we were prone. I think one of us was supposed to be a little boy, because there was a certain amount of loose talk about hair-cropping on the part of the Art Supervisor, quickly squelched by our mother. She was glad to co-operate up to a point, but that point didn't include having either of her daughters shorn of woman's crowning glory, even if that glory was of admittedly unarresting quality and quantity.

In addition to the home posings, we were frequently cut
out of the first and third grade herds during school hours to
go up to the Normal School Assembly Hall for further practice under the eye of the Art Department, a distinction to
which I attribute my present-day inability to balance my
checkbook, since these sessions always seemed to take place
during Arithmetic. By the time The Night arrived, we were
so perfect in our parts that if we came within twenty feet of
each other, we automatically fell into a Gainsborough and
held it with a kind of cataleptic ecstasy.

Do you know, the Tableaux were a great success and, believe it or not, the little Dickinson girls were acclaimed as
being especially good? The set-up was simple. The center
of the stage was occupied by a large and ornate gilt frame,
flanked by flats, floodlighted from within, and covered by a
red velvet curtain. While the models were being arranged
behind this curtain, the Art Supervisor or one of the Normals
delivered a short lecture on the artist and the painting to be
shown. Then the curtain was swept grandly aside, and the
tableaux was revealed in all its splendor. We were somewhere along toward the end of the program, so we were all
braced to receive the clapping that approved each revelation,
swelling in a rather terrifying manner when a favorite like
the Blue Boy or Whistler's Mother was on stage. We weren't
prepared, however, for the additional *oh's* and *ah's* that
floated up on a great wave of applause to greet us, and it
almost threw us. I could feel tears pricking my lids and could
see the distressed red creeping up Alice's face. In one more
minute—

The curtain swished back into place before we could dis-
grace ourselves; and then, just as we were getting our control
back, the Art Supervisor, flushed with lady-like success, told
us we'd have to do it again. The people wouldn't stop clapping unless we did, she said, and added that we should be
very pleased and proud. We were the only ones so far to get
an encore. We looked at each other, and I could see the same
gleam that I felt in my own eye developing in Alice's. We
were tasting blood, and it tasted surprisingly good. We fell

into our poses, gazing at each other like a couple of dying swans and so carried away with exhibitionistic fervor that we didn't even feel like giggling. The short remainder of the evening we spent with jealous ears bent on the applause; but nobody else got an encore, although there was a ticklish minute there in connection with Lady Hamilton, who we had to admit was looking very handsome and unlike her everyday self.

There was some discussion of a repeat performance, but it's just as well that it came to nothing. We'd have been spoiled rotten if we'd gone through that again. Even as it was, we showed a regrettable tendency to preen ourselves when people said, "Oh, you're the little Dickinson girls! Wasn't it *hard* to hold those positions so long?" But in time the Tableaux passed into history, and we reverted to normal. We were bracketed forever, though, much more conclusively than would have been accounted for by mere natural blood ties.

When I was about thirteen and Alice eleven, our mother had to have a mastoid operation. She'd never been ill before in our lives—or if she had, she'd never admitted it and certainly never spent even part of a day in bed since Alice was born—so this was a true domestic cataclysm. If our mother was sick enough to Give In, she was pretty sick, and we realized the fact. We felt lost and frightened, and we didn't know what was going to become of us.

Our father sat us down and explained to us that our mother must go to the hospital for two weeks or so, and asked us if we thought we were capable of running the house during her absence. He said that although he realized we were pretty young, he personally thought we were up to the job; but if we had any doubts about it, he'd try to get a woman to come in by the day. He told us that nobody would blame us if we refused to take on this responsibility, since no one would ordinarily expect girls of our age to assume it; but one of the things about being a Dickinson was that Dickinsons always expected more of themselves and each other than they did of other people or than other people expected of them. (We could have told him a few things about that, too. Our

teachers were always shaking their heads at us sadly and saying that they'd expected better of a Dickinson; but we were
too crushed by the immediate tragedy to rake up old, minor
grievances right then.) Our father was wise in shoving this
problem on to us, since it took our minds off our troubles by
giving us something to think about and do, and the upshot
was that we accepted the proposition. Possibly it was indeed
the Dickinson in us coming out, but I'm afraid we regarded
it as much as an opportunity as an obligation.

Our poor father! It was lucky for him that he was naturally indifferent to the creature comforts, being more interested in and preoccupied with ideas and principles and other
matters of the mind and spirit than with the mechanics of
daily living. Even so, he'd never have weathered our regime
either mentally or physically if he hadn't had the disposition
of a saint and the constitution of an ox. Our housekeeping
wasn't as bad as you might expect of eleven-and-thirteen-year-
olders, since we'd been trained in our mother's school, which
held to some fairly strict tenets. Dishes were *never* left to
soak in the sink, for example, but washed immediately after
every meal, and dishwashing included scouring the bottoms
of all pans, emptying the garbage, rinsing out the dishtowels,
cleaning the sink, properly storing the leftovers, and sweeping the kitchen floor. Beds were *always* thrown open to air
as soon as you arose, according to our mother's precepts, and
made up neatly right after breakfast. At the same time, the
bedrooms were tidied, so that you didn't have to be embarrassed by the most persnickety caller after nine o'clock at the
latest. The carpet sweeper and dry mop were run around
daily, and the place subjected to a really thorough cleaning
once a week.

That's the way we'd been brought up, and that's the way
we continued, chiefly, I guess, because we didn't know any
other way of doing things. We weren't anywhere nearly as
competent and efficient as our mother, of course, since we had
a way of skimping on the dusting because we didn't like to
dust, and a slightly careless disregard of corners and places

that didn't show; but the condition of the house didn't deteriorate too much under our attentions.

It was in the culinary department that we went hog-wild. Like most beginners in any field, we found first principles boring and were inspired to ambitious experiments way beyond our skill and experience. For instance, we didn't see why you always had to eat cucumbers, which the garden was producing by the peck, raw. So we served them stuffed and baked, or rolled in crumbs and fried in bacon fat. Our father ate them uncomplainingly, just as he ate the boiled lettuce—if spinach and chard made good greens, why not lettuce?—and the elaborate Jello dessert that didn't turn out as pretty as the picture in the magazine, and the hot potato salad that we assured him was a German dish, but that really was the consequence of our having forgotten to cook the potatoes in time for them to cool. The hens were laying well, so we ignored the one-or-two-egg cakes that we knew how to make and tried fancy eight-egg cakes that we didn't. They were supposed to cut to look like checkerboards or pinwheels, but somehow they never turned out that way. Moreover, they always slumped badly in the middle, probably because we kept opening and closing the oven door to see how they were coming along.

This didn't daunt us at all. We'd fill the depression with two inches of frosting, so that, until it was cut, the cake looked like a caterer's dream. Our father would obligingly eat a piece and then say that he didn't have much of a sweet tooth, so why didn't Alice and I finish it up between us. We were willing, and what's more surprising, able. Then we'd several times run across scenes in books where the high-life characters fortified themselves between ordeals with a cold bird and a bottle, and this seemed to us to be the very last word in elegance. So when our father brought in the inevitable chicken, plucked and dressed for Sunday dinner, we boiled it, chilled it, and served it with potato chips and bottles of homemade root beer which we'd hastily concocted on Saturday afternoon, using twice the correct amount of extract so that it would get done fast. It was a very terrible meal, but our father ate it.

Once in a while even we got discouraged with our flights of fancy, and allowed the pendulum to swing to the other extreme of Spartan simplicity. We'd have hamburg and plain boiled potatoes three days in a row, with sliced bananas and store cookies for dessert. At that, such a meal was probably a relief to our poor father. At least he had a sporting chance of living to greet the rising sun, a thing most people wouldn't have cared to bet on after some of our collations. So unswerving was his loyalty that he told not only the neighbors, whose business it wasn't, but also our mother, whose business it was, what marvelous cooks we were. It's a wonder the words didn't choke him; or maybe not, at that. Anybody who could eat our food was pretty unchokable, and that's no idle jest. Anyhow, that piece of misinformation, coupled with our mother's praise of us as immaculate housekeepers—we'd really polished up the place on the day we expected her home—gave us a widespread reputation for being Reliable Types; and that led to our first paid job.

The town, it seemed, had allocated a sum of money to be used for cleaning and refurbishing the Public Library. The two librarians, Miss Lucia Christian (Adults) and Miss Rachel Crocker (Children), considered it essential that in addition to the necessary painting and floor finishing, every book in the place should be taken down and dusted.

In those days the shelves were closed to the public. If you wanted a book, you told the librarian about it, and she went and got it for you, while you waited outside the carved wooden fence that separated the sheep from the goats. The shelves came very decidedly under the category of Sacred Ground, available only to the librarians or their duly empowered agents and assistants and jealously guarded from unlawful hands and eyes. There was no random and casual browsing around by the goats, who, if they did nothing worse, could surely be counted upon to put the books back in the wrong places. Under this system some books weren't even touched, let alone read, from one year's end to the next. It wasn't very surprising or unnatural that during that time they collected quite a coating of dust. And who better could be found to cope with the situation than the little Dickinson girls, who in addition to being Reliable, were Readers and Respecters of Books, and who, moreover, could be expected because of their tender years to work for much less than a regular cleaning woman would?

We were paid, I think, five cents an hour, which seemed like the wealth of Croesus to us. By going in right after school, we could make a dime apiece before suppertime; and on Saturdays, when we worked in the morning as well as all afternoon, we sometimes amassed as much as thirty-five cents, a truly impressive sum. We liked the money all right, but after the first day or so, we'd have worked for nothing if we'd had to.

We never knew there were so many books in the world. We tried to be honest and conscientious, we tried not to peek, but turning us loose in a library was like turning an alcoholic loose in a wine cellar. We'd open a book with the innocent intention of seeing what it was about, that's all; and fifteen minutes later we'd rouse to find ourselves perched precariously on top of the ladder, or crouched uncomfortably on the floor before a low shelf, or standing like statues in an aisle, devouring page after breathtaking page. We'd slam the book shut and do half the next section at top speed, to make up for lost time. No matter what vows of abstinence we took, sooner or later we'd slip again; and we'd go home in much the same condition as one who has ill-advisedly mixed his drinks, our minds awhirl with a heady brew compounded of a few pages of Tom Paine, a little Pascal, a verse or two of Thomas Love Peacock (What a name!), and a dash of Pepys; or if we happened to be in the F's, a stout blend of Fielding, Franklin, Fitzgerald, and Freneau. It's no wonder that we haven't got really straightened out on some of them yet, especially since we had the bad habit of reading aloud to each other particularly choice gems. It wasn't unusual at all for us to carry home the impression that somewhere in the middle of *The Oregon Trail* was a poem which began, "The world is too much with us; late and soon."

Nevertheless, those five or six weeks of dusting books contributed more to our so-called education than sixteen years, more or less, of school attendance. They gave us, first, some slight comprehension of the vast and varied extent of recorded human knowledge and speculation; but that was the less important contribution. Up to that time, we had accepted, because it never occurred to us to do otherwise, the ready-made set of ideas and attitudes that had been presented to us both at school and at home. We thought that everybody held the same opinions that were handed to us. Now we discovered that such was not the case at all. There were actually some people who didn't think that the Revolution was justified, for example, or that the Patriots—whom we had been led to believe were the finest flower of all that was brave, courteous, kind, and disinterested—were any better than ordinary men, only smarter and luckier. We were shocked and exhilarated. Why, you could believe anything you wanted to! You didn't have to accept what anyone, even teachers, told you!

I suppose that at some time in everyone's life the moment comes when he discovers his own mind and the infinite pleasure of exploring it. I suppose that there is always someone at hand to share this greatest of adventures with you. In my case the occasion happened to be the book dusting and the companion, Alice; and because we were so closely in rapport and saw so much of each other, maybe we traveled faster and further than we would ordinarily have done. We went completely overboard and became iconoclasts of the first order, for a spell there. Eventually we settled down to a middle course of a reasonable skepticism that methodically investigated any new idea before accepting or rejecting it. But it certainly was wonderful while it lasted.

Naturally, we were filled with missionary zeal to impart our discovery of new worlds to others, and events played into our hands. We finally worked ourselves out of our dusting jobs. (And none too soon, I might add. If it had lasted much longer, so violent was our love affair with books, we'd have entirely given up living our own lives in favor of the vicarious living of bookworms. It was a very real danger which we escaped by the skin of our teeth.) But we left the hallowed precincts of the library with our reputations for reliability untarnished.

The following summer, Miss Christian and Miss Crocker were obliged for personal reasons to take their two weeks' vacations at the same time. Usually they took turns, one going away to relax while the other held the fort and kept an eye on the substitute librarian, whoever she might be. Faced with the necessity of leaving their sacred trust in untested hands, they thought of the little Dickinson girls, who although rather young for the posts, were fabulously Reliable. (Yes, honestly! I, too, find it hard to believe now.) So we were approached and snapped at the chance. We went into the library for a week or so to learn the ropes; and then Miss Christian and Miss Crocker took off, leaving us in charge. If they were troubled with misgivings, they were too tactful to say so. They knew we wouldn't use the library as a place of assignation, since it was well established that we had no use for Boys; they knew we understood the regular library procedure well enough for practical purposes; and probably they thought we couldn't do much damage anyhow in two short weeks.

That's where they underestimated us. Oh, we fulfilled our technical obligations meticulously, stamping dates on charge slips with a firm flourish, sending out overdue notices on the dot, keeping at bay those members of the public who thought this would be a good chance to prowl around in the stacks, frowning at anyone who raised his voice above the lawful whisper, collecting and recording fines with the impersonal severity of cops, and shelving books with a care bordering on fussiness. No one could find basis for complaint about us on any of those scores. It was in the less easily defined realm of the cultural that we went haywire.

We decided with the arrogance of which only the psychotic or the very young and immature are capable that we would give people not what they wanted to read, but what we thought they ought, for their own good, to have. We constituted ourselves into a sort of drumhead court to hand down quick, summary, and unalterable decisions on what was wrong with various individuals and what they'd better be given to read to correct their deficiencies. Miss Babson? She wants a nice little love story? She's much too silly already. It's time she stopped thinking about moonlight and roses. (Miss Babson was incredibly old, all of thirty; it was a wonder to us that she could still get around without a wheelchair.) Let's give her *Lives of the Great Philosophers*. Mrs. Hilton, that old calamity howler? She gets *Pollyanna*. That ought to straighten her out. The mathematics teacher at the Normal School? But it's his vacation! He *can't* want Bowditch's *Practical Navigator*. He's supposed to be resting his brains. Give him a good Jack London.

We had visions of completely revolutionizing the reading habits of the town, and through the medium of the printed page, bringing about a modern Utopia. We were sure that, given time, our reformation would work. Time, fortunately—since if we'd been granted it, we'd undoubtedly have reduced Miss Christian's cherished Circulation to Absolute Zero—was what we didn't have. At the end of the two weeks, we retired to private life, and our victims went thankfully back to their former reading habits. Deprived of our Mission, we moped around for a few days; but then something else came up to absorb our energies. That was one nice thing about being so very young: no matter what our failures might be, we were conscious of the fact that we were going to live forever to correct them.

4

Houses and Horses

THE FIRST HOUSE THAT WE LIVED IN IN BRIDGEWATER WAS A
two-family affair at 27 Spring Hill Avenue, and I don't remember a thing about moving into it. It seems to me that
one morning I was looking out the window of my grandfather Dickinson's study in the house on the hill in Huntington, watching a buggy drawn by a white horse crawl along
a road on the floor of the valley below, while behind me my
grandfather sat at a table with a red-checked cloth and read
Greek, and Alice slept soundly in a wicker baby-carriage at
his side; and that afternoon I was lying in bed in the ground-
floor bedroom of the house on Spring Hill Avenue. The
sun was streaming in the window through the leaves of the
cherry tree outside, making a restless pattern on the spread,
Alice was still asleep in the baby carriage just outside the
door, and I was crying. I was being punished for playing in
a big puddle that a summer shower had left in the street in
front of the house and getting my clothes all wet and muddy;
but that wasn't why I was crying.

I was crying because the man who lived upstairs—a man
named Ike Percival, who didn't go to work because he was
sick, although not sick enough to be in bed himself; I think
he must have had tuberculosis—kept walking past the window
on the path outside and looking in and making fun of me

in a voice perfectly audible to me, but not to my mother in another room. He'd taunt me, and then if he heard my mother's footsteps approaching, he'd dodge back and the window would be empty. This infuriated me, and I was crying from sheer rage. I didn't complain to my mother, because I was well aware that I had been a naughty girl and I didn't think she'd sympathize with me particularly.

Finally Ike Percival started making faces at me, in addition to jeering at me. I flew into a frenzy, leaped out of bed, and ran to the window with the fully formed intention of scratching out his eyes; but he laughed and drifted out of reach and sight, and I was left with my fury all bottled up inside of me. I looked about for a victim on which to vent my spleen, saw Alice in the wicker carriage, and darted out into the living room. I gave her a good sharp pinch on the thigh, and she woke up with a bellow of hurt surprise. My mother's footsteps came toward me, clean and clipped and rapid on the bare kitchen floor. I ran back into the bedroom before she could discover me, jumped into bed, and pulled the covers over my head.

That's all I remember about the move from Huntington to Bridgewater.

In fact, our whole tenancy of that house comes back to me only in a series of flashes, like the glimpses from the window of a train traveling at night through a strange country in a thunderstorm, when the landscape is seen briefly and brilliantly by the lightning, and the scenes are sharp and clear, but disconnected. We didn't live there very long, and I was only a little over two when we arrived and not yet four when we moved on. The house was large and pleasant, with a small barn or carriage house attached, left over from the days when everyone had a horse, and set in a big yard full of fruit trees. The old apple trees made wonderful climbing, but I wasn't supposed to climb them, because I might fall out of them. In a corner of the back yard was a boarded-over and abandoned well, grown round with myrtle, pennyroyal and violets, which I was warned never, *never* to go near, because I might fall into it. Neither was I supposed to go into the upper story of the barn, partly because that was the Percivals' domain, but mostly because I might fall out of the big door intended for use in storing hay, which Mrs. Percival left open much of the time to expedite the drying of her washing, hung conveniently there under cover.

I wasn't supposed to go down cellar, either, and I don't remember why. There's nothing to fall into or out of in a cellar, presumably. And I never did go down cellar, not because I was forbidden to, but because Ike Percival informed his daughter Eadie and me that there was a skeleton down there. (That man must certainly have found time hanging heavy on his hands.) This wasn't any ordinary, quiescent skeleton, content to lie in a corner looking like a heap of old bones. This skeleton walked around, holding itself precariously together and balancing its skull with some difficulty on the end of its backbone. If I heard thumps in the night from the cellar, Ike Percival said, that was the skull tumbling off the spine and bouncing along the floor. And I'd better be sure, always, that the door at the top of the cellars stairs, which opened into our living room, was bolted after supper, because the skeleton had a habit of wandering around at night. If I listened carefully, I could probably hear it fumbling up the steep and narrow stairs in the dark, trying to get into the lighted rooms above. Naturally, I heard thumps, cautious, climbing footsteps, and the dry rustle of bony fingers on the cellar doorknob almost every night. Wild horses couldn't have dragged me down cellar.

When we lived in that house, we had a cat named McGinty. I remember the name, because my father—who really couldn't sing at all—often sang a song, "Down went McGinty to the bottom of the sea." (His other song was "Pop goes the weasel.") I'd never seen the sea, but I understood that, sooner or later, that's where McGinty the cat was going.

So when she disappeared, leaving two kittens in her stead— they were both males, so I assume they were the pick of the litter—I was neither surprised nor grieved. One of the kittens was a homely gray-and-white, with a black smut on his nose, so he was named Smut, and he was mine. I had him for

twelve years, and I don't believe I ever gave any living creature the wholehearted devotion that I gave Smut. He slept
with me every night, although this was strictly forbidden,
since cats were notorious for sucking your breath (whatever
that means) while you were asleep, so that you never woke
up. Smut soon caught on to my mother's views and hid
every night when putting-out time came, and then sneaked
into my bed when he thought it was safe. If he heard my
mother coming, he wormed himself down under the bedclothes and curled up at my feet. When I was a big girl in
the seventh grade, Smut still warmed my feet on winter
nights. I really loved him with all my heart, and told him all
my troubles.

The other kitten was all white, except for five black hairs
under his chin, and he was called, with remarkable originality, Whitey. He was Alice's, and she loved him as much as
I did Smut. He slept with her, too, every night for about ten
years; and during those ten years we tried spasmodically to
make a pure white cat of him, whenever we didn't have anything better to do, by pulling out with tweezers the five black
hairs. They always grew back in again, as dark as ever, a
thing that we couldn't understand then, and that I'm not sure
I understand now. How does a little patch of skin no larger
than the head of a pin know that it's supposed to put forth
black hair, when all the surrounding ocean of cat-skin is
white-fur-bearing? You'd think it would get discouraged.

One other thing made a great impression on me while we
lived at 27 Spring Hill Avenue. Aside from not going near
the well, climbing trees, exploring the cellar, or ascending
to the loft of the barn, I was allowed to wander around the
neighborhood fairly freely in the company of Eadie Percival,
who, being a Bigger Girl and under oath to hold my hand
while crossing streets in case of runaway horses, was considered good loss-and-accident insurance. One of the places we
liked to go was the Old Elwell House, on Summer Street,
across from the end of Spring Hill Avenue and within sight
of my mother's kitchen windows. This was a rambling house
with wide porches, a mansard roof, and terraced lawns, which

must have been impressive in its day. But it hadn't been occupied for a long time, its paint was peeling, its lawn overgrown and wild, and its windows boarded up. It made a wonderful place to poke around and play the aimless, endless games of early childhood, and we considered it our own private domain.

Then one day some men came and started tearing the boards off the blind windows and moving dozens of cot beds and heaps of gray blankets into the house. Eadie and I were wide-eyed with anticipation. Anybody with that number of beds must have rafts of children, some of whom were bound to be of a suitable age to play with us. A day or two later, however, two great horse-drawn buses arrived, escorted by armed and uniformed guards, and deposited a crew of shabby men, who quickly disappeared into the house. We were told not to go *near* the Old Elwell House, but to stay in our own yard where our mothers could keep a constant eye on us. Those men were Scabs!

We knew only one meaning for the word, since we were always being told to leave the scabs on our skinned knees alone or they'd never get well. Any men deserving such a horrid name must be thoroughly horrible. Every morning while we watched from behind the kitchen sash curtains, they filed out of the house under armed guard and rode away in the buses, and every evening they returned, still under guard, and went into the house. We assumed that the guards were for our protection, there to prevent these ravening wolves in human form from breaking loose on society with reeking knife and smoking gun. We were in a state of constant terror, intensified by the occasional appearance of other men, identified mysteriously by our parents as Strikers, who walked up and down in front of the house and even, once in a while, threw stones at it. A dark and terrible threat seemed to lie over our whole world.

Then one day the buses didn't come. The strike was over and the Scabs were gone. The whole thing was completely meaningless to us, having no connection with anything that came before or after; but it left an evil shadow on the Old

Elwell House. We never played there again, and we felt re-
lieved when in the spring the building was razed, the big
garden leveled and broken up into lots, and new, smaller, less
sinister houses built on them.

I don't know why we left that first house. We didn't go
far—only next door to 35 Spring Hill Avenue. I always liked
Number Thirty-five, although perhaps it was simply because
we lived there quite a long time, for us, and not only was I
getting older and more at home in the world, but Alice grew
up there from a useless baby in a carriage into my sister
whom I could play with. The house looked small, being a
low, white, Cape Cod cottage type, but the appearance was
deceptive. It had nine rooms, a long woodshed, and a barn,
but no bath. The yard was large and full of fruit trees, there
were an asparagus bed and gooseberry bushes along the fence
next to the Severances', and I wasn't afraid of the cellar. It
was a lovely cellar, under the front part of the house only,
perfectly round in shape like a big, bricked-up well, providing no corners for skeletons to hide in. Since it didn't extend
under the kitchen, the kitchen floor was always cold in
winter.

In fact, it must have been a fiendish kitchen for my mother
to work in. Not only was the floor cold, but Smut and
Whitey by this time had grown into big cats and had learned
the trick of opening the door, which had a thumb-latch instead of a knob. This saved a lot of getting up to let the cats
out, but they never could be taught to close the door after
themselves, so it was left swinging wide to cool off the whole
house. Locking it wasn't a good idea, because that left Alice
and me continually squalling on the wrong side of it. In
addition, there was a pump in the sink, although cold water
had been piped in from the town main, so that the pump just
sat there, outmoded and in the way. If you wanted hot water,
you took it out of the teakettle on the coal range. In spite of
all these inconveniences, it was a very pleasant room, with
sun all day long from the geranium-filled windows on both
sides, and a nice view of the orchard.

While we were living at Thirty-five, we grew up enough so

that we were allowed to play all over the neighborhood on our own. That was a very good neighborhood for small children. The avenue was short, with four houses on one side and six on the other, arched over by elms and maples, and almost free of traffic, since it was only a side street. All the houses had large yards, and in addition there were two vacant lots, although I hesitate to call them that. The term brings to mind dead cats and tin cans. Ours weren't like that at all. They were fields of grass with a few ornamental shrubs thrown in for good measure, and the only difference between them and the yards was that nobody bothered to trim the bushes or mow the grass, so that daisies and buttercups and goldenrod came to full flower. We weren't allowed to go off the avenue, and we didn't want to. There was enough there to fill our days.

At the top of the street lived Miss Lily Worcester and, across from her, Miss Susan Keith, maiden ladies of unbelievable age and respectability, who were, of course, a total loss as far as providing us with playmates went. We considered them as part of the scenery most of the time, scarcely seeing them as they went along the sidewalk in their black dresses with the narrow white lace collars, elbows carried primly in, toes in black buttoned shoes pointed correctly out. But in the winter one of us would be elected by the other children of the avenue to ring Miss Worcester's doorbell—an agate knob that you pulled, and after a minute a bell would jangle at the end of a wire, far in the depths of the house—and ask her permission to coast on her lawn. She had the best slope on the street, a great waste, so we thought. But she was nice about letting us use it, and we'd spend whole afternoons sitting—because only rough boys did belly-bumps—on our high, curve-ended red sleds, sliding down that gentle declivity and plodding back up again. If any fights started, Miss Worcester rapped sharply on her windowpane with a thimbled finger, and we had to go home. The one responsible for starting the fight and spoiling our fun was clapped into Coventry, and nobody would speak to him for the rest of the day.

In the spring it was Miss Keith's turn. The whole bottom

of her lawn was a mass of great purple violets, and if you rang
her doorbell and asked nicely, she'd let you pick them. She
really was a sweet old lady. She gave us gentle lectures on not
pulling the plants up by the roots in our zeal, the first intima-
tion I ever had of conservation of natural resources; and she
suggested rather diffidently that she herself thought bouquets
much prettier with a few heart-shaped leaves among the blossoms, which was my first inkling of the somewhat controversial principles of flower arrangement. We were careful
about not pulling up roots, but we weren't much impressed
with the desirability of leaves. You could pick leaves any old
time, and violets came only in the spring. We'd go home
with bunches for our mothers as big as soup bowls, and never
a smitch of green to mar the beauty of the deep gorgeous
purple. If you fought in Miss Keith's yard, you had to go
home, too; but that didn't happen as often as it did in Miss
Worcester's, since violet picking isn't as rugged and temper-
testing a sport as coasting is.

Between the two houses, at the top of the hill where Spring
Hill Avenue turned the corner and became Maple Avenue,
was the street light that marked the limit beyond which we
couldn't go in that direction. At regular intervals a man
came to change the carbon in the light, and this was a great
event. When he appeared with his ladder, children ran from
all directions and gathered at the foot of the pole; children
not only from our own street, but the alien population of
Maple Avenue as well, since they considered the street light
as much their property as it was ours. (These children, you
understand, were of the same Yankee stock all of us were,
but they were alien, suspect, and probably dangerous and
immoral simply because they didn't live on our street, but
around the corner. There's a lesson here, but I guess I won't
bother with it now.) The object of these congresses around
the light pole was to gain possession of the discarded carbon,
a perfectly useless piece of material, brown at one end and
black at the other. You couldn't even draw pictures very well
with the black end. Its value lay entirely in its scarcity and in
the convention that labeled it desirable. Alice and I never

got one for ourselves. We were too little and too shy to put
up the necessary battle. Next best to securing one yourself
was the knowledge that one of your own gang was the lucky
winner. It spoiled the whole morning if the carbon was carried off to Maple Avenue.

We usually won, because we had the Chadwicks and the
Williamses to fight for our team. The Chadwicks weren't,
strictly speaking, members of the tribe, since their front door
faced on Summer Street, at the bottom of Spring Hill Avenue. But their house was on the corner and its considerable
length extended up the avenue. Their mother made them
stay off Summer Street because of all the delivery wagons
racing up and down it at the dizzy pace of probably two miles
an hour, and they never used their front door anyhow. Like
the rest of us, they went in and out the back door, through
the kitchen, reserving the front door for company use; and
their back door opened on to Spring Hill Avenue. So we
overlooked the technicality and considered them as of us.
They were a large and energetic family. Some of the older
ones were in high school, and of course they didn't even
know Alice and I existed, no matter what shrill encouragement we gave them when they condescended to scramble for
the light carbon. Our friends were Esther and Serepta, girls
of about our ages with whom we launched various ambitious
projects.

My mother had in a border under our dining room windows some flowers that she told us were called four-o'clocks,
because the blossoms opened every afternoon at four o'clock.
Alice and I could see that the pink-and-white flowers did
indeed open at some time during the afternoon of each day,
and since we couldn't tell time anyhow, we were willing to
accept her story as gospel. Serepta Chadwick had the temer-
ity to express doubts, based on the premise that even if
flowers could tell time, which she doubted, there was no clock
where they could see it. So, while Alice and Esther acted as
lookouts, Serepta and I sneaked up the Chadwicks' back stairs
and swiped an alarm clock. We beguiled Alden's delivery
man, a gentleman named Peck who we thought was wonder-

ful because he wore white rubber hip-boots summer and winter, fair weather or foul, and who happened by on his route at the crucial moment, into setting the clock for us, so that it would go off at four o'clock. Then we placed it where the flowers couldn't see it and sat down in a row on the grass to wait. This was probably at about two or so.

Sometime during the next two hours Joe Chadwick, the biggest brother of all, the one who was going to Washington with the Senior Class of the high school the next spring, came prowling around the corner of the house and pounced on us. He shook Serepta until her teeth rattled and accused us all categorically of stealing his clock, monkeying with it, and breaking it. Understandably enraged, Serepta kicked his shins and bit his hand, while Esther jumped up and down calling him a Big Fat Liar and a Fool. Alice and I were shocked speechless. *Liar* was one of the words we weren't allowed to use—"She isn't telling the truth" was acceptable, though—and even the Bible had something to say about "He that calleth his brother a fool," we knew from the daily after-breakfast devotions. We were horrified.

Joe, nursing his lacerated hand, took his clock and went home to repeat the same base canard—we were *not* monkeying with his darned old clock and breaking it!—to his mother, who made Esther and Serepta stay in their own yard for two days and wouldn't let Alice and me go over there and play with them, either. It was a very disillusioning experience, all in all. We never did find out about the four-o'clocks, no lightning struck Esther down in her tracks for calling her brother bad names, and worst of all, Joe Chadwick—so old, so wise, so much a hero—was shown to be capable of telling things that weren't true, like an ordinary mortal, and making his mother—who like all mothers was supposed to be fair, just, and infallible—believe them. The falling of the Heavens couldn't have left us more unsettled.

The Williamses, right across the street from us, had a large family, too, since they had some cousins living with them, for some reason. Olive Williams was my friend, a quiet child with a lovely *café au lait* skin and luminous gray eyes. We made miles of dandelion chains together, getting our hands all black and gummy with dandelion juice. You picked the heads off the dandelions and thrust the smaller end of the tubular stem into the larger end. This made a ring. You looped the next ring through it, and so on and on, until you had a chain long enough to go around your neck and clear down to your knees, if you wanted. You could wear a dozen chains, and you could make bracelets to match. Then, if your passion for self-adornment was unsated, you could find some extra long and plump stems in the tall grass of one of the vacant lots, slit them, run them in and out of your mouth several times, and make dandelion curls. These could be looped over your ears and thrust into the hair around your face, so that you looked—you hoped—like a princess in a fairy tale. The only trouble with making dandelion curls was that they tasted so awful, more bitter than gall.

Olive Williams and I played a lot of flower games. We tried to blow every last bit of fluff from the white head of a dandelion-gone-to-seed in one breath, in order to get a Wish. We held buttercups under each other's chin to see if a golden reflection would prove that we liked butter. (We always did.) We plucked the petals one by one from daisies, chanting, "He loves me, he loves me not," because that's what the Big Girls did. (The chant was truly meaningless to us, as emptily ritual as "Eenie, meenie, minie, mo.") We smoked Dutchman's-pipe blossoms and touched the slender seed pods of the jewel weed back of the barn with long blades of grass, to make them snap. We bit off the ends of honeysuckle and trumpet-vine blossoms and sucked out the drop of honey, telling each other how good it was, although it really didn't taste like much.

Sometimes we made flower dolls, searching all over the neighborhood until we found twigs that were just right, about three inches long, with forked ends for legs and branches placed properly at the sides for arms. We made heads of anything we could find—large rose haws, small green apples, or horse chestnuts—and then we assembled whole wardrobes for them, using morning glories or petunias for hats, nasturtium leaves for umbrellas, big, soft peony petals for party dresses, and grape leaves for opera cloaks. We tied the clothes on with lengths of striped grass, like green-and-white ribbons; and when we had our families all outfitted, we went on to make tea-sets for them, using acorns for cups and the flat, shilling-like pods of honesty for plates.

In the fall we pinned together with their own stems the brilliant leaves of the maples into crowns and cummerbunds and cross sashes; and we spent hours trying to produce ear-splitting whistles by blowing on grass blades held taut between our thumbs. And there was a weed with soft, fleshy, silvery leaves, from which you could make little purses, known as frogs' bellies, by pressing them gently and blowing into the space between the freed outer membranes. This was fussy work and rather difficult to do, so a successful frog's belly was a prize.

I had a lovely time with Olive Williams, but it was her brother Scott that made the most lasting impression on me. He gave me an orange one day. Oranges were not very common then, and we usually had them only around Christmas at our house. But this was in the summer, and he had a whole bag full of them. I can't imagine where he got them or why he had so many of them. Maybe it was his birthday. This orange was supposed to be an especially great treat, not only because it was out of season, but also because it was a kind I'd never heard of, a blood orange. Scott cut a hole in the end of it so I could suck it, and sure enough, when I squeezed it something red came spurting out. I thought it really was blood, and I couldn't possibly have eaten it if my life had depended on it. To this day, I can't face a blood orange without feeling seasick.

Then there was Norma Sturtevant, whom Alice and I envied terribly, because she was pretty and had long yellow curls, but even more because she owned a big, good-natured dog named Max. She was an Only Child, and according to the convention of the day, should have been a spoiled brat. She wasn't. She never minded when we ordered Max around as though he were as much our dog as hers, and one winter when the Sturtevants went to Oregon—a venture which in those days before distances had been shortened so drastically put them in the class of modern Marco Polos—she didn't let it change her at all. When she got back, she just went on playing with us as before, and never once bragged about her wonderful trip. She was involved in the worst trouble we ever got into, though.

We stole some matches and set fire to the long grass in the vacant field between our houses. Fire, as I had known it, was something that crackled submissively in a stove or, well under control, filled the autumn air with the wonderful smell of burning leaves. We loved the bonfires of the fall, when neighbor called to neighbor through the blue and smoky twilight, and little red flames glowed all up and down the street. This fire of ours was different. From one disappointing little tongue of flame, pale in the afternoon sunlight, it swooshed into a racing tide that swept the field and seized hungrily upon the high board fence along the Sturtevants' back yard. I have never since been so frightened, thank the Lord, and the thing that scared me most was the sound of my own voice. I was putting everything I had into screaming, but all that came out was a noise like a cat mewing.

Just then our hero, Peck of the white rubber boots, came hurtling off his delivery wagon into the fray, and put the fire out by beating it with his jacket. He gave us a stiff talking-to, but I didn't hear a word of his lecture, so overcome by chagrin was I at appearing in such an unfavorable light in his eyes. He didn't tell our mothers, but they found out anyhow and punished us. They needn't have bothered. We'd learned for life. The worst aspect of the whole affair was that now I had to run and hide every time I saw Peck. No more for me the daily hope that he might possibly say "Hello" to me. He certainly wasn't going to speak to any such abandoned wretch as I, and I couldn't face coldness from him. I was pretty miserable. It never occurred to me that possibly he hadn't considered the whole matter worth one second thought.

The Big Girls whom we smaller fry revered and imitated

were May Something and Ina Severance. They really were sophisticated, way up in the fifth grade or so, and all of eleven or twelve years old. They couldn't be bothered with Alice and Norma and me very often, although they did have time for Olive Williams and Serepta Chadwick. We couldn't understand why. We thought we were just as good as Olive and Serepta, and we tried a lot harder to ingratiate ourselves. I was always snitching maple sugar from the big box my father received annually from an associate back in Huntington for May's delectation, and running my legs off doing errands for Ina. I was further puzzled by an abrupt change in their attitude toward Alice and me one September. Suddenly Ina and May were offering *us* pieces of cocoanut cake and volunteering to help us rake leaves. It didn't make sense. Things were as they had always been, except that my mother's youngest brother Preston, who was about fifteen at the time, had come to live with us for a while, to attend high school and help our father at the *Independent* office. I didn't connect the two things at all until one day Ina said she'd give me her best glassie—a beautiful clear marble with a twist of multi-colored threads in the middle—if I'd tell Preston she was fourteen years old.

I took the glassie, and I said I'd do it; but I didn't. Preston already knew Ina's correct age. I'd heard him ask my mother. Anyhow, the whole thing seemed a silly ado about nothing to me. However, the scales had fallen from my eyes. I knew now why the Big Girls fussed over Olive and Serepta. *They* had brothers! I wasn't even embittered by this new knowledge. I accepted it as one of the ways of the world and tried even harder to please Ina and May, since I now appreciated the serious nature of the disadvantage I was working under.

May was the one who told Alice and me the truth about Santa Claus. She was the quiet one of the two, a peaches-and-cream girl with fluffy light hair around her face and curves where she should have them. She had an insinuating little voice and she dearly loved a Secret. She used to lie on her back under a syringa bush, her softly rounded arms behind her head, staring up into the fretwork of branches

overhead, and tantalize us by intimating that she knew something we didn't know. Naturally, this drove us mad with
curiosity and longing, and we'd promise the most outrageous
things—that we'd run every errand she asked us to for a week,
or give her every single piece of candy that we got our hands
on for a month—if she'd tell us The Secret. She always did,
eventually, and that's how we learned that Santa Claus was
really only your own parents.

This piece of intelligence really bowled us over, and our
first impulse was to run and ask our mother about it. May
reminded us that we'd sworn secrecy and gave the penalties
of breaking a promise the once-over-lightly: our teeth and
tongues would fall out, we'd become bald, and nobody, ever,
would speak to us again. So we reconsidered. We went
home, sober and chastened, and held a conference under our
own spice bush. Was what May had told us true? Forgotten
little incidents came back to us. What about those packages
that appeared in the living-room closet each year before
Christmas, that we were told not to touch and never saw
again? What about the doll's tea-set I'd admired in Scotton's,
which later showed up—or one suspiciously like it did—under
our tree? And the Sunday School Santa, who we'd said at the
time looked as though he had on a mask? When the evidence
was all in, we weighed it carefully and came to our conclusion: there was no Santa Claus.

"Do you think that we ought to tell Ma that we *know?*"
Alice asked. She looked worried.

I thought it over. "I don't know," I said uncertainly.

"Let's not. She and Pa go to a lot of trouble every year—
Let's just not say anything and let them go on thinking that
we believe in"—she gulped—"*Him.*"

And that's what we did, year after year, until the fiction
died a natural death. We got a lot of satisfaction out of it,
too. It was exciting to see how good an act of simple credulity we could put on, all the time hugging to our undeveloped
bosoms our superior, grown-up knowledge. It made us feel
protective and important.

May Whatever-her-name-was and Ina Severance alternated

between being the closest of friends and the deadliest of enemies. When they were having one of their differences, each would try to enlist on her side all the younger children of the neighborhood. We would be told by May in no uncertain terms that we had to choose. We couldn't be friends with both—although we couldn't understand why not. If we chose that Ina, all right for us! We had a right to, of course, and she, May, didn't care a bit. But if we thought that she, May, was going to invite us to her birthday party next February, we had another think coming. Besides, she knew a Secret, and she certainly wasn't going to tell us, if we had anything to do with that Ina.

Ina's methods were different. She laid down no laws and gave and extracted no promises. If she saw May with a coterie of her more or less wholehearted partisans, Ina started singing at the top of her lungs taunting rhymes, like:

"Ma-ay's mad, and I am glad,
  And I know what to please her!
  A bottle of rum and a sugar plum
  And (*Here she interpolated the name of the most loathsome male she could think of*) to squeeze her!"

This was sure-fire baiting, successfully calculated to reduce May to tears. Or Ina strolled arrogantly along the sidewalk and engaged the first person she met in conversation. It might be the milkman, or Miss Worcester, or a child whom May hadn't yet corralled, or a complete stranger. It didn't make any difference who it was; soon the two of them would be having a wonderful chat, laughing and joking without a care in the world; and before long the little group around May would start melting away to re-form around Ina.

It isn't surprising that May and Ina fought. It's only surprising that they had any time at all for each other. No two people could have been less alike. May was typical of the day —pretty, feminine, devious to the point of slyness, demure, and dependent, the way girls are supposed to be. Ina was really 'way in advance of her time, so modern as to be almost a curiosity. She had long legs, slim hips, wide shoulders, and a large mobile mouth that she didn't even try to purse into a rosebud. She handled herself with a curious free and angular grace, and she said and did whatever she wanted to, openly, loudly and frankly. Even her scheming—as in the matter of the bargain about Preston—was above-board. Neither her looks or her manner was widely admired. Heads were shaken among mothers not her own over her future. It was feared that she might grow up to be *fast*. She was the first to use "Kiddo" as a form of address and "Oh, shoot!" as an expletive—and a pretty questionable one, too. One summer the tree-arched length of Spring Hill Avenue rang constantly with her deep and derisive cry of "Twenty-three, skiddoo!" which was the very latest slang that year, and not considered quite nice. When she was bored with proceedings, she'd break them up with the impatient exclamation, "A-ah, Life's too short!" which I thought was the most worldly remark I'd ever heard.

We really liked Ina better than May, but we were afraid of May. Ina might get mad at you and give you a good hard slap, but the matter ended there. May never touched you, and sometimes you didn't know she was mad at you until the next day when you learned what she'd been saying about you behind your back or discovered that she'd emptied the water out of the pan in which you kept your pollywogs, so that they were all dead. It was more fun to be friends with Ina, but we learned that it was safer not to antagonize May.

We thought, naturally, that our life on Spring Hill Avenue was going to go on just as it was forever. Or rather, we didn't think about it at all. We simply accepted it. Oh, we could see that we were growing, because our shoes kept getting too short and our mother had to let down the hems of our dresses; but we weren't changing, and our relationships weren't changing. I might have grown an inch, but Olive Williams was still exactly as tall as I. Alice's front teeth became loose, but strawberries still gave her hives. Arthur Pratt's cat died, but the Holmeses' kitten grew up to take her place. That was the way things were on our street, for now and for everlasting, world without end, amen.

It was therefore a shock, in the true, clinical sense, when one afternoon our mother told Alice and me that we were going to move. The lady who owned our house had sold it, and we'd have to find another place to live. This was the first time we'd been old enough when moving became necessary to understand what it meant, and it was the last time it bothered us.

Our first concern was *where*. *Where* could our father find a house for us to live in? We didn't know of any, which wasn't surprising, since we didn't get around much and hadn't been any more house-conscious than snails with shells on their backs. What if he couldn't find one? We remembered a story that had been read to us about a little match girl who didn't have any home to go to, so she sat out in a snowstorm lighting matches to keep herself warm and looking in windows at other more fortunate children until the matches gave out and she froze to death. (Our mother had to paste those pages in the book together with flour paste, because even looking at the pictures caused us to burst into uncontrollable sobs.) Were we going to be like that poor little girl? We didn't even have any matches, and we didn't dare to steal any after what we'd done to Sturtevants' fence. We were really worried, until we were informed that our father had found a house on School Street, which was going to be nice and convenient, since it was just around the corner from Central Square and almost next door to our school.

Then we had a new worry. Whom were we going to play with on School Street? We didn't really know the children there, but only the unnatural aspects that they wore to school. What were we going to play and where were we going to play it? That was all foreign territory, and we didn't know any of the good places. We were going to be miserable. We knew it. We made pacts with our life-long companions of Spring Hill Avenue—all of whose shortcomings had suddenly vanished like the morning dew—to exchange daily visits, and all but promised to correspond regularly and to send up smoke signals in case of emergency, although we'd be seeing each other every day at school and the two streets were just two corners and a curve apart. You could get from one to the other in three minutes easily; or less, if you cut across lots. But you'd have thought that Alice and I were about to enter a lamasery or at least move to Nova Scotia.

And as it turned out, we might as well have. At first we walked warily in the new neighborhood, conscious of being under suspicion and on trial, and when we saw the old settlers playing native games that we didn't know, our hearts were wrung for the dear mother-country of Spring Hill Avenue. We felt lost and strange, and we drew defensively together, the little Dickinson girls against a hostile world. Then relationships began to shift. We still saw our old friends at school, and we remained on good terms with them; but when school was dismissed, our feet learned to take us automatically in the direction of School Street. That's where our lives lay now, and those who had once been at the very center of our existence moved out to the periphery. What affected them was still of mild interest, but it was no longer of prime importance. There had been a time when we'd have lived through all the agonies of apprehension with Olive the week she had to go to the dentist. Now only a sense of duty made us ask to see her new filling. We were a little shocked at our own lack of feeling. Once we'd have scouted Miss Keith's lawn hourly from the time the frost was out of the ground until we could announce triumphant discovery of the first violet. Now the violets had been in bloom a week before we knew about it. It was sad, but it was true, that it no longer mattered. It didn't even seem worth while to go way over to Spring Hill Avenue—the distance had mysteriously increased with every day we spent on School Street—to pick a bunch for our mother this year. Instead, we'd pick snowdrops from the Hunts' walled garden on School Street.

This spiritual transplanting was a thing that we were to experience many times in our lives. Everybody goes through it, time and again—the "growing apart," the "losing track" of friends. It's inevitable and scarcely worth comment, except that the first time it happens to you, you feel unhappy about it, and disbelieving, and vaguely guilty, and you try to preserve the old feeling for the old things. It can't be done, and after a while you learn to accept the fact. We learned when we moved to School Street.

That was an odd street in some ways. It ran the short distance from Central Square down the hill to the Normal School campus, and was given over to more public buildings than homes. The whole lower end was the property of the state and occupied by the Normal School. At opposite sides of the upper end were the Town Hall and the New Church. The church was obviously not new, and it took us a long time to dope out that this was a shortening of its true name, the Swedenborgian Church of the New Jerusalem. It had a very steep, tall, slate roof from which the snow slid thunderously in winter to lie in a high, hard-packed drift along the sunless north side, so that we School Street kids could have the exotic experience of snowballing each other while wearing our light summer clothes and no sweaters, and while other children were playing marbles and jumping rope. It gave us a cachet. Next to the Town Hall was the Fire Station, and next to the Normal School Gymnasium was the Unitarian Church. What little space was left in the center section of the street was taken up by a few houses, and one of those didn't really count.

The house that didn't count was by far the most pretentious on the street, with a porte-cochère, a turret, and all sorts of odd-shaped windows and gables. The elaborate grounds occupied a whole square between School and Grove Streets. It belonged to Sam Gates, a banker who lived there alone with his domestic help. Unlike Miss Worcester and Miss Keith, Mr. Gates did not view the young with tolerance. He wouldn't even let us run along the top of the wall that surrounded his entire property, and he never spoke to us when we met. He walked along with downcast eyes, a very dignified gentleman, and it was said that he'd found thousands of dollars in nickels and dimes through this habit of keeping his eyes on the ground. We were afraid of him and

gave him and his a wide berth; and maybe he was the ogre
we thought him. It's equally possible, I suppose, that he was
just shy and misunderstood. I have no way of knowing, although we lived next door to him, just across the little alley
called Cedar Street.

The School Street house was a wonderful place, we found,
after we got used to it. It was in considerable disrepair, because nobody had lived there for a long time, but that didn't
bother us. It had a furnace and hardwood floors and a fire-
place and two living rooms, one of which had a bay window.
It had a summer as well as a winter kitchen, and a garret as
well as a five-room attic that we played in on rainy days.
There was still no bathroom, though, although that was the
house with the butler's pantry. Alice and I particularly appreciated the back porch, because, instead of a roof, it had a
grape arbor over it. We very soon discovered that it was only
about twice as much work to enter our common bedroom by
climbing up the arbor and crawling in the window as it was
to use the more conventional approach of door and stairs,
and a thousand times more interesting. Smut and Whitey
made the same discovery, and whipped in and out of our
room all night long.

The yard was good, too. In addition to the usual trees, it
contained a horse chestnut tree, and this gave Alice and
me considerable prestige. Not everybody had a personal
horse chestnut tree, and we were pretty choosy about whom
we allowed to pick up *our* horse chestnuts, come fall. A high
arbor vitae hedge grew along the entire length of the lot on
Cedar Street, and this provided wonderful hiding places and
playhouses. It looked smooth and solid on the outside, but
if you knew which branches to swing aside, you could open
up marvelous green and aromatic caves. When the branch
whipped back into place, nobody would suspect that you
were inside the hedge, and you could hear every word people
walking along Cedar Street were saying. I know that eavesdropping is frowned upon, and we knew it then, too; but we
indulged in it constantly, just the same. It was fascinating
to learn what people talked about when they were off-guard.

We never heard anything very interesting, but we lived in hope; and while we were waiting for the great revelation that would make our vigil worth while, we derived a certain amount of satisfaction from the fact that Miss Burnell, the eighth grade teacher, didn't know that we knew that her corn was killing her. It gave us a hold over her in the same way that sticking pins into wax dolls gives voodoo practitioners a hold over their victims.

At the back of the lot, separating it from the grounds of the Methodist Church, was a high board fence that was good to play tightrope walker on; and if the Methodists were at worship, you could sit on the fence and listen to the sermon and the unfamiliar hymns. Going to our own church was a wearisome business, but kibitzing on the Methodists was fun. On the third side of the yard, between it and the Bowmans' lovely garden, was a white picket fence that wasn't good for anything from our standpoint, although the Bowmans may have felt differently. And in front, along School Street, there was just a lawn and a catalpa tree.

But in the angle of the kitchen ell there was the tree that every child dreams of—the low-branched, tall-reaching tree that is easy to climb, and that will take you step by preordained step off the ground and into the clouds. Ours happened to be a cedar tree, and climbing it was as much a spiritual as a physical experience to me. Up and up I'd go, past the kitchen windows, past the bedroom windows, to the level of the roof and higher. Then I could look down over the house into Cedar Street and Sam Gates' kingdom, where his cook was hanging out dishtowels in the latticed drying enclosure. I could see Brud Hunt in his yard across the street playing with his collie dog, and Elise and Barbara Aldrich crossing Grove Street with their mother, and Bert Duckworth and Wilfred Thomas talking on the Duckworths' wall. I thought, with true reverence and a little awe, that now I knew how God must feel, with the whole world under His eye. Like God, I could count the hens, foreshortened and small in the hen run, and I could look down on Smut, curled up behind a bridal wreath bush where he thought he was hidden. I could see Alice trying to bounce a ball on the sidewalk a hundred times without missing, and Bertha Bartlett's mother coming around Town Hall corner with a bundle of groceries, and Marion Hunt reading in a hammock between two trees. All was proceeding according to schedule in the neighborhood, and only God and I were aware of it.

Our mother let us climb that tree all we wanted to. Either she'd decided that we were old enough to be trusted in trees, or she saw the wisdom of not making laws that she couldn't enforce. She had too much to do, now, to keep us under constant supervision. It was along about then that she started putting in a great deal of time at the *Independent* office. There had been two weekly papers in Bridgewater, the *Independent* and the *Advertiser,* owned and published by a Mr. Willis. I don't see how the town supported two local weeklies for two minutes, but it did, for years. Eventually, though, the going apparently became too tough, and some deal was made whereby our father took over and merged the two papers. This meant increased circulation and more work, obviously, and it probably meant a tying up of any available funds—I wouldn't know, since business was one of the things not discussed before children—so that it was impossible to hire more help to carry the extra load. So instead of helping out just on publication day, our mother spent more and more time at the *Independent* office. This left us free to climb the cedar tree.

We also spent a lot of time at the town stables, out behind the Fire Station. It sounds like anything but the proper environment for Little Ladies (Rough Men! Lewd Talk! Foul Oaths!), but actually it was a wonderful place to play, and all the kids of the neighborhood gravitated to it. The stableman, as far as I can testify from experience, was a model of clean-mouthed decorum. All the town equipment for road work was parked in the stableyard, and we'd sit on the seats of the dump carts, whoa-backing teams of imaginary horses, or manipulate the big wings of the snow plows to fling up great waves of imaginary snow. We played hide-and-seek all over the rambling barn, and jumped from the rafters into the haymow.

Best of all were the horses, though. We simply *loved* the horses, and were perfectly willing to clean out the stalls if the stableman would let us feed and water them as a reward. They were work teams, slow and ponderous, but to us they were as fleet and beautiful as the most fabulous Arabian mares. They were more important, more real personalities, to us than most of the adults we knew. We dreamed of them nights and were positive that they recognized us whenever and wherever we encountered them around town during the day, earning their keep. Sometimes after a snowfall we'd meet the little one-horse plow used to clear the sidewalks, and we'd greet by name the heavy gray that drew it. He, we were certain, nodded and smiled to us, and for the next block we walked on air. Not everybody was on speaking terms with a public horse!

When there was a fire, we nearly burst with pride. The same horses that worked on the roads served as fire horses. When a fire broke out, the bell in the Fire Station tower and the whistle of one of the shoe factories sounded alternately, "Dang-*hoo!* Dang-*hoo!*" in a clarion tocsin that could be heard all over town and miles out into the country, in the direction of the wind. Living as we did practically on the Fire Station threshold, we were lifted out of our chairs and brought up standing every time there was a fire, and we'd snatch sweaters and rush outdoors to watch proceedings. If the fire occurred during the working day, the horses were unhitched from whatever piece of equipment they were currently hauling and turned loose to gallop back to the station under their own cognizance, with their human custodians panting far in the rear. We'd hear the drum-roll of urgent hooves in the distance, and then our darlings would wheel into School Street, great legs pounding like pistons, knees thrown high, manes and tails straight out in the wind of their passage, and eyes glowing like huge jewels. They might have seemed to be dying on their feet from boredom the moment before, harnessed to a gravel spreader; but the first "Dang-*hoo!*" changed all that. They loved fires.

I'm sure that present-day motorized equipment is much more efficient than the old horse-drawn apparatus; but fires have never been as thrilling since the old town horses were put out to pasture. The old apparatus even looked more exciting, all red and dazzling brass, with the steamer pouring smoke from its gleaming stack and spewing live coals behind it, and the hook-and-ladder rounding the corner by the Town Hall with firemen clinging precariously to the sides with one hand and holding their helmets with the other. There seemed to be a lot more shouting connected with fires then than there is now. Everybody shouted at everybody else, and at the horses. Instead of a siren there was a big brass bell on the hook-and-ladder wagon; and while a siren's moan is fairly blood-chilling, it isn't in the class with a bell's strident clangor for quickening the pulses.

But it was the horses that really gave *élan* to the spectacle of the fire department tearing to a fire. I know that probably a motor truck gets there quicker, but it doesn't seem to be going as fast—undoubtedly because it covers ground without apparent effort; and it doesn't seem to be participating the way the horses did. A truck is just driven to the fire. The horses were straining their legs and breaking their hearts in a personal effort to get there. They *knew* that much depended on them, while a truck doesn't know anything. I don't think it would be very practical to go back to horse-powered fire departments, but I do think they were more glamorous.

After the fire department had gotten safely away in the direction of the fire, Alice and I would look at each other and sigh, spent and drained with emotion. Our horses had acquitted themselves with credit again. Wasn't it *lucky* we'd had to move from Spring Hill Avenue? Just think, we might never have known the town horses! It was a thought too dreadful to be entertained.

But do you know, incredible as it would have seemed had we been told so at the height of our affair with them, we began to outgrow the horses. We didn't love them any the less, but we just didn't seem to have the time for them that we used to have. We helped our mother around the house more, now that we were bigger and she busier; we read more and more, having graduated from baby books to real stories; we went to the homes of other girls more after school, and entertained at our house girls who would have thought it childish to talk to horses, so that we concealed that facet of our lives from them. (We felt like Benedict Arnolds about it, too, every time we gave a town horse the cut direct.) And we were involved with those darned Montmorency sisters in the butler's pantry, who had begun to make our lives thoroughly uncomfortable. So we weren't sorry when the landlady died and left the house to the Methodists, who decided to move it and build a new church on the site, putting us again in the position of little match girls.

This didn't worry us at all, this time. We'd developed a philosophy about moving by now. When you had to move, you had to move; nobody we knew was without a house, so why should we be? The Lord would provide, and what He would provide was not a matter for apprehension, but of lively interest. Anyhow, the School Street neighborhood was going to the dogs. The Fullers, Lena and Charles, great friends of ours, had moved to Connecticut and out of our lives forever. The town had bought the land next to the Unitarian Church and was about to tear down the three houses there and erect a junior high school, so that the Thomases, the Hunts, and the Bartletts had to move, too. Sam Gates died and left his property to the state, which was going to expand the Normal School so that it would have lapped our very doorstep, if the Methodists had left any doorstep to lap. There were going to be only three houses left on the street, and in none of them were there any children of our age. A fine thing, a street given over almost entirely to Church, School, and State! We certainly wouldn't have stayed voluntarily in any such sterile and deteriorated environment, even if we'd had a choice in the matter.

We moved to Broad Street, which led off the lower end of

Central Square, into an old colonial house that had seen
better days. Before the town had grown up around it, it
must have been a lovely old place, set in wide grounds; and
even with the land whittled down to a small yard, it still
retained some of its former dignity. It was a big, square
house with a fan-lighted doorway, in bad repair and with no
improvements, except that the fireplaces in every room had
been blocked up and pipes for stoves put in. Even this
desecration couldn't spoil the cool proportions of the rooms.

The ceilings were low, as was usual in colonial days to
make heating easier, and the first few days we lived there I
was constantly opening doors and windows wide, in spite of
the chilly autumn weather. Our mother would order me in
no very gentle a manner to close them, what was I trying to
do, heat all outdoors? I'd say that I *had* to have them open, I
was smothering, I was *scared!* She told me tartly not to talk
silly, I was *not* smothering, and what was there to be scared
of? I didn't know, and after a while I got over feeling that
way. But it was genuine enough while it lasted. I really did
feel as though I were smothering, and I really was frightened. I report this only as evidence, if any is needed, that
claustrophobia is a fact. I'd never heard of such a thing, and
neither had any other layman at that time. Yet I certainly
had a case of it, and it wasn't all my imagination. I recovered
bravely under a stern and stop-your-nonsense treatment,
which sometimes makes me wonder.

The yard was disappointing. It was small, with only two
grapevines and two trees, a maple and a cherry, neither one
fit for climbing. But the neighborhood more than made up
for that deficiency. It was the sort of neighborhood that I
suppose can be found only in a small town like Bridgewater,
where growth has been completely unplanned and without
benefit of zoning. Between us and the Square was a solid
block of rather ramshackle stores and other business buildings, looking somewhat like a western boom-town, minus the
saloons and hitching rails. Yet behind us and the stores was
a big field with a brook and trees and bushes, as unspoiled as
open country. At the foot of Broad Street Hill was the rail-

road station, called the Dee-po, and some shoe factories; and
yet the middle stretch of the street was lined with good, well-
kept residences where members of the old families lived
quietly. Right spang in the center of it all was a blacksmith's
shop, still in operation as such.

Of course, there was nothing like the Fire Station on
Broad Street, but to tell the truth, fires had begun to pall at
about the time we began to outgrow horses, and Broad Street
offered such an infinite variety of diversions that we didn't
miss the Fire Station as much as we would have in the long
ago days of our childishness—say, six months before. Right
next door to us was a Cloverdale Store which dealt chiefly in
dairy products. The manager threw all his packing cases out
behind the store until he had enough to warrant calling the
trash man; and we systematically threw them in turn over the
fence into our yard, so that we could build a hut in the field
behind. We always had a hut under construction. As soon
as it was nearly done, we had a better idea and pulled it down
and started all over again. These edifices had a tendency to
wobble in a light breeze and the roofs always leaked when it
rained, but we got a great deal of satisfaction out of them.
We kept them stocked with stale doughnuts and boxes of
raisins against the day when we had to run away from home
for some reason, or in case we should have to hide out from
the police.

Further along in back of the stores was the rear exit of the
new and palatial—or so it seemed to us—moving picture theater, The Princess. If we were very good and helped our
mother without too much argument, we were given a nickel
apiece every Saturday to go to the matinée, which always
consisted of a Western and the current episode of the Pearl
White serial. That comprised our entire legitimate movie
experience. But in warm weather when the rear exit was left
open for ventilation, we could go along behind the stores, sit
on the back steps of the theater, and listen to the music. This
was almost as good as seeing the picture. Over the threshold
we could just glimpse the piano player—a young man named
Ralph McCarthy who had supplanted Peck of the white rub-

ber boots as Our Ideal—sitting on the middle of his spine with his head against the rail of the piano pit, watching the action on the screen and supplying appropriate background music. (These were silent movies, of course.) The Overture from *William Tell* meant that a cavalry rescue was in progress, and we could always tell when the picture was almost over and the lovers about to melt into each others arms by "Hearts and Flowers."

There was always a hiatus while the reels were being changed, and then slides were thrown on the screen, bearing the words of popular songs which Ralph McCarthy played and the audience was supposed to sing. Usually the co-operation was fairly good. Then in the big break between pictures professional entertainers sang, danced, told stories, or whatever. These entertainers apparently traveled a circuit, going from town to town and staying in each a week or so. Often a favorite would come back time and again for repeat engagements. We thought these people were the most talented and glamorous in the world, and sometimes when they came out onto the back steps to smoke during the movie, they'd say hello to us. We'd be paralyzed with ecstasy and incapable of uttering a word, no matter how determined we had been beforehand to dazzle them with scintillating small-talk. The one we liked best was a singer called Lili Byron. We hoped she'd marry Ralph McCarthy, but I don't think she did.

We weren't the only ones who cheated the movies. The Chinaman did it, too. Most towns then had a Chinese laundry, which usually was just a single Chinaman who did up shirts better than anybody, and who must have—although nobody worried about it—lived a very lonely life. I don't know what adults felt about the Chinaman—nothing, probably—but children were afraid of him. He was rumored to eat rats and to love nothing better than slitting the throats of young Occidentals with a long, thin, wicked knife, as a sacrifice to his heathen god. Alice and I knew better. We already had a slight acquaintance with our Chinaman, whose name was Harry Hong and who had a round, serious and pleasant face. He wore a pigtail pinned around his head to keep it out of the way, and the light, clean, pajama-like costume of his country. Before he moved on to Broad Street, he had conducted his business in a room under the *Independent* office, and had occasionally used our father's telephone. So we weren't afraid of him to start with, and we ended by being friends with him. He'd sit on the back steps of the theater with us and shake his head over the music of the Western world, making comments in his peculiar singsong voice that was incapable of sounding the letter R.

In the laundry, which was also his home, he had an old phonograph with a horn like a morning-glory flower and cylinder-type records of Chinese music. Sometimes he played them to us. They sounded awful, like drums and cats and wailing women all mixed up; but we didn't say so. He had a cricket in a bamboo cage not much bigger than a walnut shell, which we thought was the most charming thing we'd ever seen. He could draw delicate, lively caricatures with the slender brushes and India ink he used for marking the laundry. He told us about sending money to his parents in China, and about how he was saving so his little brother could come to visit him, since the law wouldn't let him come to stay. We thought that was sad, and I guess it was. At Christmas he gave us lichi nuts and sacred lily bulbs wrapped in red-and-gold paper with Chinese characters on it. He was a very nice man.

When we walked past the laundry on the sidewalk, he was often busy sprinkling clothes by spraying water from his mouth onto them, or ironing shirts with sad-irons, and if he happened to look up and see us through the window, he smiled and waved. We smiled and waved back. One day, though, we were with a group of girls of our own age—the silly age—and they broke into screams of derision. Once we were beyond the laundry, they started dancing in circles around Alice and me, rubbing their forefingers together in the gesture that I consider the most obscene and objectionable possible, the gesture that means "Shame!"

"Ooo-oo! Shame on Alice and Louise!" they chanted.

"They smiled at the *Chinaman!* Ooo-ooo, I'm going to tell my mo-other!"

We were consumed with anguish. We couldn't tell them that he was a friend of ours. They wouldn't have understood. We couldn't explain about the cricket and the lichi nuts and the brother in China. They'd have laughed all the louder. We felt terrible—somehow disgraced and guilty, although we didn't know why. Everything was spoiled. After that, we waved at the Chinaman only if we were alone. Otherwise we pretended to see something of interest on the other side of the street when we passed the laundry. I'm glad to say that this didn't make us feel a bit better, but worse, if anything. We hoped he didn't understand, but we were afraid that he did, and when he gave us lichi nuts as usual at Christmas we felt like bawling. Only the fact that we had now adopted our We Don't Cry policy prevented us from doing so.

There was another fascinating institution on Broad Street, the trolley car. This wasn't the Brockton or Taunton trolley that started from Central Square. This was the preliminary East Bridgewater trolley, and it started at the top of Broad Street, by Casey's Ice Cream Parlor. The real East Bridgewater trolley started on the other side of the railroad crossing, down by the Dee-po. Probably as a precaution against grade-crossing accidents, the first trolley—which was a little bobbed-off thing like the Toonerville Trolley—went only to the crossing gate, a distance of about one long city block. There the passengers detrained, crossed the tracks on foot, and boarded the real, life-sized trolley on the other side. They took off over Sprague's Hill, and the little trolley went back up the hill to wait an hour for the next load. It must have been a monotonous job for the motorman, just riding up and down the street all day long or killing time between trips; and sometimes when he was feeling good-natured, he'd let us ride with him for free. This was considered fun, although we could have walked the distance quicker if we had any business at the other end of the street, which we never did. I guess it was just the idea of a free ride that intrigued us. We'd waste three quarters of an hour waiting for that little trip that took us nowhere and back to where we'd started. But after all, I suppose that's what a trip around the world does, too, if you want to look at it that way.

It was while we lived on Broad Street that we started hating boys. Before that, we'd played with the children we lived near and liked, without thought of their sex, and disregarded those we didn't like. But the inevitable phase caught up with us on Broad Street, and we wouldn't speak to a boy, no matter what our previous relationship had been. Instead, we became much, much chummier with the girls of our acquaintance. We walked around with our arms about their waists, giggling and whispering secrets. There was a hollow stump in our yard, and we converted it into a mailbox. Alice and I wrote long letters to each other and to our very, *very* best and bosom friends, Ruth Hunt and Bernice Sherman, several times a day. We saw nothing incongruous in the fact that very often—almost always, really—the recipient of the letter was present when it was put into the stump, took it out immediately, and read it in the writer's presence as we strolled to school, frequently asking for help in translation when the penmanship, syntax, or spelling proved baffling.

I don't remember why we left Broad Street. Probably I never knew, being too flitter-brained and otherworldly at that point to pay attention to the mundane. We moved to Dean Street, on the outskirts of the village, into a small, new house in what would be called today, I suppose, a development. Alice and I didn't feel at home in the comparatively cramped quarters, and neither did Smut, I guess. At any rate, after being shifted from pillar to post for years, he suddenly dug in his heels and refused to move. We went to Broad Street and got him a dozen times, and we tried all the recommended methods, like putting butter on his feet and locking him in the cellar for three days, but they didn't work. So we gave him to the blacksmith, who had always admired him and promised to take good care of him. I missed him terribly for a long time. Our mother liked the new house, though. It must have been a relief to her not to have to struggle with an ark of an old place, with everything else she had to do. She could whip through her housework in no time flat, now that the front door wasn't half a day's journey from the kitchen, and going upstairs a minor conquest of Everest.

Dean Street was a dead-end street, very different from busy Broad Street, but it died in a meadow of daisies and rue, beyond which there was a great field, then a creek, then woods, then Carver's Pond. It didn't make any difference that the yard was small and barren of trees—until our father planted some he got from a nursery that couldn't pay its advertising bill in cash—because we had all outdoors past the end of the macadam in which to roam. So influential is environment that we almost immediately changed from the rather urban types who doted on trolley rides and movie mood-music into students and lovers of nature. We grew to know those fields and woods like the palms of our hands. We knew where to get partridge berries for terrariums, where the meadow larks nested, where to find pussy willows in the early spring, and later, frogs' eggs and the big, flat bird-foot violets. We knew the best places for dandelion greens and watercress and low-bush blueberries, and we could find trillium and ladys' slippers when no one else could. We even admired skunk cabbage blossoms, which everyone else fled from in disgust. We brought home cattails to soak in kerosene for torches to use in burning tent caterpillar nests, an invention of which we were proud.

We became completely enamored of and absorbed in the outdoors, and I think perhaps that's one of the reasons we grew up so slowly. When other girls of our age were going to dancing school, we were brushing out and blazing a trail through the underbrush to the hut we'd built on the edge of the creek. We refused flatly to have any part of dancing school, a silly waste of time and money. When other girls were spending cold winter afternoons stewing in the house and talking about clothes and boys, we were down at the pond skating, or out in the woods tracking rabbits; or on a hot summer day, instead of sitting in hammocks and preserving our complexions, we were in the sun-drenched fields or shadowy woods, looking, listening, tasting, smelling. It was a phase we should have succumbed to and recovered from at a much earlier age, probably, but we didn't, because of circumstances beyond our control. So I guess it was like measles: we had it late, so we had it hard.

There is a poem by Robert Frost that starts:

> Whose woods these are I think I know.
> His house is in the village though;
> He will not see me stopping here
> To watch his woods fill up with snow.*

That's exactly the way we felt about our woods. We knew the legal owner, a Mr. Burrill. But his house was in the village and he was busy with his own affairs. He didn't know, as we did, the special fresh and fragile look of a cove full of white water lilies in the slanting morning sun. He wasn't familiar with every step of the narrow path that led from his field through a little swamp and onto a low ridge overlooking the pond, so that he could walk it with his eyes shut and never stumble over a root or get his feet wet. He could call the woods his, and pay the taxes on them; but they were really ours, bought and paid for in love and knowledge.

I have often wondered how we'd have turned out if we'd lived always in any one of our domiciles. Each one must have left its impression on us, shaped us in some way, altered the direction of our growth. What would we have become if we'd stayed on Spring Hill Avenue, if we'd never left School Street, if we'd come to rest on Broad Street? I don't know, but I believe we'd have been unlike what we are, whatever that is. I do know that during the years we lived on Dean Street, I was set in a mold that has not changed during all the rest of my life to date, and won't change now, in all probability. It's simply this: there are some who can live without grass under their feet, and trees murmuring over their heads, and a loam-scented wind in their nostrils, and some who cannot. I cannot. To me the right to step out of my house

---

* From "New Hampshire" by Robert Frost. Copyright, 1923, by Henry Holt & Company, Inc.

directly onto the living earth is something to be worked for
and guarded more jealously than fame or a million dollars;
and to see a sunset over a field of snow or the first star
through the branches of a tree is a thousand times more thrilling and beautiful than watching the most elaborate man-
made spectacle on the biggest stage in the world.

That's the way I learned to feel when I was a green girl
on Dean Street, and that's the way I feel now.

5

Star Bright and Last Look

WHEN I'M CLEANING OUT THE ATTIC OR CELLAR AND MOVING all the equipment my children seem to think they have to have in order to live fully—all the skis and skates and tennis racquets and bicycles and outboard motors and frogman flippers and golf clubs—I wonder how the sporting goods business made out at all when I was their age. There must have been some sadly undernourished and ill-clothed individuals among the salesmen and manufacturers of the outfitting companies, if they were depending on the pigtail and knee-pants trade. We played a great many games that my children never heard of, but they were all games requiring no equipment at all, or just things we could pick up around any old place, or at most a ball and something to use for a bat.

There was Ten-step, for example, a game that could be played with no paraphernalia whatsoever, and no physical or mental qualifications beyond the ability to move around on your feet and count to ten. Any number of people exceeding two could play, from the age where they could walk and count, up to the age when they couldn't any longer, because of arthritis or senility. Usually, though, the players were under fourteen or so. After that, the game began to seem kiddish.

It was really a very simple game, but some good fights

sometimes grew out of it, and that was roughly the test of the goodness of a game. If enough interest couldn't be generated to make a fight conceivable, the game didn't amount to much. I'll have to admit, though, that in those days Peace At Any Price was not our watchword, and it didn't take much to start a fight. We were very touchy indeed about our honor, our rights, unfairness, and any real or fancied cheating or discrimination. Possibly we just liked to fight—or argue, since most of the fights turned out to be mere battles of words. Blood was seldom spilled, and certainly almost never in the playing of Ten-step, which was not a personal contact game.

First, one person had to be It. There were several ways of determining who this was to be. Someone might say, "Let's play Ten-step. NOT IT!" Everybody else would then shout, "NOT IT!" and the one whose reflexes were slowest and who therefore said "NOT IT" last, was It. This was often good for an argument, when two or more people said "Not It" last together; but usually that question could be settled by the drawing of lots (twigs held in a ringleader's hand with the ends even; the one who drew the shortest twig was elected) or by Toss-up. In Toss-up, since nobody ever had even a plugged penny in his pocket, let alone a coin of respectable value, a reasonably flat pebble was found, and someone either scratched or spit on one side. That was heads, and the unmarked side was tails. The Toss-up then proceeded according to immemorial custom, best two out of three.

Or someone, being sure first to get a good head-start, would shout, "Last one to the corner (or over the fence) is It," and the last one—the one with the shortest legs, poorest wind, or slowest start—would indeed be It. Or if one member of the group was out of favor at the moment—and someone always was, but it didn't mean anything, since the condition was only temporary and the onus shifted hourly, according to the whim of the masses—there would be a spontaneous cry of "Mary's (or Wilfred, or Stanley, or Kitty) IT!" and Mary or Wilfred, or whoever, would be.

Another method that we ourselves didn't use very much,

but that we ran into once in a while when we went to play in a strange neighborhood, where they had their own peculiar folkways, was Holders. One person suddenly shouted "Picker-up!" and picked up a pebble. Immediately there were cries of "Wiper-off!" and "Holder!" Picker-up handed the stone to the first to have shouted "Wiper-off," and that eliminated Picker-up at once. Wiper-off made a great play of wiping off the pebble on the seat of his pants, if he were a boy, or the front of her dress, if she were a girl, and handed it to the first one who had shouted "Holder," and that put Wiper-off out of the running. Then Holder put his hands behind him, and everyone else had to guess which hand held the stone. If you guessed correctly, you, too, were Out, and Holder kept on holding. If you missed, you took the pebble and became Holder until someone failed to guess in which hand you held it. Eventually, after a certain amount of bickering and bitter accusations of shifting the stone from hand to hand after a successful guess had been made, someone was left holding the bag—or pebble—and was It.

These, however, were more or less slapdash methods. A more formal procedure was Counting Out. Someone, usually self-appointed, would be the counter, the others would line up, and the counter would chant one of several traditional verses, pointing to each person in turn to accent the rhyme. The one to whom the last syllable fell was Out, the counting was repeated until there was only one individual left, and he was It. The counter always started with himself, according to some dark rule, and if someone against whom he had a grudge was about to be counted Out, it was possible to cheat within limits, by adding one of the traditionally acceptable tags to bring the count beyond him. For example, the counter might be using the most common count in our circles, supposedly derived from the ancient Latin:

> Eenie, meenie, minie, mo
> Catch a nigger by the toe
> If he hollers, let him go.
> Eenie, meenie, minie, mo.

If the last syllable fell to the comrade whom he suspected of tattling on him to teacher last week, he'd add, "O-U-T goes Y-O-U"; or if that would bring the count around again to his enemy, "Out goes you." This was recognized as sharp practice, but nothing could be done about it, except grumblings and recriminations, to which no one paid any attention. When you were being discriminated against, you were expected to complain; and if you didn't, either you were sick or a Fraidy-cat, ye olden equivalent of Chicken.

Another counting out rhyme that Alice and I, at least, used with a great sense of daring was

> Monkey, monkey, bottle of beer
> How many monkeys are there here?
> One, two, three,
> And Out goes he.

We were careful not to let our mother hear us. One did not mention bottles of beer with impunity; or so we thought. The one that I myself liked best was

> Wash the lady's dishes
> Hang them on the bushes
> When the bushes begin to crack
> Hang them on the nigger's back
> When the nigger begins to run
> Shoot him with a leather gun
> Out to Y-O-U.

This wasn't the easiest count to use, because of the weak ultimate syllables of the first two lines, but it fascinated me.

There are more complicated versions of Ten-step, involving running and hiding, but this is the simple way we played it. The person who was It sat alone at the end of an open space, and the rest of the players lined up behind a line roughly fifty feet away. It covered his eyes and counted to ten, at the top of his lungs, while the rest of the players started moving as fast as they safely could toward him. At "Ten!" everyone froze, It unblinded himself, and if he saw anyone in motion, he said so with a great deal of satisfaction, and the guilty party had to go back behind the line and start all over again. The object of the game was to reach It first—or at least not to be last—and tag him, thus putting yourself out of the game. The last one to reach the goal was It next time. By counting in an erratic manner—very slowly until you got to eight and then fast; or fast until you got to nine and allowing so long a time to elapse before ten that impatient players were lulled into false security and risked another step or two—a crafty counter could catch the unwary very often. Of course, there were always hot denials of "You did not see me move! Ask Norman! Did she see me, Norm, huh? Did she?" and protestations of "I did so! I guess I know what I saw. How does Norm know what I saw, huh? How does he?"; but all in all, Ten-step was an orderly game.

The same cannot be said of Stealing Eggs, a variant of Prisoners' Base. I think they're both descendants of the days of the border warfare between Scotland and England. Anyhow, they're very old games, and during the reign of Edward the Third, there was issued a proclamation by Parliament prohibiting the playing of Prisoners' Base in the avenues surrounding Westminster Abbey during the sessions of Parliament, because the Members, passing to and fro, were constantly getting fouled up in the games and delayed in the performing of their duties, even if nothing worse—like being knocked down and having their hats stepped on—happened to them. We didn't know all that when we played it, and we wouldn't have been interested in any case. We just thought it was a good game, better than Prisoners' Base, because the capture of property, as well as the freeing of prisoners, was involved. In retrospect, I can see what Edward's Parliament was up against, though. I'll bet even Sir Winston Churchill couldn't have crossed Dean Street when a good, hot game of Stealing Eggs was in progress.

The equipment consisted of a dozen stones, as nearly egg-shaped as possible for easy handling; and to make a good game, there should be at least a dozen players, but the more the merrier. Dean Street was the best street we ever lived on for team games, because it had the largest juvenile popula-

tion. Almost everybody had at least two children, and the
Hamlins, who moved there from Sandwich at about the same
time we arrived from Broad Street, had ten. Of the ten, only
Ruth and the baby, Albert, were too little to play. The rest,
starting at the top with Clifton and Lester, ranging down
through Elizabeth, Wilfred, Mary, Raymond and Richard to
Leona, were all old enough but not too old to play games.
Take the Hamlins and the little Dickinson girls, add Kitty
Cushman and the four Lords—Dorothy, Sabin, Emil and Arthur—and Emory Garney and the Harding boys, Lawrence
and Kenneth, and Amelia Clement and the Snow girls,
Beulah and Thelma, and you had plenty for a good game of
Stealing Eggs. If we played after supper—as we often did in
summer, when it didn't get dark until late—then two men
of the neighborhood who were old enough to be our fathers
but very young at heart, Henry Worcester and Martin
Coombs, would play with us. That was wonderful. They
automatically, because of their adult status, became the captains of the teams and settled all arguments by the simple
method of pronouncement. I'll have to admit that it was
more fun to play under established and unquestioned authority than it was under the more democratic method of
arriving at decisions by wrangling, which probably proved
something, but I'm not quite sure what.

The captains chose their sides, taking turns naming their
players and making their selections on the basis of ability.
Friendship went by the board when it came to picking teams.
Players were chosen on their merits; but it's a fact that not
only in Stealing Eggs, but in any other team game, character
counted, too. In Stealing Eggs, the important qualifications
were ability to run fast and dodge agilely and boldness in
taking risks, while in another game they might be the ability
to catch a ball, throw a stone accurately, or move quietly.
No matter what skills were demanded, the cry-babies, the
cheats, the show-offs and the "No-fair" howlers always went
last off the block.

Teams chosen, the playing area—which should be about
a hundred feet long, and a dead-end, no-traffic street like

Dean Street serves very well—is divided into two parts by a line drawn across the middle, and at the back of each territory a rectangle about three by six feet is drawn on the ground. This is both nest for the eggs and prison for any captives. Six eggs are put in each nest, and the game is ready to begin. The idea is to cross over into enemy territory, steal an egg, and get safely back into your own territory with it. If you're tagged on foreign soil, you're a prisoner and have to stand in the rectangle until released by one of your teammates. If you succeed in stealing an egg, you may not be captured on your return trip, and the same holds true if you succeed in releasing a prisoner by tagging him. You can steal only one egg or free only one prisoner at a time, and you can't do both on one trip; and you can't steal any eggs while one of your men is still in prison. Your first obligation is to him. When one side has swiped all the eggs belonging to the other, the game is over and that side has won.

Stealing Eggs is a darn good game. We used to develop some pretty complicated strategy, making a show of force at one end of the line while a sneak raid got under way at the other, or luring the enemy guard away from his post by goofing around and giving the false impression—we hoped— that any old grandmother snail could catch us. I haven't played for over a quarter of a century, but I feel just like going out and trying to pick up two teams this very minute.

Another game we especially liked, that required only stones for equipment, was Duck on a Rock. There should be at least a half-dozen players, I should think. We always had more than that, our neighborhood being as prolific as it was, and we usually played after dark, under the street light that the town had benevolently placed for our convenience at the corner of Dean and Worcester Streets. When it was too dark for anything else, but not yet going-in-the-house time, we could always get up a game of Duck on a Rock. Each player found a good rock, called a duck, of a convenient size to handle and throw and preferably fairly flat on one side. Finding the perfect duck, one balanced just right and exactly suited to your personality, was a serious business. Once you found it, you saved it over from game to game and wouldn't let anyone else use it. The really effete went so far as to scratch their monograms on their ducks and hide them under the Clements' privet hedge between games.

After each player had found a satisfactory duck, a large rock was placed under the street light, about twenty-five feet from a throwing line drawn on the earth. This was the duck-rock. Everybody stood behind the line and threw his duck at the rock, and the one whose duck lay furthest from the rock was It, or guard. He placed his duck on the rock, and the others stood behind the line and tried, by throwing their own ducks, to knock the guard's duck off the rock. After you'd thrown your duck, you had to recover it without being tagged by the guard. As long as you didn't touch your duck, you were safe; but once you'd picked it up, even if you dropped it again, you were fair game. If you were tagged before you crossed the line, and couldn't get your duck onto the rock before the guard snatched his off, then you were It. The guard couldn't tag anyone unless his own duck was sitting on the rock, and that's why it was desirable to have a flat-faced duck. It was harder to knock off, and you were spared the frustration of having your hand lifted to tag a runner, only to have a general lifting of voices in glee apprise you of the fact that your duck was off the rock. We had a lot of fun playing Duck on a Rock. It was a good game.

It was also, however, a fairly dangerous game. The air was frequently full of flying rocks, and it's a wonder someone didn't get killed, or at least suffer a bad concussion. Nobody did, although I once picked up my duck just as a fellow player launched his with considerable velocity. My hand was squashed between the two, and I had four stitches taken in it. I still bear the scar.

Then there was Scrub, a form of sandlot baseball that I suppose almost all American children of the last seventy-five years or more have played. We called our Dean Street sand-lot the Sandhill and we played Scrub there from the time the frost was out of the ground until October. Everyone played, not only the kids, but all the young men and men not so young, who fancied themselves in the role of undiscovered Big League material. It was not at all unusual to have the game disrupted by an irritated wife calling her husband home to fix the leaky faucet that he'd been promising for a week to attend to after work. When that happened, we'd suspend the game until he got back, whiling the time away by passing the ball rapidly around the bases, or practicing fielding the flies and grounders someone knocked out to us. When the faucet-fixer came back from his domestic duties, we went on where we'd left off. Everyone *loved* the game, and I still think it's the best in the world, involving so many skills—running, throwing, catching, batting—as well as the prettiest to watch. There is nothing more graceful than a good infielder at work, scooping up a hot grounder and pegging it over to first. It's a performance as full of style and disciplined elegance as ballet.

Everyone knows how to play Scrub. (Three o'Cat is a more technical name for it. One o'Cat and Two o'Cat are variations requiring fewer players.) It is—as is probably not necessary to explain—not a team game. Three players comprise the batting list—in raps, we called it—and the rest distribute themselves in the usual fielding positions of baseball, as far as they'll go. If there aren't enough to fill the outfield, that's all right. The basemen play deep, or well back of their conventional positions, to cover the outfield. If there are too many players, that's all right, too. You can put four or five in raps, or use extra outfielders. A player can stay in raps until he is struck, thrown, or fielded out, according to the regular baseball rules. Then he takes his place in left field, and all the other players move up one place, catcher to raps, pitcher to catching box, first baseman to pitching box, and so on, working themselves toward raps. Usually a sandlot has its own ground rules, in addition to those blessed by the Big Leagues. Ours were (1) if you hit the ball into the road when a car was passing, so that the fielder couldn't chase it, the hit was good for only two bases; and (2) if anyone broke a window in the Cushmans' house, the only house within batting range, all players were mutually responsible and had to chip in and pay for it.

Alice and I were pretty good baseball players. We could throw a ball as fast and accurately as most boys, we weren't afraid of fast grounders, we could hang onto a sizzling pitch, and she, at least, could run like a deer. But it wouldn't have made any difference if we'd been the worst dubs on the Sandhill. We'd still have been allowed to play. We were the proud owners of the only good ball, the best bat, and both a pitcher's and a first baseman's glove. And how did we come by this unusual—for adolescent little ladies and chronically impoverished Dickinsons—treasure? Through the peculiar business practices of the *Independent,* of course. One of our father's best advertisers was Fairbanks', which purported to be a hardware store, but which also sold many other things, among them sporting goods. Mr. Fairbanks and the *Independent* had the usual arrangement that advertising charges should be taken out in trade, as it was called; and there is a certain limit beyond which you need no more hammers, nails, wood screws, sandpaper, flower seeds, agate sauce pans, iron skillets, twine, paint, spading forks, chicken wire, or anything else that Fairbanks' sold. After that limit was reached, Fairbanks' still continued to advertise, and our parents were hard put to it to think up items with which to use up the credit. Of course, there were a few score things we really needed, like new shoes or a couple of tons of coal; but Fairbanks' didn't stock those.

Therefore, when we were asked what we wanted for our birthday and said a little diffidently that we'd like a baseball and bat—our diffidence stemmed not from any sense of the inappropriateness of the choice, but from the knowledge that those things cost money—our father didn't boggle a bit. He told us to stop in at his office after school and he'd go over to Fairbanks' with us and get them. Once we had him in the store, we went to work on him to give us our Christmas presents, too, six months in advance: the gloves. Since he could see the sweet reason of this request—the gloves wouldn't do us any good in December; we wanted them badly and we wanted them now, in June—and since Fairbanks' account had been running for some time and piling up a debit while the *Independent* shilly-shallied around, making up its mind, the indebtedness covered the cost, and we got the works.

It was a wonderful feeling to be in the position where everybody's evening's entertainment waited upon our convenience. We were even mean enough to dawdle over the dishwashing after supper, for the exquisite pleasure of hearing a chorus of voices from the lawn pleading with us to hurry *up* and come *out*, everyone was *waiting* for us. It gave us the illusion of being popular and much sought after.

Another game that we played quite a lot after school was one the Hamlins brought up from Sandwich. This was called Tally-oh and required a small building in the open so you could run around it, and a ball or bean bag. (Whatever became of bean bags? Every child used to own at least one, and I well remember mine, that I thought was beautiful, made of colored string crocheted around and around in brilliant stripes.) In Tally-oh, the two teams stood on opposite sides of the shed, out of sight of each other and so disposed as to cover their respective territories as fully as possible. The ball was heaved over the barrier with a warning cry of "Tally-over!" and a player on the receiving side caught it if he could. If no one caught it, it was heaved back. If it was caught, the catcher ran as fast as he could around the building and tried to hit one of his opponents with the thrown ball. If he was successful, the player hit had to leave his own side and join the other. When everybody on one side had been captured, the game was over.

This was a game requiring great alertness. You had to keep your eye on the top of the shed, in case the ball came sailing over, and at the same time you had to watch both ends and be ready to dodge, since you never knew whether or not the ball had been caught, or from which side, in case it had, the attack would come. If, as sometimes happened, you were the last person left on your side, you were busier than a one-armed paperhanger, covering the whole area all alone and keeping a snug watch out for raiders.

It seems to me that we did an awful lot of running when we were kids. Using a conservative average of four miles a day as a base of estimate, I'll bet I ran fifteen thousand miles before I was sixteen. Nobody had cars, or if they did, they were too important and sacred possessions to wear out taxiing perfectly able-bodied children around. We didn't own bicycles, and anywhere we wanted to go, we went on our own two feet. We either ran or strolled, depending on how urgent we considered the case. I don't think we ever employed a sane, three-mile-an-hour walking pace, except possibly when church-bound on Sundays with our parents, who exercised a restraining influence. Either we were dragging along at the speed of cold molasses or we were racing like whippets. It sometimes took us a good half-hour to walk to school, because we were not consumed with any burning desire to get there; but after school we could and usually did get home in two minutes flat, the sooner to change into our old clothes and start the real business of the day. Walking wore us out. We were always exhausted if we had to proceed at the rate adults found reasonable. But running didn't. We liked to run, to feel our legs stretch to eat up distance and the wind brushing past our faces, and to watch the ground flow smoothly and easily backward under our feet.

In addition to the running necessary to transport ourselves from place to place, we played a lot of running games, as distinguished from those games which involved running but of which running was not the main feature, such as Tally-oh or Duck on a Rock. Chief among the running games, of course, was tag. There were a dozen kinds, some involving goals—pronounced gools—and some not. In the simplest, there were two goals, which might be the side of a building and a fence, the opposite sides of the street, or just two lines drawn on the ground. Everybody lined up along the two goals, and the person who was It stood in the No-man's-land between. When he shouted, "One, two, three, and *o*-ver!" everyone ran like crazy to the opposite goal; and if It could tag you en route, then you were It. There was tag with no goals at all, when It just kept chasing around until he tagged

someone who'd either been caught off-guard or had run himself out of breath. We played this on the way to school sometimes, and the aim of it then was to outflank someone so that
he had to run in the wrong direction, away from school. If
you could time it right, so that he'd be late and have to Stay
After, but you yourself just squeaked in under the wire and
didn't, you could count the day well spent.

Then there was squat-tag, when you might escape being
tagged by suddenly squatting on the ground, and if It
couldn't put on the brakes quickly enough to avoid sprawling
over you and falling flat on his face, so much the better. (We
really were charming young things, so full of good will toward our fellow man.) And there was wood-tag, where im-
munity was gained by touching wood. Bushes and trees or
any other growing wood didn't count, though, and It could
make you leave your sanctuary by standing ten paces from
you and shouting, "Parley out!" Then you had to run, and
you couldn't go back to that piece of wood until after you'd
touched another. Someone told me once that this is a very
ancient game, which evidently derived from the old and universal superstition that touching wood warded off evil spirits.
This I didn't know at the time when I had the physical
stamina to play it with zest; but I now find it a rather engag-
ing thought that little cave boys and girls, from the Andes to
Siberia and into darkest Africa, and the children of the
Pharaohs' Egypt and the Renaissance and Elizabethan England, all ran shouting and looking for wood to touch, just as
we did on Spring Hill Avenue. It makes the world seem
small and friendly, and the ages short.

There was a cross-tag, too, where It had to call the name
of the player he'd marked down to catch; but if another
player ran between It and his victim, then It had to chase the
new quarry until that trail in turn was crossed. With a little
co-operation, the members of the gang could reduce an unpopular individual, by continual crossing, to that state of
collapse where his eyes rolled up and his tongue hung out.
And there was a kind of tag called Fox and Geese which
could be played only in the snow. First, in a field as yet un-

sullied, you made a big circle, as large as the area permitted, by running in single file through the snow until it was trampled down in a clear track. Then cross trails were made, like the spokes of a wheel. The point where the spokes crossed was the fox-den, and It was the fox. The other players were the geese. The fox tried to catch a goose, who would then be It. You had to keep on the trails, of course, and the geese could cross the circle only on a straight line, while the fox could angle anywhere.

Whenever I now think of winters of long ago, I see a sort of Grandma Moses scene, with blue wood-smoke rising from chimneys that are now dead and cold, no matter how much warmer the house may be inside, thanks to the new oil burner, and in the foreground a dozen children laying out a game of Fox and Geese. They are running in Indian file, silhouetted black and featureless against the glaring snow, with scarves of vapor streaming back over their shoulders and glittering little clouds of snow dust rising around their feet like the bright wings of Apollo, as they swing around the great circle. It's a pretty picture.

We played other games where you ran in circles, too, possibly as training for later life, if that isn't too cynical an observation. There was Drop the Handkerchief, one of the oldest known games, played by Cossacks and Japanese and Mayans and Italians and other children all over the world since time began. It's also the first game I remember playing, at Ruth Hunt's birthday party, when she was four and I wasn't quite. My next oldest game was Three Deep, where all the players except two stood in two concentric circles, one person in back of another, facing inwards. One of the two odd persons was It and the other was the runner. It chased the runner, who could save himself by stopping in front of any of the couples in the ring. At this point, obviously, the circle became three deep, and the outside player became the runner. If It tagged a runner, they changed places.

I don't know when we first began to play Follow the Leader, but it was at a fairly early age. At first, when we lived on Spring Hill Avenue, the feats of derring-do demanded by even the most audacious leader weren't particularly hair-raising, although sometimes we thought they were. When Ina Severance led the way across a corner of Mrs. Gurney's lawn, our blood ran cold. Mrs. Gurney was very fussy about her lawn, and she'd certainly knock on her window at us. If she ever came out and hollered—not that anybody had ever heard Mrs. Gurney holler; she was a lady of the old school—we knew that we'd die. But as we grew older, the game became more arduous. On Broad Street, once, I got stuck on Bernice Sherman's barn roof. I followed the leader up there all right, but for the life of me, I couldn't get down again. The man next door finally had to come with a ladder. I was eaten with shame.

When we weren't running, we were jumping. Boys didn't play jump rope. For some reason it was considered sissy. I can't imagine why. It required the manly virtues of strength and endurance, and prize fighters weren't above it. But be that as it may, jumping rope was positively a girls' pastime. Every little girl had her own short jump rope, suitable for jumping alone. If you were lucky, you had a bought jump rope, woven of colored strands and furnished with wooden handles, usually painted red. But a short length of any old rope would do, and that's what Alice and I usually had, until one spring when Fairbanks' indebtedness to the *Independent* exceeded the vegetable garden seed demands, and the balance of trade was taken out in jump ropes. During the season, you were never without your jump rope. You jumped rope to school, wore it tied around your waist during school hours, and jumped back home. I don't know what determined the beginning and end of the jump rope season. I guess it was just in the air, like a virus. One day it was still winter, and you were pretty fed-up with rubbers and mittens and the fourth grade teacher; and the next, everyone was suddenly, as at a secret signal, jumping rope and shooting marbles. The fever was self-limiting, apparently. After a time-lapse of two or three weeks, all the ropes and marbles disappeared, and everybody was doing something else.

The individual short ropes were all right for getting yourself to school or on errands for your mother, or for seeing if you could jump a hundred times without missing, or for doing "Salt, vinegar, mustard, *pepper!*" when you started on salt at a reasonable rate, accelerated on vinegar and mustard, and at *pepper* went as fast as you possibly could, until you were all tangled up in the rope or completely breathless. But for real fun, there were the long ropes which required two turners. You were very lucky indeed to own a long rope, and Alice and I were among those fortunate souls who did. Our mother's clothesline gave up the ghost one windy April day, parting and letting a two weeks' wash down to wallow around in the mud. She was so discouraged and annoyed—and nothing is more maddening than to have your clothesline break just after you've got the laundry out and are feeling smug and relaxed—that she didn't even try to fix it, but gave it to us and went up to Fairbanks' and got a new one. We were overjoyed. This put us in the enviable position of dictators. We could say who should and who should not play with our rope, what games were to be played, and who had to take first turns at being ends, or rope turners.

There were lots of games you could play with a long rope, and the penalty for missing was the same in all of them: you took an end and freed that turner to jump. There was Chase the Fox, where everyone lined up on one side of the turning rope and followed the leader, or fox, who first ran through under the rope without jumping, then, when everyone had done that, ran back, jumping once. The next round she jumped twice, and the next, three times, until she'd built it up to twenty-five. We stopped there, because someone said that the Visiting Nurse had told her mother that it wasn't safe to jump more than twenty-five times. You were apt to drop dead or develop athlete's heart, which we understood to be something like athlete's foot, only more serious. And possibly she was right, although with the short ropes some people frequently jumped to a hundred. Not me, though. I had shot up too fast, as the saying went, and outgrown my strength, so that I ran out of breath at about fifty.

There was Calling In, when one girl ran in and jumped

three times. On the second jump, she called the name of another girl, who joined her in the turning cage of the rope. They jumped together once, the first girl ran out, and the second called in a third. There were various rhyme games, the only one of which I remember was

> Daisy, Daisy, turn around
> Daisy, Daisy, touch the ground
> Daisy, Daisy, touch your knee
> Daisy, Daisy, one, two, *three!*

You suited your actions to the words, all the while jumping the rope, which was turned to the rhythm of the verse. On *three,* if you got that far without missing, the turners started giving you *pepper*—turning as fast as ever they could—and finally wore you out.

Maybe it was this wearing out that put a natural end to the jump rope season each year. We couldn't have kept it up indefinitely. In the beginning, we felt so light and airy in our sweaters and thin spring dresses after the confining bundling-up that went with a New England winter that we practically floated over and under and through the arching rope. But as the weather grew warmer, we grew less energetic and simmered down to hopscotch, which involved some jumping around, but not as much as jump rope.

There were lots of hopscotches, but the best was Boiler. The diagram was a rectangle about four by eight feet, with a semicircle added to one end. It was divided into boxes: two boxes at the squared end, two boxes just under the semicircle, four triangular boxes made by drawing diagonals through the middle section, and the one rounded box at the top. These boxes were numbered from one to nine, the figures scratched in them in the dirt. To play this you had to have a small, flat pebble that you could toss and pick up easily and that wouldn't roll; or a piece of worn colored glass was excellent. You tossed your pebble into One, hopped in on one foot, picked it up, turned around, and hopped out. Then you tossed it into Two and did the same thing, going through One. That was simple enough, but it got harder as

you worked up to Eight and Nine. If you missed the box you
were aiming at, or stepped on a line, or lost your balance and
put both feet down, your turn was over and the next player
started. Boiler was something like golf. If you couldn't find
anyone to play with or had had a fight with the rest of the
gang, you could play by yourself, competing with your own
score. It was a lot cheaper than golf, too.

These were only some of the games we played. There were
many others: Hide and Seek, which everyone knows, and
Run, Sheep, Run, and Hare and Hounds, where the hare
lays a scent of torn-up paper and exercises great cunning in
back-tracking and finding windy places where the paper will
be blown away, to throw off the hounds. There were many
games of marbles; and all the games we learned at school,
like Dodge Ball and Volley Ball, which we never played at
home. They bore about them a disagreeable odor of Organized Activity, which was anathema to us. The fact that a
game was smiled on by school authorities ruined it for us
forever. We'd never heard of regimentation, but we didn't
care for it, just the same.

Some of the things we did to amuse ourselves weren't
games at all, although they were recognized forms of entertainment. The first that I remember was Cat's Cradle, which
was introduced to me by Great-aunt Julia Dickinson, when
she came to stay with us the time Alice and I had chicken
pox, so our mother could be free to help our father. Great-
aunt Julia took a piece of string about a yard long, tied the
ends together, and wove it over her fingers so that it formed a
basket, or Cat's Cradle, between her little white hands. Then
she instructed me how, by grasping it at the proper places
with my thumbs and forefingers, I could turn it wrong-side-
out and transfer it in a differently constructed cradle to my
own hands. She in turn took it back in still another shape.
I thought this was marvelous and kept her at it by the hour.
It took my mind off my itching. She also bought us each a
large scrapbook and blunt-ended kindergarten scissors, made
up a quart jar of flour paste, and collected all the old maga-

zines and catalogues she could lay her hands on. Then she told us that the scrapbooks were houses, each double page being a room, and helped us cut hinged doors between them, that would really open and shut. We drew lines to divide the walls from the floors, sketched in windows where we wanted them, and painted pictures on the walls. Then we cut out furniture from the magazines and pasted it into the proper rooms. We loved our scrapbook houses and worked on them for years, whenever it rained or we were sick, until they were crammed with furnishings. Great-aunt Julia would have made a wonderful primary grade teacher, if she hadn't unfortunately had Independent Means, so that she didn't have to work.

Bridgewater was a town famous for its lovely old trees. All the streets were arched with them, and everybody had a yard full. The whole town drowsed in summer beneath a murmuring tent of green. But in the fall the leaves came raining down, and for weeks everyone was raking. We loved the fall. There were leaf-fires burning everywhere, and if we could manage to swipe a few potatoes, we found a good fire and roasted them. They never got done, because we never could wait long enough, but we ate them half raw and wholly black and thought they were delicious. We loved to scuff in the long, deep windrows of leaves that lay against walls and in gutters. They smelled so good—dry and sweet—and made a lovely whispering sound. We piled them into mountains and jumped and turned somersaults in them, or we raked them into the walls of forts or castles and had leaf-fights. We got them down our necks and into our shoes, and we probably breathed in enough dust and germs to kill a herd of buffalo; but we had a lot of fun. I guess we were pretty simple.

And like all simple peoples, we lived lives bound round and controlled by a network of spells and superstitions. We were governed by signs and portents, propitiated strange powers, and observed esoteric rituals. Even the art of insult was stylized and conventional. If one of our number gave

way to tears of grief, pain, or rage, we chanted in unison and
as offensively as possible—and we could be pretty offensive—

> Cry, Baby, cry!
> Stick your finger in your eye
> And tell your mother it was I!

This obnoxious little ditty succinctly and unmistakably accused the tearful one of (1) lack of manhood, (2) inflicting
wounds on self for the purpose of getting his associates into
trouble, (3) lying, and (4) talebearing. It was rightly resented,
but since there is little the individual can do when mob spirit
moves against him, the victim, if he was wise, went home and
waited it out. If he did nothing to further aggravate the
gang, the matter blew over in an hour or less.

If a boy was suspected of entertaining the tenderer emotion
toward one of the little girls, the other little girls took
umbrage. Possibly this was rooted in envy, but I don't think
that was the chief cause. I think it stemmed more from a
vague sensing of a threat to our solidarity. Girls stuck together at that stage and had nothing to do with boys as such,
although they were tolerated as sexless players on teams. Individual preference of one boy for one girl boded ill to our
close sisterhood, and the members joined forces to protect the
endangered one. Our weapon of defense was a chant which
we hurled at the love-smitten boy, running after him and
screaming it at the top of our lungs:

> Georgie, Porgy, pudden-pie,
> Kissed the girls and made them cry.
> When the boys came out to play,
> Georgie Porgy ran away.

The swain was understandably embarrassed, especially if
by some happy chance his name really was George. His face
would get red, and he'd threaten us with everything he could
lay tongue to. If, goaded beyond endurance, he started throwing stones at us or chasing us with the idea of inflicting
bodily injury, we became all self-righteousness and called him
a big bully, picking on the girls, and threatened to tell our

mothers on him. I'm not happy to have to say this, but the young of my sex can be the world's absolutely worst stinkers. We weren't any exceptions. The smart boy refused to play into our hands by getting mad. He either ignored us or fell back on the counter-cry

> Sticks and stones
> May break my bones
> But names will never hurt me!

This was putting the shoe on the other foot with a vengeance, and drove us crazy. There was no particular reason why it should, except that tradition labeled that retort as unanswerable.

Or if some poor unfortunate child moved to town and made a civilized effort to win new friends by the quite acceptable method of asking one of us his name, maybe he'd get a straight answer and maybe he wouldn't. We were quite capable of mimicking him in a high falsetto,

> *What's your name?*
> Pudden Taine.
> *Where do you live?*
> Down the lane.
> *What's your number?*
> Cucumber.

Why didn't somebody murder us? Talk about the law of the jungle! Any half decent hyena would have been ashamed to act the way we did sometimes. I wonder we had any friends at all

Besides being full of bad manners, we were riddled with superstition and misinformation. My grandmother Stewart was responsible for some of this. When she was a child, tomatoes were called love apples and were supposed to be poison. Although she revised her views later in life, after seeing her descendants survive unbridled tomato-eating, when we were small children she still held to her original opinion. She succeeded in proselyting Alice and me, so that for years I had hives if my mother made me eat tomatoes.

(All right so they were psychosomatic hives. They itched just the same.) Grandma Stewart also believed that the tiny black seeds in bananas caused appendicitis, so we always scraped them out with a teaspoon; and that soda crackers dried up your blood, so we rationed ourselves strictly and drank a lot of water after eating one, to counteract its evil effects. Cocoa was supposed to dry up your blood, too, and we never had it at Grandma Stewart's house. Instead we had cocoa shells. I haven't thought of them in years. They were thin, dark brown shells, looking something like dried butternut husks, only more fragile. You steeped them into a tea and added sugar and milk. The result tasted a little—a very little—like bitter cocoa. It wasn't very good.

For purposes of her own, our mother caused us to believe for a while that eating bread crusts and carrots, which we didn't like very well, would make our hair curl. We wanted curly hair more than anything, so we gave them both a fair trial. They didn't do a thing for us, so we tossed that particular creed overboard fairly early. There were a few beliefs that everybody subscribed to, and it took us longer to get rid of those. One was that dragonflies, or darning needles, would sew up your lips if they got a chance. Whenever we saw one flying around in the sun on its own business, glinting and quick and beautiful, we clapped our hands over our mouths and kept them there until it had gone away. Another was that handling toads made warts on your hands. We liked toads. There were always two or three in the garden, and we spent hours watching them. They camouflaged themselves so well, squatting in their holes and blending with the mottled earth, motionless except for the pulsing of their creamy throats. Their eyes were so dark and mysterious, and their slender tongues, attached at the front of their mouths, so quick to flick up an insect as far as two inches away. They fascinated us and we caught flies for them; but we wouldn't have dreamed of picking one up.

We'd early exploded the theory that cats suck your breath while you sleep, by taking our own cats nightly to bed with us, in spite of our mother; but we believed for a long time that if you killed a spider, it would rain within twenty-four hours. That faith died hard and amid great disillusionment. We spent a whole day, once, catching and killing spiders so that it would rain and we wouldn't have to go to the Sunday School picnic. Picnic day was perfect and we had to attend. It was a bitter blow. We disproved the notion, too, that if you held your breath when a mosquito had his proboscis stuck in you, he couldn't pull it out and you could swat him at your leisure. I don't suppose that snakes' tails really do continue to wiggle until sunset of the day you kill them, either, although that's one I haven't had occasion to subject to test, since I've never lived where there were poisonous snakes, and I don't kill the other kind. I know that you don't immediately develop galloping consumption, as tuberculosis was called, if you get your feet wet. However, it's probably just as well not to wade in puddles unless you have to. It ruins your shoes, if nothing else; which is probably what our mother had in mind when she imparted that bit of medical lore. Nor do I imagine that carrying a horse chestnut in your pocket will help your arthritis, as was commonly believed in my youth; or that wearing a silver coin on a black silk string around your neck will ward off fits.

When we lived on School Street, the stableman at the town barn told us that if we put long hairs from the horses' tails and manes into water, they'd turn into snakes. We collected a whole skein of them and soaked them in a bucket of water all one summer. We were going to take them to school on the first day in the fall and let them loose in the room of a teacher whom we didn't like. It didn't work, though. They never changed a bit, except to get rather slimy. We had to think up some other method of getting even with the teacher. We finally enticed the Fullers' coal-black cat into crossing her path, but I don't know that anything particularly horrible happened to her, unless you want to count having to deal with the likes of us for ten months of the year.

While we were calling down disaster upon the heads of our many enemies, we were concurrently observing all the proper rites to guard our own persons from ill fortune. We always carried lucky stones in our pockets, pebbles with one or more bands or rings around them. The more rings, the more efficacious the spell. Some of the sidewalks in town were made of concrete, which heaved and cracked in the frost. It was very bad luck to step on one of the cracks, and we avoided it grimly even if it made progress up the street a ridiculous combination of mincing and striding. We were always on the lookout for four-leaf clovers, which had to be worn in your left shoe for the best results. You had to find your own, too. If you had one given you, you might as well throw it away, for all the good it would do you. If you could find two, one for each shoe, you were practically invincible. You could dare anything. I once walked the whole length of a barn ridgepole and back, so protected, a thing I'd never ordinarily have attempted. If I'd fallen off, I'd have broken my worthless neck. But I didn't; and probably the four-leaf clovers really were responsible through giving me complete confidence, a nice handy thing to have when you're balanced on a knife-edge fifty unbroken feet above the ground.

It was very bad luck indeed to kill a ladybug—one of those small orange beetles with tiny black spots. Instead you were supposed to say

> Ladybug, Ladybug, fly away home.
> Your house is on fire; your children will burn.

The ladybug would fly away, especially if you flapped your hand at her, so full of gratitude for this false warning, presumably, that she'd exercise her mystic powers in your behalf. Grasshoppers were almost as powerful as ladybugs, if you treated them right. You must never kill them, naturally. But if you caught one, held it in your fist, and intoned, "Grasshopper, Grasshopper, give me some molasses," it might see fit to expel a molasses-like fluid, probably as a defense reaction. This augured well for you. It was bad luck, too, when you were walking with a friend, to pass on opposite sides of any obstacle, such as a tree or hitching post. One of you had to go back and run around the post three times.

Walking under ladders or raising umbrellas in the house, of course, were unthinkable.

There were countless ways of getting your wishes to come true. You could wish on a new moon, or on a load of hay drawn by a white horse, or on the first star. In the last case, you had to say

> Star light, star bright,
> First star I've seen tonight,
> I wish I may, I wish I might
> Have the wish I wish tonight.

Then you had to close your eyes, turn your back on the first star, and look for another. If you spotted one before you looked again at the first, you'd probably get your wish. It was rather fascinating. You'd see the first star, bright on the horizon in an apple-green western sky, the only one in the whole pale field of Heaven. You'd make your wish, turn your back, and search all above you vainly for another star. There wouldn't be a single one in sight. But as you stared and the light drained away, out they'd come, one by one, dim at first, but slowly brightening until the whole sky was full. They'd been there all the time, you realized with a sense of wonder; and it was safe to turn back to the first.

None of these were sure-fire wish-granters, though. They were only hopes or precautions. The best opportunity for getting a wish granted came when you accidentally and without collusion said something in exact chorus with another person. If someone made a remark, for example, and you and a friend answered in unison, "Oh, no, it isn't," then the first step had been taken. But that was by no means the end of it. There was a lot more to it than that, and if you spoke one word other than those of the ritual before the ceremony was completed, all bets were off and you didn't get your wish.

So you buttoned your lips tightly, as soon as you realized the situation, linked the little finger of your right hand with the little finger of your friend's right hand, and pressed the balls of your two right thumbs together. Thus joined, you stood in silence while each made her wish. Then one of you asked, "What goes up the chimney?" and the other answered, "Smoke." Together you said, more earnestly than grammatically, "Our wish will never be broke." To doubly insure this, the first said, "Longfellow," and the other replied, "Shortfellow." Then you could relax. You never told your wish in any of these rituals, because if you did, you certainly couldn't expect it to be fulfilled.

There was one rite we always performed at the end of each day, when the shadows of the trees lengthened across lawns and gardens, and the smoke from chimneys all up and down the street swelled and billowed as fires were freshened for preparing the evening meal, and the voices of our mothers sounded high and clear in the quiet air, like Angelus bells, calling us in to supper and a long night's sleep. It was the rite of Last Look. "Antoinette, Antoinette," we'd call, "turn around!" And when she did, "Last Look!" we'd carol, and turn toward home. Only under great temptation, no matter what inducements she offered, would we look at Antoinette again that day. Last Look was a way of writing finis to and setting a seal upon the events of the day now dying, and of insuring the happiness of the morrow, when we'd meet again. All over town the voices floated lightly in the stillness of the evening, near at hand and sweetly diminished by distance: "Last Look, Lillian; Elizabeth, Last Look."

I hear them now in memory with a sense of deep nostalgia. Last Look, oh little girls who loved to run, who trusted in striped pebbles to preserve them from all evil, who believed in wishing on a star, who had nothing, and everything!

6

The Evening of the Amateur

I SUPPOSE THAT YOU MIGHT CALL THE DECADES IN WHICH I
grew up the Age of the Amateur. I'm not sure that the word
professional, in its modern sense of making a business of
something not properly to be regarded as a business, or of
developing a very high degree of skill and competence in any
ordinary line of endeavor, was known. Certainly I never
knew it and never heard it so used. There were the Professions, of course—the law, medicine, the church, or teaching—
which were highly respected. It was assumed that men who
embraced them cared more about serving mankind than
about making money, and that they had chosen their respective fields through a feeling of responsibility and continued
in them at a sacrifice of themselves. They were supposed to
be governed by a sense of duty and to possess and observe
codes of professional ethics that put their conduct on a
higher plane than that of ordinary people. My father, as
editor of the local newspaper, was considered a professional
man, although lower on the scale than a doctor or a minister,
whereas a mere reporter or printer—and my father was those,
too—would not have been so considered, but only as the plier
of a trade. It was assumed that the men in the Professions
not only set up and personally maintained a high standard of
behavior, but that they possessed and used influence to raise

the general level of the community thought and attitudes.

By and large, I would say that all these assumptions were correct. These men really were, with few exceptions, the conscientious, selfless, dedicated members of society. That's what *professional* meant. A woman on the stage was simply an actress, and a writer was an author, unqualified by any adjective like professional. Nobody ever heard of a professional tennis player or politician or house-painter. The word just wasn't used that way. It would be a contradiction of terms, since politics or writing or tennis playing weren't professions in the first place.

By the same token, no one ever talked about someone's being practically professional in the fields of cookery, sport, singing, harness-mending, or what have you; or about amateur standings, performances, and attitudes, or about amateurs. If you inherited a plumbing establishment, you either sold it or became a plumber. If you were asked to recite at a church sociable, you picked out a suitable poem, learned it, and recited it loudly, slowly, clearly, and with gestures, but without thought to possible talent scouts in the audience; and if you felt like going swimming, you went and had a good time dog-paddling around, careless of polishing up your crawl to professional standards. I guess we were a bunch of terrible dubs in all departments, intent on nothing except passing time as enjoyably as possible. Perhaps that's the mark of the amateur: that he stops performing when he stops having fun, while the professional keeps on after the activity involved has become drudgery, in the interests of fulfilling a stated or implied contract.

That's why I say that, although the word amateur never crossed our feckless minds, we nevertheless lived in the Age of the Amateur.

You should have seen us down at Carver's Pond on a winter afternoon. I hesitate to call what we were doing skating, but that's what we thought it was. We were on ice, and we had some things other than our shoes fastened onto our feet. Otherwise we were clothed in our usual winter outfits—no crimson-lined skating skirts, no shoe-skates, no ski-pants, not even any wool slacks. After all, skating wasn't even a sport. It was something we did for fun, just as we played hopscotch in summer for fun; and we certainly wouldn't buy a special hopscotch costume and go to all the trouble of changing into it.

Anyhow, changing your clothes in winter was a major operation and not to be undertaken lightly. Unless you wanted to run the risk of having a caller or deliveryman barge into the living room or kitchen in the middle of your toilette, you had to disrobe in an icy bedroom, and it just wasn't worth it for any trivial cause. You got dressed for the whole day in the morning and simply skinned out of your school dress and into your old one after school, without disturbing the basic layers.

The foundation layer was a shirt of heavy combed cotton, with long sleeves and a high neck. The lower extremities were taken care of by a pair of long-legged underdrawers with a drop seat. Forgive me for going into such intimate detail, but those long drawers were a source of great annoyance, not to say pain. The buttons were always coming off in school, and you had to ask the teacher for a safety pin, a very embarrassing necessity. Pulling on your long, ribbed, black cotton stockings over the long, stretched out pant-legs took more time and trouble than all the rest of getting dressed put together. You folded the pant-leg tightly about your ankle and tried to work your stocking on over it smoothly, so that your leg would look like something faintly human. You were never very successful, and when you finally put on your high laced or button shoes, you seemed to be a victim of elephantiasis, in spite of your best efforts.

Over the shirt and drawers you wore a Ferris waist, a sort of heavy knit, tape-reinforced vest with various buttons placed strategically upon it, and long elastic garters at the bottom to hold up the stockings. This might be boned lightly, if your mother thought you were Developing and beginning to look Immodest; but when you were very young, the Ferris waist was just something on which to hitch other things. The first of the other things was another pair of drawers, short ones, this time, of white cambric with lace or Hamburg edging on the legs. Over this came a flannel petticoat with feather-stitching around the hem, for warmth; and over that came a white cotton petticoat trimmed with lace or Hamburg, for decency and style. (Style! Jeepers!) All these depended on the overworked buttons of the Ferris waist; and what's more, if the weather was unusually cold, one or more petticoats were added. Above your waist, buttoned down at the bottom to the Ferris waist, you wore a camisole of white cotton, with lace or eyelet embroidery at the neck.

We were always having terrible underwear trouble, the least of which was the aforementioned having to ask teacher for a pin. That request could be made in decent privacy, and she could be trusted to be discreet and understanding in her part of the transaction. Often you were less fortunate. A key button would pop, and—oh, shame never to be lived down!—you'd lose your petticoat. All the girls would laugh at you, as though they didn't live in glass houses themselves. If there were boys around—well, I have no words to tell you what an awful and devastating experience that was. Don't ask me why. Most boys knew about petticoats. They must have been blind on washdays if they didn't, even with respectable and modest matrons taking care to hang the more personal bits of laundry on the inside lines, where they'd be well shielded from profane gaze by the sheets and bath towels. In any case, the garments in question were always clean, whole, and (I think I may safely say) far from suggestive, lewd, or obscene in cut or material. They were about as crammed with aphrodisiac qualities as a pillow case.

When we weren't worrying about our petticoats falling off at the bottom, we were concerned about our camisoles showing at the top. It was a dreadful thing to have a little lace exposed at the neckline of your dress. If a friend of yours was walking around all unconscious that her camisole showed, you apprised her of the fact in a whisper, and she turned red and commenced a clutching and hauling maneuver to remedy the situation. It was even more terrible to have your garter break and let your stocking sag in unlovely folds about your undeveloped calves.

But, of course, the worst thing that could possibly happen to you in your whole life would be to lose your pants. I remember one time, when we were living on Broad Street, sitting in the sewing room window at the front of the house and watching the passers-by. The street was almost deserted, since it was neither train-time nor factory-letting-out time; and a young woman whom I knew slightly went swinging briskly down the hill. I could see a line of white creeping lower and lower beneath her modestly long skirt, unmistakably her underdrawers, and I'm not exaggerating when I say that I became paralyzed with horror. I felt that I ought to warn her about what was happening, since she was evidently unconscious of it; but I was incapable of raising my hand to knock on the window. As I stood there with my face flaming for her and my mouth wide open, she became aware of the situation. She stopped short, looked around quickly and furtively, and gave herself a shake like a dog coming out of water. The you-know-whats dropped around her feet, she stepped neatly out of them, scooped them up with one lightning motion, and went on her way.

My heart bled for her, although I don't think a single soul except me saw the incident; and for weeks I lay awake nights in anguished contemplation of the fact that the same thing might happen to me any day. If it did, I would gladly have changed places with Joan of Arc at the stake, and that's no fooling. I took to wearing so many safety pin reinforcements to my Ferris waist buttons that it's a marvel I ever got dressed in the morning or undressed at night.

But that's enough about underwear. Even thinking about it makes me as nervous as a witch to this day. All I can say is that things are ordered better nowadays.

To get back: Underwear in order, you were now ready to don the things that showed. All winter dresses were wool. They had to be. Houses weren't heated very well—or at least ours wasn't—so you had to dress warmly. And over the dresses we very often wore printed cotton pinafores, not for warmth or chic, but to keep our dresses clean. Bridgewater boasted no dry-cleaning establishment, and washing a wool dress was a hazardous project. Sanforizing was unknown, and dyes were not as dependable as they might have been; so your dress very likely would emerge from the wash a sad shrunken and faded object, fit for nothing but to be cut up into rug rags. Therefore you kept it as clean as possible by wearing a pinafore, or apron, and by basting detachable and washable collars and cuffs onto it. Any spots you sponged off weekly.

That's what you wore in the house. When you went out, you put on a heavy winter coat, a wool scarf, wool cap, homemade mittens, and probably leggings; and, if the temperature made it advisable, you wore a sweater underneath the coat. By this time, you looked and felt like a pouter pigeon, but one thing was certain: you weren't going to freeze to death. How we found it possible to move around enough to indulge in what we called skating I don't know; but we managed. You can see, though, why we didn't have time between the dismissal of school and the early winter sunset to change into special skating outfits.

Nobody had shoe-skates. Our skates were hellish contraptions with heel straps and toe clamps that kept coming off, so that we spent as much time sitting on the ice putting them on again as we did on our feet. Even when our skates were temporarily firm, we fell down an awful lot. None of us ever became what you might call even fair skaters, and it's no great wonder, considering the quality of our equipment. The wonder is that we bothered to go skating at all.

We went because in winter Carver's Pond was the gay place. Even adults went skating, progressing in a stately manner around the main body of the pond, the ladies carrying muffs, the men in business clothes, but wearing bright scarfs around their necks as a concession to the occasion. The young blades of the town played hockey on rinks defined by the placing of stones on the ice, and we played, too, on our own rinks, using homemade sticks and an old rubber heel for a puck. There was plenty of room for everyone on the pond. Long lines of school kids played snap-the-whip, and you could always attach yourself to one of the whips. Why someone didn't get killed, I'll never know. When the anchor man dug in and snapped, the end man came around at express-train speed. It was terrifying. Usually some traitor let go, and the last few persons on the whip went caroming off to pile up in a tangled heap on the shore. Or we played tag, just chasing each other around and falling down and shrieking from sheer animal spirits. Usually there were several fires burning, one at the ice house, one on the island, and one where the creek emptied into the pond. If you grew cold, you could warm yourself sketchily at one of the fires. But you almost never did get cold. You were too active with all the falling down and getting up again. But you joined a group around a fire anyhow, occasionally, for sociability's sake.

Once or twice every winter someone fell in. This usually happened down by the ice house, where the employees of McNeeland's Ice, Coal and Coke Company were cutting ice. The ice was scored by a horse-drawn machine, then hand-sawn into blocks which were poked along a channel by men with poles to where an endless cable hoisted it up to the different levels of the enormous, hangar-like ice house for storage in sawdust against the coming summer. It was quite an operation, getting in enough ice to last the town from June until October. It fascinated us at both ends: the cutting in winter and the delivery in July, when the slow teams of great horses paced the streets, hauling the dripping red ice-wagons, and the iceman weighed the blocks on a scale at the tailboard and chipped off pieces that we picked up out of the dust, wiped off sketchily, and sucked. Ice was better in those days. It didn't come in neat, cloudy cubes, but in crystal-clear splinters. It seemed colder and more refreshing.

It was into this hole left by the ice-cutting that people sometimes fell. No one ever was drowned, because the ice-cutters always pulled them out at once; but I can think of no more miserable sight than a poor wretch streaming water from every fold of his stiffening clothes, his lips turning blue and his teeth chattering horribly, while his friends got him off his skates and headed home. There was no shelter to which you could repair to dry out. If you fell in, there was just one thing you could do: run home as fast as your legs would carry you, trusting to the exercise to ward off pneumonia. I guess it did, because I never heard of anyone's catching worse than a cold from falling into Carver's Pond. Alice and I kept well away from the environs of the ice-cutting, though. We thought our mother wouldn't appreciate it if we fell in and ruined our clothes.

It was nice down there at Carver's Pond in the winter. The ice shone like a gray steel mirror in the frame of the snow-powdered shore, and the woods stood up black and bare all around, etched against the high, blue winter sky. The snow slowly changed to gold under the westering sun, and the purple shadows stretched longer and longer across the ice. A nip came into the air, and the fires, that had been marked only by columns of blue smoke rising above them, gleamed with a deepening red-gold of their own against the woods as twilight fell over the countryside. We knew we should be starting home, but we couldn't tear ourselves away. "One more turn around the island," we'd tell each other, and "Just one more." Finally we knew we *had* to leave, and we'd take off our skates reluctantly, to tramp over the frozen fields on clumsy feet that still felt the pressure of the blades, toward the glimmering lights of the village.

Our skiing prowess was on a level with our skating. We'd never laid eyes on a pair of real skis or heard of harnesses and waxes. We'd seen pictures, though, and to us the things the people in the pictures had on their feet looked enough like barrel staves as to make no never-mind. So we made our own skis by tacking toe straps onto hogshead staves. If they didn't work very well, we didn't know it, since we had no idea of what you were supposed to be able to accomplish on skis. They got us from the tops of the gentle declivities which were all that Bridgewater had to offer in the way of slopes to the bottoms, and that was all we asked. What's more, we were sometimes able to stand up all the way down. We coasted a lot, too, on our little high, red sleds—boys had low, flat sleds, and nobody had Flexible Flyers—and sometimes we got hold of some old pans or trays and slid down hill on them, going round and round and holding our feet up at a painful and awkward angle. Anything for the thrill of going down hill without effort, I guess, for the privilege of trudging back up again.

I remember something rather dreadful, though, that happened once while we were coasting on the Normal School Campus Hill, even if I didn't realize until twenty-five years later the full implications of the little incident. As I have said before, a great many immigrants settled across the tracks in Bridgewater, and their children attended the same school, the Model School, that we did. When they arrived in this country, the foreign children couldn't speak any English, so there was a special class for them, officially called the Non-English-Speaking Group, but commonly known as the Nonesuch English. Here the immigrant children stayed until they had learned enough of the language of the country of their adoption to join their proper grades. Then the rest of us acknowledged their existence, at least. Before that, while they were still in the Nonesuch English, they might just as well have been shadows on running water, as far as we were concerned.

My fifth grade teacher, Miss Jenniebennett (to distinguish her from her sister, the sixth grade teacher, Miss Nelliebennett), was a woman of great heart and imagination, and she evidently deplored our attitude. One morning she tried to make us see what a lonely and terrifying thing it was to be a child in a strange land, where the language and the customs of the people and the very stones of the street were unfamiliar. Just a smile would mean much under those circumstances, Miss Bennett said, or any act of simple friendliness. She spoke simply and with genuine feeling, and at the end we were all fired with determination to be nice to the Nonesuch English.

That very afternoon, when we were coasting as usual, I saw this little Nonesuch English boy watching us. He was standing there with his bare hands in the pockets of his too-thin jacket, but his black eyes were quick and bright as they followed the swoop of the coasters, and when someone spilled, his dark, Mediterranean face would light up and he'd laugh softly to himself. He wasn't hoping for a chance to coast himself. He was happy just to be watching the others. I remembered Miss Bennett's words, so I touched his arm and handed him the rope of my sled. Never have I seen a face so full of incredulous joy. He stammered something in his own tongue and was off like a bird. I saw him at intervals during the next hour, while I was sharing Alice's sled, laughing and shouting and having a completely wonderful time. I'm afraid I felt very smug and self-righteous.

Then suddenly he wasn't there any more. I looked and looked, but he had gone and my sled had gone with him. Finally I had to go home, full of rage and hatred, vowing never to try to be nice to anyone again.

The scene in the Principal's office the next day was painful and, I came to realize years later, plain ugly. The boy and his parents were there, and the Principal and the Nonesuch English teacher, acting as interpreter, although she admitted freely that their dialect was beyond her. However, the facts spoke for themselves. I, out of the goodness of my heart, had loaned him my sled, and he had stolen it. He'd returned evil for good. All the talk of these Foreigners couldn't alter that. Finally the three of them stopped trying to argue and just stood there, a swart, fierce little man with bowed shoulders, a puzzled woman with a shawl over her bright hair, and a little boy with a tear-smudged face. I got my sled back, and that was that.

That was that until just a few years ago, when I was waiting for a train on the Dee-po platform, and a sailor came up to me. "I'm Garabed Blank," he blurted, "and I got to say something to you. I never stole your sled. Honest. It was like this." And he told me how it was.

When I had put the sled rope into his hand, it had been a miracle as great as the miracle of snow, which he had never seen before. He'd been so transported with joy that he hadn't even looked at me. He'd been in Seventh Heaven as he'd coasted and coasted the afternoon away. "And then it come time when my mother was expecting me home, and was I ever on a spot! I didn't know who the sled belonged to, and I didn't dare to just dump it there for some other kid to swipe. So I took it home. I didn't know what else to do. And then we couldn't explain, and everything got fouled up —" He sighed. "Anyhow, I'm glad I seen you now. I been ashamed every time I heard your name for the past twenty-five years, knowing you had me taped for a dirty thief. If only we could of spoke English— But things are okey-doke now. Ain't they?"

I said sure, of course things were okey-doke; but they weren't. I don't like the idea at all of one of my fellow men walking around for a quarter of a century and being made ashamed of himself by the sound of my name. It makes me feel like the Gestapo, and that's not a good way to feel. It wasn't Garabed's fault that he couldn't speak English; but the rest of us should have had enough sympathy and under-standing to recognize decency and honesty in any language. I'm glad he feels all right now, but I feel like a louse. Oh, well, it's only simple justice that I should take my turn.

The only other forms of winter entertainment were oc-casional stereopticon lectures at the church, when some missionary from the foreign field came to talk about his ex-periences and to show his slides. And the movies. We went to the stereopticon lectures because we had to, as members in good, though reluctant, standing of the Central Square Congregational Sunday School. The visiting missionary usu-ally wore a rusty cutaway, although not always, and he stood on the platform beside the pulpit, below a screen stretched across the arch of the organ loft. Our own minister led us in a hymn and a prayer, and introduced his spiritual brother. Then the church was darkened and a great beam of light cut down through the blackness from the rear gallery, where the lantern was set up. Bad boys, present under duress, took this opportunity to throw on the screen gigantic shadow pictures of rabbits wiggling their ears, by thrusting their hands up into the path of light, thumbs and two fingers pinched together into a nose, the other two fingers standing up like ears. They really did look like rabbits, and we laughed with a heartiness bordering on hysteria. Barring the accident of one of the pictures being inadvertently shown upside down, as happily chanced once in a while, it was the last laugh we were going to get, and it was too bad it couldn't last longer. But an outraged deacon always nailed the offenders at once and made them sit in the pew with him, out of temptation's way.

The missionary speaker was always sincere and earnest, but he was seldom silver-tongued. Not to put too fine a point on it, he was usually a colossal bore. His pictures were not much better. They stressed heavily the results, in the form of shapeless Mother Hubbards and ugly little frame schoolhouses, of toil in the faraway vineyards of the Lord. All the redeemed natives looked sad and discouraged and unbeautiful, and it was hard to imagine their state, if this were an improvement, before they'd been salvaged. He never showed pictures of them in their pre-redemption condition, because they would have shocked us; but sometimes he gave us cryptic verbal hints. We gathered that they had been an unregenerate crew, running around with nothing on except garlands of flowers and frittering their days away in swimming, sailing, laughing, and singing pagan songs. Unquestionably, the man was wise to suppress pictorial evidence of this deplorable state of affairs.

Occasionally the lecturer mislaid the clicker with which he signaled the operator of the lantern that it was time to change pictures and had to resort to finger-snapping or whistling; but by that time we were ordinarily too dispirited to enjoy his discomfort. When the lights came back on again, we dutifully dropped into the collection plate the dimes we'd been supplied with by our parents, toward the buying of more Mother Hubbards, wearily dragged ourselves through the closing hymn and went home.

The movies were something else again. We went there because we wanted to. At first they were shown in the upper part of the Town Hall, one day a week, under the impresario-ship of Fred Waite, who was also Chief of the Fire Department. This was definitely a catch-as-catch-can performance, liable to all manner of catastrophe, such as the breaking-down of the projector, the leaking of light around the blackout shields at the windows so that the pictures dimmed almost to invisibility, or the outbreak of fire somewhere in town, so that the entire personnel had to leave in a hurry to attend, accompanied by the large percentage of the audience who were members of the Volunteer Fire Department or just plain sublimated pyromaniacs. These contretemps didn't dismay us at all or lessen our enjoyment of the pictures. Just the fact that the actors really moved was enough to hold us spellbound through all improbabilities of plot or action. We were really living, those rare days when we were allowed to go to the movies.

But we hadn't seen anything until the Princess Theatre was built down on Broad Street. At the Grand Gala Opening we were stricken dumb, as captive barbarians from the wild tribes of Outer Gaul must have been stricken amid the decadent luxury of Imperial Rome. First of all, every patron on that first day was given a rosebud—not a paper rose, but an honest-to-God real live hothouse flower. Never had we heard of such a thing. Roses in winter were strictly for funerals. Then the seats! We were accustomed to the collapsible wooden chairs of the Town Hall, which weren't hitched down, so that the floor could be cleared for other purposes such as voting or a Women's Relief Corps Whist Party. In the event of a fire, when there was a hasty mass exodus, the Town Hall chairs fell to the floor like wheat before a scythe, only with a lot more noise. The Princess seats were indecently comfortable, leather-upholstered and possessing springs; and they were fastened down. Nobody behind you could shove you into the row ahead by putting his feet on the back of your chair and straightening his knees.

When the piano player—for the movies were silent, of course—Ralph McCarthy, walked down the aisle amid popular acclaim in the form of clapping, whistling, and the stamping of feet, the lights didn't just go out, leaving a semi-gloom pierced by arrows of sunlight from ill-shuttered windows. They faded slowly and dramatically, leaving an absolute pitch blackness, except for one little gleam from the light over the music rack, way down front. It made the first offering on the screen—a notice which read "Ladies will please remove their hats"—much clearer and brighter than the same request on the Town Hall screen. As a matter of fact, it wasn't necessary at the Princess for ladies to remove their hats at all. The floor inclined, unlike the Town Hall floor, so that you could see over the biggest Merry Widow. Oh, I tell you, the Princess was Lucullan!

There were always slides first, advertising the wares of the various merchants around town. We applauded these vigorously, because we were there to have a good time, and noise was implicit in enjoyment. There was usually a one-reel comedy, in which Keystone Cops made fools of themselves side-splittingly. We laughed until we were almost sick. At Saturday matinées, which were the only shows we were allowed to attend, there was always an installment of the current serial, usually featuring Pearl White. That woman certainly took a beating. Everything happened to her. She was tied to railroad tracks or the carriages of saw mills, lashed to wild horses, shut up in cellars with poisonous snakes, ambushed by homicidal maniacs, and tossed into water-filled quarries, to mention only a very few of her tribulations. We screamed our lungs out, warning her of impending perils, and when the screen said "Continued Next Week," leaving her dangling over a cliff, we were as limp and weak as she was. Limper and weaker. She had a strange talent for coming out of lakes bone-dry, being snatched from runaway horses with every blonde hair in immaculate place, and emerging from attacks upon her virtue—never, need I tell you, successful—with her respiration normal. It never occurred to us to criticize this flying in the face of natural laws, or to doubt the eye's evidence.

Very often the main feature was *Sad*. Children got lost, dogs died, mortgaged homes were lost to unspeakable villains, and feeble old parents went over the hill to the poorhouse.

We cried. For some reason, even though we made a cult of not crying over our own affairs, it was all right to cry over movies. So we enjoyed ourselves thoroughly, confident that things would come out all right in the end, in time for us to dry our tears and present our usual stoic countenances to the everyday world. When Ralph McCarthy went into "Hearts and Flowers," we started mopping up and were our own women by the time the last clinch was over and the lights went up. Then we'd go home feeling fine, thank you, purged and uplifted, the gamut of the emotions having been given a workout from A to Z and back, and the catharsis complete. We spent the week until the next Saturday re-enacting with improvements the dramas we'd seen, taking turns being Miss White and using the porch roof for a cliff. We certainly got our money's worth out of our movie nickels.

That's about all there was to do in the winter except read. It's a wonder we didn't read ourselves blind. I don't even know whether ours was a very good children's library or not. Probably it wasn't, since the town didn't allot a staggering sum for the purchase of books for the young. It seemed wonderful to us, though. We could always find something to read there, and that's what we went for. Of course, we weren't very fussy. We'd read anything, provided it was printed in English; and we weren't at all averse to re-reading over and over, a book we especially liked, until we had it practically memorized. We adored the Little Colonel series, and read the book again and again. We wanted to be just like the heroine, a Kentucky girl named Lloyd Sherman who lived with her mother and grandfather in a pillared white mansion. I'll bet I remember to this day almost everything about her. She had a friend named Nancy, and— But you can read the books yourself, if you're interested. I wonder, though, if any children's books being written today will be remembered in the loving detail with which I recall the Little Colonel.

Dorothy Dainty we didn't care for. She was too holy to be true, and showed us up in a bad light. We loved Mark Tidd —Marcus Aurelius Fortunatus Tidd, an ingenius fat boy of Clarence B. Kelland's creation; and all the other boys' books, like *Stover at Yale* and the Frank Merriwell Series. Oddly enough, we liked equally well the Andrew Lang collections of fairy tales—the *Blue Fairy Book*, the *Red Fairy Book*, and all the rest. Just the sight of the words *"Once upon a time there lived a king—"* swung us into the world of abused princesses, wicked stepmothers, animals who could talk and weave spells, and prospects of living happily ever after.

If we couldn't find any book that we wanted to read right then, we could always take home a volume of bound *St. Nicholases*. *St. Nicholas* was a monthly magazine for boys and girls, full of wonderful stories. There was a letterbox in the back, in which letters from readers were published. I entered into a correspondence with a girl in Hilo, Hawaii, through that letterbox once, and kept it up for years; and once I even had a letter of my own published, my first appearance in print. Nobody could have touched me with a ten-foot pole for days after that; not that anybody tried. I got some fan mail, too: a letter from a girl in Binghamton, New York. Her name was Ruby Merrill, and she seemed like a very nice girl. Intelligent, too. She liked my letter.

The other magazine that we read religiously was the *Youth's Companion*. This was supposed to be for boys, but that didn't make any difference to us. If anything, it was a recommendation. By and large, we considered stories for boys better than stories for girls. More action and less mush. A contributing author whom we especially esteemed was C. A. Stevens, who wrote about adventures in the woods of Maine. I swore that when I was grown-up, I was going to live in the woods of Maine myself. Improbable as it sounds, youthful oaths being ordinarily ephemeral and quickly outgrown, I finally made it and came to rest for about fifteen years smack in the middle of the C. A. Stevens country. It was just exactly as represented, too.

Another service that the library offered was the loan of stereoscopes. These were optical instruments for the viewing of educational pictures. There was an eyepiece with a red velvet edge, from which extended a tongue of wood supporting a rack to hold the pictures. The pictures came in boxes, assorted by subject ("Views of Yellowstone National Park," or "A Trip Through India," or "Well-known English Cathedrals"); and on each card the picture was printed twice, one print right beside the other. They looked like ordinary, flat sepia photographs, but when you put them into the racks and peered at them through the lenses, the scene leaped out in three dimensions. It was marvelous to our unsophisticated eyes. We kept one of the stereoscopes on permanent loan at home, and changed the boxes of views two or three times a week. We ran through the limited available supply in short order, but then we started at the beginning and took them all out again. I guess the stereoscope really did educate us to some degree, in spite of ourselves. We weren't aiming at Culture. We were just being entertained.

Besides the books that we withdrew from the library, we read everything else, appropriate or inappropriate, that we could lay hands on. The only thing I was never able to get through was the *Pickwick Papers;* and I haven't succeeded to this day. I found it dull then, and I find it dull now. It looked for a while there as though I'd have to add another book to the list of those I hadn't finished. For some reason it was a matter of honor to read a book through, if once you started it; and our long-range program was eventually to read every book in the world. (Age must have softened my fiber. I no longer keep on reading a book I don't care for, and I long ago admitted I was licked when it came to giving man's published works full coverage.) But the second book I almost didn't finish was an opus by Hall Caine called *The Woman Thou Gavest Me,* and the reason I stopped reading it for a time was not failure of intent but Censorship.

I think one of my mother's sisters gave her the book. It appeared on the living-room table, and as involuntarily as a chicken picks up corn and eats it, I picked up the book and started reading it. My interest at this point was mild. The book was readable—anything in print except *Pickwick Papers* was readable—but there was an awful lot of talk in it, and not much action. Having begun, however, I was honor-

bound to continue. Then my mother livened things up considerably by telling me that I was to put that book down at
once. It was not fit for a young girl to read. After she'd
caught me taking a sneak-read a couple of times, the book
disappeared.

Naturally my curiosity was whetted to the point of fever.
I hadn't yet found anything bad in the book, although I'd
looked hard enough, and I lived and read in hope. There
was a woman who was married to one man and was always
kissing another, but as far as I was concerned that only went
to show that she was a pretty silly type. Her husband had a
whole stable full of saddle horses, and here she was wasting
her time kissing.

I finished it standing on one foot and then the other,
fifteen or twenty minutes at a time, in Faxon's little stationery store up on Central Square. Of course, I was reading
pretty fast, because I didn't know when Mr. Faxon would
clamp down and tell me either to buy the book or leave it
alone, and maybe I missed the bad part in my haste. But I
learned something about the way censorship works.

There was a lot to do in summer, over and above our
standard pursuits of building huts, playing games, helping
our mother, and just ramming around the neighborhood,
keeping an eye on things, and exploring the woods and fields
about the village. Summer was better than winter anyhow,
in every respect. We didn't have to go to school, to begin
with; and we didn't have to wear all those tiresome clothes.
Starting about April, we tapered off by discarding a layer of
underwear at a time, at intervals, until we were down to just
the short cotton summer drawers, sleeveless summer under-
shirts, the Ferris waists, lightweight now, and two cotton
petticoats under our thin, washable cotton dresses. The second petticoat was worn so that we wouldn't Show Through,
as it was disapprovingly called: so that when we stood against
the light, we wouldn't be silhouetted to reveal the fact that
we possessed legs above the knee. She who was careless about
Showing Through was shameless and abandoned indeed. We
went from coats to sweaters and finally to that heavenly con-

dition where we could go outdoors without any wrap at all and, in full summer, could even go barefooted.

I can't tell you how wonderful it was not to be weighted down and constricted by all those layers and layers of bundling. We felt so free and bodiless, so light and graceful and airy, so careless and enraptured, that it affected our minds as well as our bodies. We became even more bemused and flighty than was inferential in our age and sex. We giggled at anything or nothing, broke from immobility into a leaping canter for no reason, forgot errands on which we had been sent, lifted our bare arms like weightless, slow wings, and stood for long moments in mindless trances. It was almost worth living in a climate that demanded winter clothing for the joy of getting rid of it. We felt like gorgeous great butterflies coming out of cocoons, although the physical resemblance was not likely to strike the beholder as startling.

Even the natural world was better in summer than in winter. The days were longer and the sun high-riding and hot. No more did we rise in a dark and icy predawn, but to a world beautiful with long shadows across dewy, diamond-strewn lawns. Far from eating our suppers by lamplight, we ate them while the sun was still aloft and had long hours of sunshine still to play before bedtime. Lawns were green and gardens bright, where all winter there had been dun stretches of dead grass and frozen earth. The trees that had made a delicate winter tracery against a cold sky put forth leaves and became massive and heavy-headed. They were no longer harps giving forth a faint and eerie music under the fingers of the biting wind, but ships in full sail tugging at their anchoring roots, the high branches tossing and turning with a murmurous, rushing sound. Our New England puritanism approved the clean austerity of the cold winter landscape; but something deep within, decadent and traitorous to our upbringing, responded hungrily to the lushness, the brilliance, the languor and the heat of summer.

Perhaps that's why we were willing to eschew our Saturday afternoon sessions with Pearl White in favor of the ball games. Our mother wouldn't let us go to the movies in summer unless it rained, on the grounds that we were much better off out in the nice fresh air, a fact that cannot be gainsaid. For once we didn't mind doing something that was good for us. Seeing someone else run around energetically in the hot sun underlined our lotus-eating mood of lazy leisure. Besides, we were deliciously and hopelessly in love with several of the players and seized upon this opportunity to worship from afar. We never spoke to one of them in our lives, and I'm sure I don't have to add that they were completely unaware not only of our adoration but indeed of our very existence. They were, I feel safe in saying, perfectly normal young men, possessing their quota of human frailties; but we endowed them with the somewhat divergent virtues of Galahads, Lancelots, and Arthurs, and enshrined them in our hearts accordingly.

Possibly I am not in a position to judge dispassionately, my views being colored by romanticism, but I think that the Saturday afternoon ball games would have been fun anyhow. They were played on South Field, which had nothing whatsoever in common with Braves Field or the Yankee Stadium except a diamond laid out on it for the same general purpose. South Field was, during the months from September to June, the Model School playground, where we whiled away our recess-times at dodge ball and other teacher-motivated games of doubtful origin and interest. There was no fence around it and no bleachers. Anyone who wanted to go to the ball game—and they were well attended—just wandered onto the field from any point of the compass and stood or sat on the grass along the first and third baselines. No attempt was made to collect an admission fee, and that fact alone would indicate the non-professional nature of the games. The town team, which traveled under the name of the Bridgewater Club, was made up of young-men-about-town who liked to play baseball and who played it, actually, on a level that would nowadays be considered semi-professional. The games were good, not with the practiced, machine-like perfection of the Big League games, but liable to unforeseeable errors and failures in crucial moments that made them all the more exciting.

In summer, too, we always had a week of Chautauqua. This was a tent-show, sent out from the annual assembly at Lake Chautauqua, New York. The summer sessions at Chautauqua were brought into being not too long after the Civil War by Bishop John Vincent and Henry Lewis for the avowed purpose of raising the general cultural and educational level of the country by means of lectures and talks. By our day, the project had become considerably expanded and elaborated, so that the meetings at Chautauqua were only a small part of it. The entertainers were trained there, but then they went on the road in companies, following various circuits and spreading the light of Culture far and wide. It would be very easy now to hold up for ridicule the Chautauqua shows and the whole idea behind them, but it would be unfair, false, and unjust, a cheaply smart attempt at cynical humor. Possibly they would seem corny to us now, but then they seemed wonderful, and were wonderful, considering the times and the difficulties the troupes had to work under. Perhaps we lived in a corny era. Certainly we had no background for comparison—only home-talent shows and the dreadful, badly conceived and acted, rudimentary movies. In comparison and according to our tastes, the Chautauqua productions were polished, cosmopolitan, and worth while. They gave us a glimpse of a whole world, the existence of which we would otherwise never have known.

The procedure for securing Chautauqua was routine. A group of civic-minded and responsible citizens guaranteed a certain sum of money if the show would include our town in its circuit. This money was raised by advance sale of tickets, and if there was a deficit, the individual guarantors and interested organizations such as churches and civic clubs dipped into their pockets to make it up. This came under the heading of Civic Improvement. Our father was always a guarantor, as editor of the local paper, so we always had tickets to some of the shows. He had to buy them, both because of his position on the committee and because of his editorship. He also, by virtue of this dual role, had to give the show free publicity and free advertising space, as his personal contribution to the endeavor.

We went two or three times each season, and the whole of Chautauqua Week was a period of alternate feverish anticipation and gratified review. The tent was set up on South Field—the Bridgewater Club had to schedule an out-of-town game for Chautauqua Week—and just the sight of it there, mammoth and brown and weathered, was exciting. It really wasn't such a big tent, but it seemed big to us. It was wonderful inside, rather dim except where lances of afternoon sunlight shot in through the cracks, or the footlights of the makeshift stage—a wire was run in from a telephone pole on Grove Street—reflected over the rows of funeral-parlor-type chairs, set up on the worn, familiar grass. The canvas rippled and sighed gently in the wind, stirring with a lazy life of its own around and above us, secret, mysterious, thrilling. Once in a while it showered, and then the tent was full of a sound like the faraway muffled hoofbeats of the horses of imagination. It's too bad that the meaning of the phrase "out of this world" has been so distorted and vulgarized, because it exactly describes what it was like, virtually, inside the Chautauqua tent.

I'm not going to try to tell you about the shows themselves. I can only tell you about their effect on us. You must remember that this was in the day before television or even radio and sound movies, so we had not acquired the experienced, critical, and sophisticated eye and ear of today's young. Ours were simple, fresh, and innocent minds, ready and eager for miracles. And so the miracles occurred: miracles of beauty and skill and ingenuity. Our musical education had been confined to listening to the efforts of the choir at church, the local band concerts, and the Normal School Glee Club annual concert. So the fare offered by Chautauqua —the Negro Male Quartet with its deep-toned, heartbreaking spirituals, the Swiss Yodelers and Bell-ringers, the Stringed Octette which played chamber music—fed some deep and previously unrecognized craving in us. We hadn't known that we loved music—in fact, we'd have denied the charge as smacking of the affected—but we found ourselves moved and uplifted. Perhaps the performances were not first rate. Perhaps they were third or even fourth rate. I have no idea, and it doesn't matter anyhow, since the sweetness of music lies entirely in the ear of the listener, and in our ears these were celestial harmonies.

Chautauqua programs were by no means confined to music. They were, as a matter of fact, very well balanced and must have been the result of careful planning. There was, for example, a glass blower, who, with no more equipment than a flame, some molten glass, and a little tube, fashioned lovely and delicate flowers and birds and animals which were given away to lucky members of the audience. Oh, the joy of cradling a tiny, perfect glass sparrow, still warm as with life, in fearfully careful, cupped hands! There was a magician who really could pull rabbits out of hats and pennies out of ears; and folk dancers of gaiety and agility and grace, in bright, quaint foreign costumes. There were the lecturers and story tellers on which the movement had been founded; and it was at Chautauqua that I saw my first real live play, a production of *The Man from Home,* which left me consumed with a desire to grow up quick and tread the boards myself.

We haven't had Chautauqua in Bridgewater for a long time, and trying to bring it back would be an experiment foredoomed to failure. There's too much high-powered, precooked, easily digested competition now. It's too bad. No super-colossal, wide-screen spectacle can possibly rouse in the breasts of presentday youthful viewers the great emotions of wonder and discovery that claimed Alice and me in that beat-up little tent on South Field.

Thursday evenings in summer were Band Concert nights in Bridgewater. These were held from the bandstand on the Common in Central Square, from eight until ten. Everybody attended, and just before eight o'clock the streets were full of people, Common-bound, some carrying sweaters in case the evening turned chill, some carrying rugs or pillows to sit on, some empty-handed, but all full of a holiday spirit. The few who owned cars arrived a little earlier, in order to secure vantage points along the iron rail fence, from which to see as well as hear. Not that the selections were going to be any novelty or surprise to them. All week long, anybody passing through the Square after working hours—for the bandsmen were wage-earning citizens who happened to play some instrument—could hear all too well, unless he was literally stone deaf, the painful progress toward perfection emanating from rehearsals, held upstairs in the Bowman Block, over Scotton's Dry Goods Store. Excepting possibly the travails of a beginner on the violin, there is nothing more trying to the sensitive ear than the gropings of a brass band on unsure ground. The very leaves of the Common trees quivered in nightly agony until Thursday.

But on Thursday the performance had been polished sufficiently to be creditable; or else new numbers had been replaced by old familiars and put off until a later date, when the rough spots would have been ironed out; or else the presence of a Mr. Edson from East Bridgewater, who played what would be called today a hot cornet, served to pull the rest of the band together. Mr. Edson led the band and played two solos during the course of the evening. He was good. Chills used to run down our spines during his solos, when the silver-gilt notes climbed higher and higher, clear and pure, rising impossibly to new heights, up through the tops of the trees, up past the weathervane on the white Congregational spire, up to the high-riding, listening moon. The Square was very quiet while Mr. Edson played; and then it rocked with a pandemonium of applause from a thousand throats and from raucous automobile horns.

The rest of the time I'm afraid we weren't too attentive to the music. We ran around in packs, annoying those who really wanted to listen and spending our weekly dimes according to convention: five cents for an ice cream cone at Hayes' and five cents for a bag of popcorn from the little horse-drawn cart that came weekly down from Brockton. That popcorn was a feature of Band Concert Night. The man made it right there before your eyes and drenched it with melted butter after he'd scooped it into the little paper bag. It was hot and fresh and tasted much better than popcorn at home.

During the concert the wagon stood beside the fence like a little, brightly lighted, glass house, the center of a milling swarm of customers. The horse had long since been safely quartered in Atkinson's Livery Stable for the duration of the festivities. I suppose that when I was very, very little, I thought that the popcorn cart just sprang up like a mushroom on Band Concert nights and withered away when the affair was over. I can remember the birth of my realization that such was not the case. We were riding down from Brockton on the trolley car in the late afternoon and, looking out the window, saw the popcorn wagon on its way to its weekly rendezvous in Bridgewater. The little brown horse was trotting along between the daisy fields at a steady and businesslike clip in the broad daylight, and the popcorn man, in an old gray sweater instead of the white coat I'd always associated with him, was sitting on a stool with his legs crossed, reins loose in his hands and route left to the horse's discretion, reading the Brockton *Enterprise*. I felt as though I shouldn't look, as though I were spying on something I wasn't meant to see and invading his privacy unwarrantably in thus catching him off guard and *on déshabille,* as it were. And I felt like crying for the little horse who was trotting along so cheerfully and bravely, not knowing that he wasn't going to get home to his own bed until it was late and dark.

I can't imagine what we were doing on the Brockton trolley on a Thursday afternoon, nor who was in charge of us. It couldn't have been our mother. Thursday was Publication Day, and she went to the *Independent* office as soon as the breakfast dishes were done and the house put to rights, and stayed there until the paper was off the press, which might be any time between eight o'clock and midnight. Alice and I shifted home-base from the house we happened to be occupying to the *Independent* office on Thursdays. That is, we ate there the lunches and suppers our mother put up for the whole family before leaving home, and we took our problems, complaints, and requests there for judgment.

Whether we could attend the Band Concert when we were small depended upon the progress being made with the *Independent*. If things were going well, we'd be able to stay for only a few numbers, or none at all. Our mother considered the place for us after dark to be bed, if possible; and in any case, she wasn't going to have us running wild and unsupervised all over Central Square at that hour of the night. She wasn't in any mood or condition, after a twelve- or fourteen-hour day of hard nerve-testing work, to lallygag around there with us, either. She wanted nothing but to go home. If things were going from fair to badly, we'd hear more or all of the concert. Between selections, we raced into the office to check on progress, and out again if there was time to hear another rendition.

So maybe we appreciated the concert even more than the mine-run listener. We never knew which number was going to be our last. It lent a certain element of suspense and obliged us to wring from each moment its final drop of enjoyment.

Going home when the concert was just getting well under way was a desolating experience. We walked staidly along the dark and quiet streets, the whole family of us, out of step with the evening. The few people we met were hurrying in the opposite direction, latecomers to the concert, their approaching footsteps eager and their greetings carelessly flung and hasty. Ahead of us stretched the long empty tunnel of the leafy street, leading away from the excitement and the bustle and the lights. Behind us we could hear the music and the mutter of the crowd, growing fainter and fainter as we followed the casually spaced beacons of the street lamps to a house that offered nothing of excitement but only the undesired benison of a quiet night's sleep. This was what it would be like to die young, we felt, to have to leave before anything had happened, before we'd learned how anything came out. Other kids were having fun up there in Central Square, and we—

But perhaps that's the way you feel no matter when it comes your time to die.

7

The Three R's and William Tell

THE ONLY TIME DURING MY CHILDHOOD WHEN I DID NOT FEEL
the grim shadow of school hanging over me was for about
three weeks each summer during July. It took me that long
to shake off the effect of the school year just completed; and
then August loomed. By any calendar I had ever seen, the
end of August meant the first of September, and September
meant hated, inevitable school. I loathed school so much that
just thinking about it gave me a stomachache; and sometimes
during February I would wonder with a sick despair whether
I could ever live out the time until June. I always had, but
I'd feel that this year was the straw that was going to break
this camel's back.

This wasn't any attitude that I *took*. On the contrary, it
took me. In some subjects—reading and composition especially—I did as well as anybody did, and better than most. I
was poor in arithmetic, but history and geography offered no
special problems. In general, I got pretty good report cards,
although not as good as Alice did. Having that fact periodically pointed out at home didn't further endear school to
me, in all probability; but it wasn't bad enough to account
for my bone-deep and abiding hatred.

I guess it was primarily a matter of the Dickinson temperament. Dickinsons are not and never have been group-minded.

They prefer to operate on their own. They function better alone than with others. They resent—and this is a bad fault —being told anything; and while you can sometimes influence them if you know the right spell to say—for all true Dickinsons have a fatal weakness for words—you can neither drive nor lead them. They won't go where the flock goes, even if wandering off to the other end of the range by themselves means that they are going to be hungry and cold. They're not going to be lonesome, that's one sure thing. You can't ever punish a Dickinson by shutting her up in a paddock alone. She enjoys her own company too much. The only time Dickinsons are lonely is when they are in crowds, trying to adjust their slightly off-beat thinking to the accepted trend. They are eccentric in the purely mechanical sense of being a little bit off center.

Emily Dickinson is an extreme example of Dickinson behavior, but there are plenty of others to illustrate my point. John Dickinson signed the Declaration of Independence, I feel sure, partly because he was seduced by the fine sound of the name of the document, but more because it was at the time the less popular political course to take.

The old stock has become considerably watered down and weakened of later days; but enough of the former stubborn, nonconformist flavor remains so that I couldn't bear to be shut up with a lot of other kids, being bossed around. I wanted out.

That's the only way I can account for my first, instinctive, and deathless revolt against going to school. My initial experience was pleasant enough so that I should, had it not been for this heritage, have loved school very much. Bridgewater had one of the few school systems anywhere around in those days to boast a kindergarten. This was because of a set-up peculiar to those towns in which Normal Schools were located. The grade school was partly supported by the state and operated in connection with the State Normal School as a training ground for would-be teachers, and also as a sort of laboratory in which to try out, or to demonstrate to visitors, new ideas in the field of education. It was, although a far cry from the later Progressive schools, a very progressive school for the times. In comparison with the ordinary schools, it was run along extremely informal, relaxed, and flexible lines, a fact for which I should be thankful, even if I didn't realize it and appreciate it at the time. It was called the Model School because it was supposed to be a model school. It seemed more like Devil's Island to me. I honestly wonder what would have happened to me if I'd been subjected to the strict regimentation of the average school of the day. I think I'd have gone completely haywire, although there is always the possibility that it would have made a better woman of me.

Kindergarten should have been enjoyable. It was conducted by Miss Keyes and Miss Wells, two gently firm, placid, even-tempered women who liked children genuinely. The two large rooms in which it was held were sunny and pleasant, connected by an enormously wide double door, and full of plants and birds in cages and fish in a tank. There were interesting pictures, and educational toys designed to encourage the constructive and creative talents, and a big dollhouse with a whole family of dolls, not for display, but for dressing and undressing and holding in laps. Each morning we opened the session by standing with linked hands, toes neatly aligned on the big circle painted on the floor, and singing "Good Morning, Merry Sunshine" if it was a pleasant day, or "Good Morning, Dear Teachers" if it wasn't. Then we scattered into small groups, taking our little chairs to the low tables, and there learned to weave and sew with bright yarns, or to say the alphabet, or to count to one hundred. We colored pictures, too, and cut them out and mounted them. The kindergarten paste smelled and looked good enough to eat, and it was. I ate some once, to find out. We made butter and ate it on common crackers, and we played singing games like London Bridge and Farmer in the Dell. In the spring we planted a little garden out underneath the kindergarten windows. I guess it really was a model kindergarten; but I would rather have been at home.

After this comparatively idyllic existence, the first grade came as a rude awakening to the facts of life. I was so miserable there that if psychosomatic ailments had been invented then, I'd surely have died of some obscure, psyche-rooted illness. My fear and hatred of the teacher was something that I haven't got over yet, and the fact that she is now dead fails to make me remorseful over all the time I spent praying for her early and painful demise. Oh, sure, *de mortuis nil nisi bonum,* but I never did see why. Death can do a lot of things, but it can't alter the facts of the past or undo old acts of cruelty and injustice. What's the point of trying to behave decently if, after death—which neither saint nor sinner escapes—only good is going to be spoken of you no matter how well or badly you acted? It makes no sense. So I'll speak as ill of the dead as I think they deserve, and expect the same treatment after I'm gone.

My first grade teacher used to pinch me until I was black and blue. I wasn't used to being pinched. Spanked, yes. Shaken by the shoulders, yes. But pinched, no. The first time it happened I was so shocked and outraged that I couldn't believe the evidence of my senses. *This* happening to *me?* I guessed she didn't know who I was! (I didn't either, naturally; but I did have an inbred notion of personal inviolability.) She did know, though, exactly. She knew I was just a frightened little mutt who couldn't and wouldn't dare to fight back.

The standard punishment of first and second graders for run-of-the-mine offenses and dilatoriness was something called Standing in the Archway. The two grades shared the exclusive use of an entrance, other than that used by the upper grades, which had a steep flight of stone steps leading to a sort of deep, sheltered porch under a stone arch. It was a cold, sunless cave of a place, and if you'd been a bad or lazy girl or boy, you spent your recess-time standing there instead of playing out in the yard with the others. It really was a punishment, since the archway was chilly and boring, and you weren't allowed to talk to any others in the same boat. There was always a line of sad little apples lined up there at recess-time, wistfully watching their friends running around in the sun. In addition to having your freedom curtailed, you were made to feel disgraced; and that should have been enough.

But not for Miss Stuart it wasn't! I well remember the first time I ever had to Stand in the Archway. It later became my Home Away from Home, and I spent more time there than I did on the playground, usually for some offense the nature of which I had only a very hazy notion; and eventually I came to accept Standing in the Archway as my lot in life and developed a protective numbness about it, too discouraged to care any more. But the first time it happened, I did care. We had been given some boxes of letters, and we were supposed to arrange them on our desk-tops in reverse alphabetical order, starting with Z and working back to A. I got ZYX done all right, but I couldn't find W. I searched for a while, and then I glanced out the window and saw some pigeons on one of the Normal School dormitory roofs. They were walking around, preening themselves and taking sudden short flights into the air, like tossed scarfs against the blue of the sky and the crimson and gold of an autumn maple tree—I can see that tree yet, and the white birds blowing across it!— so I forgot all about the alphabet and just sat there watching.

Reckoning day came, of course, and everybody except me had his seatwork done; so it was the Archway for me. I felt terribly, particularly since I knew I'd been a bad, lazy no-good and deserved to be punished. I was standing there, staring straight ahead and trying not to cry, when Miss Stuart and the second grade teacher, Miss Lockwood, started down the line. Miss Stuart was happily rubbing salt into open wounds for Miss Lockwood's benefit. She was making each first grader tell for what heinous crime he was doing penance.

When she came to me, I failed to answer at once because I wasn't sure I could speak. It was then, while I was fighting for control, that she grasped my arm and started pinching. Startled, I looked up at her, confident that it was a mistake and that she didn't realize how much she was hurting me. She looked right straight back, and her fingers twisted a fold of my skin; and I knew with a sick horror that she meant to hurt. From that time on, I was lost. I spent all the rest of that year and the next trying to make myself small and silent, so that the teacher wouldn't notice me.

It didn't work very well. My very anxiety to avoid attention trapped me into pitfalls, and I was always giving silly answers and doing stupid things, so that I was made more conspicuous than ever. Everybody else seemed to get along all right, and I developed a horrible feeling that all the other kids were privy to some secret knowledge that was denied me. They were so facile and successful and seemed to be having so much fun, while I was so awkward and wretched. I thought there must be some key-word, some magic formula, that would set things right and open up the world's oyster for me; but I couldn't find it.

All I found was a small core of cold, stubborn pride inside me that refused to let me whimper, no matter how badly I was hurt. It has stood me in very good stead, too. I also learned another valuable lesson: that trying to guess what teacher wants you to say is a hopeless gamble, so you might as well say what you think, admit you don't know, or keep quiet. All courses get you into about the same amount of trouble, and any one of the last three is easier and more satisfying than the first.

I never did find out what the secret was, although to this day I sometimes have indications that it still exists, and that everybody else knows something I don't know. But I don't care any more. I started learning not to care down in the grade school. Let them have their secrets. I've got secrets, too. That was my attitude, a whistling in the dark if ever there was one.

I guess I was stir crazy by the time I got out of the first grade. I don't remember much about the second grade except that I was put into the group called the Crows, who couldn't carry a tune. The good singers were Canaries, Bluebirds, and Robins, in a descending scale of tunefulness. And I remember a poem we had to learn, starting

> So here hath been dawning another blue day.
> Think! Wilt thou let it slip useless away?
> Out of Eternity this new day was born,
> Into Eternity at night will return—

I could say it with great expression and feeling, but I hadn't the faintest idea what it meant.

It wasn't until I was in Miss Jenniebennett's fifth grade that I really emerged from my state of shock. Love for Miss Bennett crept up on me. I felt like a traitor to a cause, and I fought my finer feelings doggedly, but it was a losing battle. I couldn't help myself. Miss Bennett wasn't young or pretty. She was an energetic, middle-aged woman who looked like a schoolteacher; but she acted like a human being. She laughed occasionally, and when she was cross, you knew what she was cross about and so could try to improve the situation. She conducted her classes with a businesslike ease, giving the impression—which may or may not have been true—that she was as anxious as you were to get the stupid business over, but that since we were all obliged to go through these motions, we might as well get what we could out of them. She was an excellent teacher and so altered my thinking on the subject of school that I finished the grammar grades, if not in a state of euphoria, at least with an attitude of passive acceptance of the inevitable rather than in the active and self-destructive bitterness of hopeless revolt.

It really wasn't so bad all the time. There were aspects that gave respite from the general chain-gang atmosphere. One of these was the periodic Changing of the Normals. While this was not as impressive as the Changing of the Guard at Buckingham Palace, it was still of interest and importance to us and carried with it its own little traditions. The Normals were, of course, the students at the Normal School, who at a certain point of the preparation for their careers as teachers were adjudged to be stuffed full enough of method and theory to try their hands at real teaching. The Model School was their practice ground and we were their guinea pigs. They were always under the direction and supervision of the regular teacher whose grade it was supposed to be, so they didn't do as much damage as they might have, I guess. But it is my possibly mistaken opinion that it doesn't help one who—like me—couldn't do arithmetic and was decidedly shaky in spelling to be exposed to a dozen or more instructors, with their varying methods, disciplines and personalities, in the course of one school year, particularly if that instructor is shaking in her own boots. Nobody feels secure, except probably the regular teacher; and she was often so irked at having to sit by with her hands folded, watching some neophyte make a mess of a lesson she could have taught well in her sleep and would have much preferred to be teaching now, that she was of no help to anybody.

But I didn't realize any of that at the time. At the time, I was interested along with the rest of the grade in seeing what we were going to draw this trip. We had new Normals about every six weeks or so, three or four at a clip, and we spent the first few days with our horns drawn in, spying out any suggestions of vulnerability. Any poor Normal who seemed unduly nervous or who had a speech defect or a characteristic mannerism was our meat. Most of us, taken individually and alone, were reasonably well-behaved and polite children; but in a pack we were a bunch of little wolves, hot on the scent of any weakness. We were fairly subtle about it—we had to be, because our real teacher was no fool, ever, and she certainly had no desire to let her grade get out of hand; but we were effective, nevertheless. One Normal I remember had a long neck and a habit of tossing her head around on the end of it in what I suppose someone had once told her was a graceful manner. We called her the Dying Swan and we all took to tossing our heads in an affected and exaggerated way at the least excuse until it was a wonder they didn't fall off. We finally achieved our aim. We reduced her to tears. All right; so we were little brutes. I couldn't agree with you more wholeheartedly. But one thing was certain: we sure cured her of that silly-looking habit in jig time, and if she didn't thank us, she should have.

Sometimes the Normals were pretty or cute or lively or possessed of some other attribute that we found fetching. Then we developed crushes on them, and I'm not sure that that wasn't worse for the victim than incurring our enmity. We'd languish in their presence in school and follow them around all over town during their free time. If there was

Romance in their lives, we knew all about it, or if we didn't, we rounded out the facts in our possession with imaginary details tailored to suit our fancy. I should have thought that it would have been enough to cool the ardor of the most devoted swain to discover that, while he was walking his inamorata down by Carver's Pond in the twilight of a nice spring evening, he was being tailed by a covey of giggling sixth graders, very obviously avid for a little sentimental action on his part. Probably many a romance was nipped in the bud this way. But strangely enough, a few came to maturity in spite of our encouragement; and in our eyes it always added stature to a local boy if he succeeded in winning the hand of one of these out-of-town and therefore exotic girls. He took on glamour; and to this day, silly as it may sound, if I ask whatever became of Jack Jenkins, a contemporary of mine of whom I had lost track, and am told "Oh, he married a Normal," I wonder with some chagrin if I wasn't overlooking something in Jack, back there in the eighth grade.

There were things other than Normals to discombobulate a hard-working Model School teacher's day. There were what we knew as Observers. That's what they were, too; but it seems a little odd to me now that I could come home from a day in the third grade and inform my mother in a blasé manner, "We got out of spelling today. We had Observers." Kids in other schools didn't know what the word meant, I'm sure; or if they did, it didn't hold the connotations it had for us. Observers were serious-faced people with notebooks who were shepherded into the room by the Principal, and who, after an exchange of the amenities with the teacher, took chairs at the back and sat there very quietly all through the session. We knew that they came from schools all over everywhere to study the famous advanced methods of the Model School, and we knew what to expect.

First of all, we knew better than to trust the change in the teacher's manner. She might suddenly seem to emanate sweetness and light, but God help you when she got us alone, after the Observers had gone, if you tried to take advantage of this false aspect. The two big boys who sit at the back of

every classroom in the world, the ones who never know the
answers to anything and are just sweating out their time, always jumped up with a promptness and courtesy never displayed at other times, as soon as it was apparent that the
Observers were going to stay, and placed chairs for them.
They also inquired solicitously whether the chairs were too
near the radiator and whether the visitors would be more
comfortable with the Venetian blind lowered a little. That
ceremony completed, Miss Davis (for example) could take
her eye and ear off them. They'd said their pieces according
to training, and she could alert with an eagle glance the three
girls whose tour of duty it was this week to be ready upon
signal with books turned to the correct pages, to offer to the
Observers when the time came. It was a privilege to be a
book loaner. It meant that you could share a book with another pupil, sitting on half her small seat. It was uncomfortable, but it made a change and broke the monotony
peculiar to school.

Now we were ready to get down to business. The fiction
was—and it was reinforced and underlined by the Observers'
saying, "Don't let us disturb you," and the teacher's answering, "Oh, no, we won't"—that we'd just go on with our regular lessons as though they weren't there at all. We knew
better, through long experience. So we sat with our hands
clasped on the edges of our desks, our feet primly together
under them, our backs straight and our eyes on the teacher's
face, waiting for her to tip her mitt, as it were. However she
wanted to play it, we'd string along with her; for it was an
odd thing that once Observers reared their ugly heads, an
armistice between us and our natural enemy, the teacher,
went into effect. Temporarily at least, we'd co-operate to the
hilt not to let her down, to impress the Observers with the
special abilities of the pupils and teachers of the Model
School.

Instead of arithmetic, we might dramatize a scene from
Pyramus and Thisbe or from *William Tell*. This latter was
an old standby, and we did it very well. We should have,
considering the number of times we'd been through it. We

even managed the spur-of-the-moment effect, unfounded in truth, which seemed to be desirable to the teacher and impressive to the Observers. The teacher let her eye roam over the room in a pretty play of being undecided upon whom to call to take the various parts, although half the cast were halfway out of their seats while their names were still on the tip of her tongue. We all knew well who did what best. I was usually a ferryman—sex was disregarded in the assigning of roles—resting on the shore of a Swiss lake and chatting with a friend of mine, a herdsman of goats. As the scene opened, we were discussing the fact that it was going to rain. I remember after all these years one of my speeches, although we were supposed to be reading and not reciting them, in the interests of seeming to give an impromptu presentation. It went, "The fish are springing and the waterhen dives deep. A tempest sure is brewing fast."

We batted that about for a bit, and then the great Tell himself came dashing down from the back of the room, out of breath and staggering from exhaustion. He had just crossed the Alps on the dead run, and some of the boys could give really remarkable performances, with their tongues hanging out, eyes rolling, and knees wobbling like jelly. He'd come reeling up to us bucolic characters, gasping, "In God's name, Ferryman, your boat, your boat!" This line alone made being chosen to play Tell worth while, because you could swear in school and get away with it. I, as ferryman, would become coy, drawling with aggravating slowness, "How, now, what sudden haste is this?" apparently all unaware that Gessler's foot soldiers were thundering down the aisle near the blackboards, out for Tell's blood. In the meantime, the unchosen members of the class, serving as extras and sound-effects, made noises like wind and thunder to indicate the increasing violence of the storm, while Tell continued to plead, I continued to act stupid, and the soldiers began to close in. In the nick of time, however, I got it through my thick head what was expected of me, leaped onto a desk, stowed Tell away in the seat, and bent my back to imaginary oars, wafting him away from certain death across the stormy waters of Geneva, while Gessler's men raved and swore on the shore, as defined by a certain crack in the floor. It was pretty tense there for a few minutes, and Observers were always favorably impressed with the way we threw ourselves into our roles.

Sometimes we sang our Part Songs—the parts being soprano, alto, and rhythm—for the Observers. Those who sang rhythm were the ex-Crows. We still couldn't carry a tune, so instead we now sang *bong, bong, bong* in a monotone to accent the beat, as a sort of accompaniment. This allowed us to participate, kept us out of mischief, and probably didn't impair the general harmony too much. Sometimes we did folk dances, and sometimes we drew pictures or maps. Once in a while we did the flashier types of drill-work, the kinds involving contests or playing games rather than the simple and unadorned giving of the correct answers. It's possible that a particularly tenacious Observer did once in a while stay with us long enough so that the teacher was reduced to conducting a regular lesson; but if so, I don't remember it. I retain a very definite impression of treating all Observers to a demonstration of well-organized, mass showing-off. It's a wonder that more of us didn't turn out to be grandstanders, adept at giving a brilliant, superficial performance at the drop of an Observer's—any old observer's—hat, to conceal the abysmal depths of ignorance below. That's all right in a pinch, and there's nothing I now admire more than the ability to rise to an occasion; but for the long drag, there's nothing like a good foundation. We were trained to be spectacular, but we weren't very sound.

As if the poor teachers of the Model School didn't have enough of a handicap with us, the Normals and the Observers, there was yet another scourge, the Supervisors. We were Supervisor-ridden. Each department in the Normal School had its Head, and her stamping-ground extended down into the partially state-supported Model School. I think perhaps the idea was that she should keep her eye on what the Normals were doing with their practice teaching; but the Supervisors weren't content to let it stop there. They slopped over onto us, frequently sailing in without notice and taking over. After all, the Normal School classrooms were in the same building as the Model School, so it was the easiest thing in the world for a Department Head just to walk down a corridor and turn in to a grade room, to kill a little time. This nasty habit kept everyone—teachers, Normals and pupils alike—constantly on their toes. There was no advance warning in the form of cars drawing up to curbs to be spotted from a window or Supervisors checking in at the Principal's office, so that word could be sent out over the grapevine. When the doorknob turned, it might be only some boy coming back from the Basement—as the lavatory was always called, even if it was on the third floor of the building, except when it was called the Sanitary, which sometimes wasn't too apt a name, either; or it might be a Supervisor. You never knew, and it was fair-to-middling nerve-racking.

When a Supervisor honored us—and we averaged three or four visits a week, from one or another—we had to stop whatever we were doing and swing over to her field of interest. The doorknob would rattle, the door would open, and Miss Prince of the Music Department would be revealed in all her rather bosomy splendor. We'd close our arithmetic books, and the fog would come down thicker than ever between me and common fractions.

When Miss Prince came, we sang slips. I don't know whether other schools had this form of torture, or whether it was a practice peculiar to the advanced methods of the Model School. It had nothing to do with either scat or calypso singing, no matter what it sounds like. In a rack there were hundreds of slips of paper, each one a bar of music consisting of about eight measures, ranging from easy, in the first slot, up to very hard, in the last. The slot one slips were all in the key of C, written in 2/2 time, containing only quarter notes, and requiring a voice range of perhaps six tones. Those in the last slot could be written with five sharps or six flats in 6/8 time, and contained half, eighth, full, dotted-quarter, or grace notes, as well as rests, and they might skip all over the place. You worked your way from the first slot toward the last. After you had successfully sung a slip out of one slot, the next time we had slip singing you were supposed to take one from the next. It was sight reading, and was intended to teach us to read music easily. It did, too. Even I could read any slip correctly, but singing them was something else again for such as I. You sang alone and unaccompanied, except in my case, when I was accompanied by the sad shaking of Miss Prince's head.

Eventually I licked the system, or else Miss Prince tacitly admitted herself licked. I found a slip in slot one, by the trial and error method, that I could get through, if not creditably, at least recognizably. It was the easiest slip in the bunch, being nothing more than the first five notes of the scale, up and back. I clung to that slip grimly through grade after grade, and if some double-crossing rat got to it first, I sang that tune off the strange and impossible slip with which I'd been stuck. Long after everyone else was way up in the fancy slots, I was still croaking my slip from slot one.

The Penmanship Supervisor was Mr. Doner, who came regularly at a set time, once a week, and occasionally when he felt like it. He had dark hair that we suspected was dyed, wrote a beautiful hand, and was very nervous, as anybody who has given his life to the teaching of penmanship has every right to be. When Mr. Doner was in the room, you couldn't just pick up a pen and start writing. Oh my, no. First he had to check on Position. Position included the disposition of feet, knees, buttocks, back, neck, head, arms, hands, fingers, and thumbs, and, as far as I know, the part in your hair. When he had satisfied himself that all was as it should be by prowling up and down aisles and taking cross sightings of rigid backs, we went through limbering-up exercises, rolling our right arms, hands in loose fists, on the tops of our desks, using the forearm muscle as a cushion. Then, and only then, could we pick up our pens (in unison and to count), dip them in ink (at another count), and put them to paper.

First we did drills, lines of ovals (to count: "*Round,* two, three, four, five," et cetera) and lines of up-and-down strokes (also to count: "Push-pull, push-pull, push-pull"). Then we got down to letters, filling whole pages with t's, a's, or whatever that day's lesson might be, while Mr. Doner paced the aisles, commenting on individual work. I had trouble with the capital D, having a tendency to leave it gapping at the top. Mr. Doner clucked at me about that and told me I'd better be careful or else bugs would crawl into that space I'd left and lay their eggs. After that, every time I wrote my name hastily and failed to close the D, which was pretty often—it was too bad that I didn't have a name starting with M, which I could make fairly well—I'd think about those bugs and feel them crawling around and laying eggs in my head. All right, it doesn't make sense; but it's a fact, just the same. And it's useless to say that adults should be careful what they say to children, because the only way I can think of to avoid planting harmful suggestions in impressionable and zany little minds is to stop talking altogether within their hearing.

Mrs. Little was the Art Supervisor. I liked Art—the sketching of heads of Timothy grass or goldenrod in crayon, or the making of color-wheels in watercolors to show the relationship of primary and secondary colors. After we'd mastered these preliminary aspects of Art, we went into Still Lifes, and there I got in over my depth. I'm not sure what the object of the lesson was that day. Probably Mrs. Little was trying to teach us some principles of design. At any rate, the subject we were to draw and color was an arrangement of bananas and lemons in a yellow bowl. After we'd blocked them in to Mrs. Little's satisfaction, she said we were to color the bowl yellow, but the bananas were to be blue and the lemons lavender. That threw me. I was perfectly willing to concede that the result might be a more pleasing and colorful picture; but I'd never heard of a lavender lemon, and I didn't think anybody else had, either. In my book, you painted things the way you saw them, and I didn't see blue when I looked at a banana. Being a docile type, I did as Mrs. Little said; but I thought my own thoughts about modern art, and I still think them. Blue bananas, indeed!

These weren't all the Supervisors, by any means. There was Miss Gordon, the Physical Culture Supervisor, who informed us in hushed tones that the Body was a Temple; and Miss Moffatt of the Dramatics Department, who taught us to lead with our wrists when making gestures and was thereby responsible for a great deal of affectation in some quarters. Miss Soper of Arts and Crafts initiated us into the mysteries of making lopsided baskets, and Mr. Kelly of Manual Training taught us to pound a nail straight. In fact, we had a Supervisor for about anything you'd care to mention, except possibly putting on our rubbers or breathing, and sometimes even those activities were given a close scrutiny with a view to getting them standardized.

We had a lot of fancy things besides Normals, Observers and Supervisors that other poor, underprivileged brats whose schools stuck to the three R's didn't have. For example, we had Voice Charts, and we had them every day from about the third grade through the eighth. These were large charts of about twenty pages, hung at the front of the room. At the top was printed the symbol of the sound we were going to work on that day, and underneath came the exercises. I remember the *oo* chart best. It said *oo* at the top, and the first line read *pool, poor, loon, loom*. First we all intoned, *"Oo,"* and then we read, *"Pool, poor, loon, loom"* in a level tone. Then we read each word with a rising note, as if asking a question; and then we read them on descending notes, as if finishing a sentence. Then we read, *"Oo, pool* (level), *pool* (up), *pool* (down)" and so on for *poor, loon,* and *loom.* This was supposed to give us flexible voices and to improve our enunciation and inflection. I don't know whether it did or not. I can't hear myself, and all of my friends who were subjected to this treatment sound to me about like those who were not. One thing is sure: those who were not know a lot more about the fundamentals than we Voice Chart graduates do.

One of the things I really liked about school was Memorial Day. Of course, all holidays were observed in one way or another. Before Thanksgiving we drew and cut out turkeys and pumpkins and pasted them on the windows, and at Easter we did the same with chicks and daffodils. All schools do that now, but at that time they didn't, and we were considered pretty advanced and radical, not to say time-frittering. Sometimes at Christmas, if we happened to have a foreign-born child recently transferred from the Nonesuch English into our grade, the teacher would ask him to tell us about Christmas customs in his native country. In spite of the fact that the child was usually consumed with embarrassment and far from at home in English, we narrow little Yankees got some fascinating glimpses of a broader world, where there were live storks, and herds of cattle with bells at their throats, and olive trees, and where people really did wear wooden shoes and had porcelain stoves with pictures on them. In this day when almost every family has a world-traveled member of the armed forces, these things are common talk. But then the world was larger and unfamiliar, and we were really more privileged in this respect than we knew. We couldn't understand why anybody would leave those lovely places for the rather doubtful advantages of Bridge-water.

But Memorial Day was the best holiday of all. Every year old Mr. Kirmayer, a Civil War veteran, would come and tell us about how he lost his leg in battle, as a soldier in the Grand Army of the Republic. That name alone sent chills down my back, it was so noble and resounding. The Grand Army of the Republic! I saw it as a body of strong and shining-faced young men in blue uniforms like Mr. Kirmayer's swinging joyfully into the fight against slavery. I should have listened more heedfully. Mr. Kirmayer was a realist and portrayed the state of war honestly and detachedly, with no gilding of any lilies, and with the seamy side exposed. (And if anybody can mix speech figures any more thoroughly, I'd admire to know how.) But my mind was so bemused by the sound of that wonderful name that I let the grimmer details go in one ear and out the other.

Then, on the afternoon of May twenty-ninth, we were excused from school to go out into the woods and fields to gather wild flowers. These we took to the Town Hall, where the members of the Women's Relief Corps made them into wreaths and sprays and bouquets to be placed on the graves of the dead of all our wars in the nine cemeteries in town. Some of these cemeteries, in the center of town, were large; and some, on the outskirts, were just little family plots, but they all got their share of flowers and a new flag for each soldier's grave. We didn't have any florist in town in those days, and anyhow, custom dictated that on this day bought flowers were not offered. They were for the newly dead. On Memorial Day the flowers were supposed to be native, either wild or from old-fashioned gardens around the village, flowers that the men might have seen and taken pleasure in, in life.

The Town Hall was like an old-world flower market on the afternoon before Memorial Day, with the flowers piled in drifts all over the floor, and the Relief Corps women moving about among them with their aprons on and their hands full of blossoms. There were compact bunches of the feathery little false Solomon's seal, with its twin, waxy leaves; and the pink lady's slippers; and violets, white and blue; and gold-hearted, white-petaled daisies by the sheaf. There was spice bush, not very showy, but smelling like Heaven; and silvery shag-bush; and heaps of heavy-headed lilacs, white and lavender and deep, deep purple; and mountains of the greenish-white blooms of the snowball bush. There were sprays of tight, sweet, old-fashioned early roses; and great bunches of syringa and mock-orange and flowering quince; and a few late tulips and daffodils. And the worn old stairs of the Town Hall throbbed under the feet of more and more children, from first grade toddlers to the big boys and girls of the high school, bringing more and more flowers. I wish that the custom of Memorial Day flower gathering still held. There was something special about it that had nothing to do with getting out of school to search the yet boggy fields and just leafing woods, to the sound of the peepers and the lately returned birds, for tributary blossoms.

Memorial Day itself was wonderful in a subdued and dedicated way. There was a parade, led by the Civil War veterans in open carriages—old men, many too feeble to walk the long route any more. They sat there in their clean, worn uniforms behind the slow-pacing horses, their faces grave and composed. As they passed, there was quiet, and heads bowed in a respect compounded of recognition of their age, and of their great service to the Union, and of their private memories of comrades long since dead. Each year the number of survivors of the Grand Army of the Republic dwindled, until only old Mr. Kirmayer was left; and then one year he too had passed on, and something that Memorial Day stood for went with him. There are still Memorial Day parades, but they aren't the same.

After the old veterans came the Sons of Veterans, on foot, and the veterans of the Spanish War, and the town band; and after them came the ranks of any organizations that chose to march—the Boy Scouts, the Campfire Girls, the Red Men, anybody. The parade went from cemetery to cemetery, and everyone in town who could put one foot before the other trailed along. There was a short service at each cemetery, with a prayer and a speech on the meaning of the occasion, and then came the part that never failed to shake my composure, the firing of a volley of arms and the sounding of taps. It really wasn't outwardly impressive. There was nothing of the finished production about it. The shots were apt to be ragged and the bugler not too sure of himself. The parade itself was, I suppose, actually rather straggling, and the background was just the same scenery that we saw every day, dimmed and softened by the warm gray mist that seemed always to fall gently on Memorial Day. Dogs and small children milled around through the crowd, detracting from the solemnity of the occasion. But nevertheless—perhaps because of the very lack of polish and because of the obvious sincerity of the participants—when the guns were fired and the notes of the bugle rose through the quiet air and drifted, slow and clear and searching, over the ordered graves, I thought that my heart would break. And today, when I'm too old and have been through too much for empty sentimentality, I'm afraid I'd feel the same way.

After Memorial Day, it wasn't long to the end of the school year, but it seemed like ages. The end was at last in sight, but time dragged interminably. The remaining two weeks seemed like two years, and a wasted two years, at that. I hadn't penetrated the mystery of long division or mastered the rule governing the dropping or retaining of *e* in such words as tim(e)ing or unmistak(e)ably in the nine months past (and haven't yet), and it seemed highly improbable that a mere two weeks more would alter that situation. Besides, it was nice outdoors now, and my frogs' eggs in the bucket in the back yard at home were coming along nicely into tadpoles and needed my attention. The eggs in the robin's nest in the apple tree had hatched and I should be there to guard the fledglings from Smut's cattish curiosity, and I wanted to replant my garden. Against wiser counsel, I'd dug it up a couple of times to see if the seeds were sprouting, and it had never really recovered. School was bad enough during the cold, raw, sunless days of January, but now, when the soft air was moving sweetly in through open windows, and the sky was silky, and everything was blossoming and hatching and growing, it was insupportable. I'd had school. Enough was enough.

Yet I do retain the memory of certain fleeting moments of beauty and pleasure. In the seventh grade, I was assigned a seat near a window that looked out obliquely on to an ivy-covered brick wall. In the fall, the leaves of the ivy turned to the deepest, richest red I have ever seen, smooth and waxy and both light-absorbent and light-reflecting. When the sun shone on that wall and the wind riffled the leaves, the whole surface gave off a dancing, living, ruby-hearted glow, so that you could feel yourself drowning in light and color. I warmed my heart at that wall through many an autumn day. And from the top-floor windows of the fifth grade, you couldn't see the ground at all or the roofs of any houses, but only the treetops and the clouds drifting lazily over. If you stared long enough with half-closed eyes, making your mind a blank, you could capture the feeling of being air-borne. It was wonderful to feel the earth dropping away and all the boredom and restrictions of school with it.

Then there was the way the snow slid off the steep slate roof during a thaw, avalanching thunderously down past the windows in a curtain of white that shut off briefly all view of the outer world. The light in the room became coldly dim, so that the startled faces turned toward the window were drained of color and oddly and sharply shadowed. For an instant I'd seem to be in a room full of strangers, none of whom was as warm and sentient and living as I was. I should have been frightened, I suppose, at any such notion; but I wasn't. I felt strong and blessedly alone and tolerant, although of what I don't know.

There was the way I felt about a quire of new paper, coming fresh out of the wrapper under the teacher's hands. My fingers itched to get at it. I had no ideas about these being new pages on which great thoughts could be written, or any of that nonsense. Clean paper held no moral or philosophical implications for me at all. I simply liked the way it looked, so unsullied and sharp-edged. I was a miser of new pencils, too. I'd struggle along with a horrible old stub, in order to prolong the period of anticipation of the high and perfect moment when I put my new pencil into the sharpener and watched the bright, cedar-scented shavings roll away. This simple pleasure is probably symptomatic of some unspeakable psychiatric disturbance, but if so, I don't want to know about it. I'm perfectly happy enjoying the memory of the way a new pencil looked and smelled the first time you sharpened it.

But the most abiding pleasure I discovered in school was the collecting of information. This is not the same as the acquiring of knowledge. Great truths would completely escape me, the laws of the universe would remain so much double-talk, and I'd wander lost as a loon through the labyrinths of man's cultural heritage. But let any odd little useless fact cross my path—and the more useless the better—and I'd pounce on it like a hawk and gobble it up. My head is stuffed full to this day of bits of absolutely worthless information that I wouldn't part with for anything. Who cares that the name of a place on the west coast of the United States, Anacortes, was derived not from the Spanish, as would seem, but from the name of a girl, Anna Curtis? Nobody, except maybe the people who live there—and me. If I got nothing else out of school, I got a fine collection of treasures like that, to gloat over in my mind on nights when I can't sleep.

8

How Firm a Foundation

THERE USED TO BE—AND PROBABLY STILL IS—A COUPLET OF
sorts that Alice and I muttered to each other with a fearful
sense of defying the lightning to strike:

> Minister's son and Deacon's daughter
> Don't act any better than they orter.

Where we picked that up I don't remember; but we said it
ironically. Our father and mother were minister's son and
deacon's daughter, and we wished they'd cut loose and raise
a little Cain as they were supposed, according to tradition, to
do. We felt that we could use some depravity around our
house, that we were altogether too clean-living and high-
thinking for comfort. What we had in mind specifically as a
manifestation of immorality was a suggestion of laxity in
church and Sunday School attendance, a little less faithful-
ness in showing up at Central Square Congregational Church
every blessed Sunday morning in the world. That's about as
far as our dream-world excursions into vice would take us.

Dream world is right. We hadn't a hope of our dreams'
coming true. Both our parents had been brought up to go to
church regularly, they believed in going to church, and they
thought that the way to make regular churchgoers of us was
to start us young and keep us at it until an unbreakable habit

had been formed. Social custom was on their side, too. In those days, nice people all went to one church or another. People who didn't attend church regularly— Well. No matter how acceptable they might appear in other respects, they were eyed a little askance. There was bound to be something unsound about them, something unreliable and off-color. We ought to be thankful, our mother told us, that we had parents who *cared* how we were brought up! Why, when she was our age, she'd had to go not only to church and Sunday School, but to the Sunday evening service *and* Wednesday night Prayer Meeting as well. If she were really fulfilling her duty to us, we'd be doing the same. We just ought to be *thankful—*

We weren't. However, we usually shut up at that point, before we talked ourselves into a more intensive course of religious education than we were already undergoing. We'd learned early to recognize when we were licked, and in the matter of churchgoing, we were licked before we started. But if, by any improbable chance, we succeeded in living through all the Sundays until we were twenty-one—an age we'd somehow arrived at as representing freedom from parental jurisdiction—*then* we'd see who went to church! It was going to be a long and almost impossible drag, but maybe we'd manage, for the pure bliss of sitting on the porch in our old clothes, with our feet on the rail, watching others in their Sunday-best wend their sedate way churchward. We'd be swigging root beer, what was more. It was a vision of bonnet-flinging-over-mills that carried us through countless Sunday mornings.

To be perfectly fair to us, I don't think that we were to be blamed too much for our attitude. In most matters I find that my accumulating years and own parenthood swing me more and more to the right wing viewpoints held by my mother and father, unreasonable as I thought them at the time. When my mother said, as she frequently did, "You'll look at this differently when you're older," she was right, ridiculous as it seemed then. But I still think that she was expecting a little too much of us when she expected us to derive any benefit from church attendance, aside, possibly, from the benefit to be derived from any form of discipline or exercise in self-control. Church was worse than plain dull. We were too immature to understand the significance of the service, and we were too young and active to sit still and silent for so long without undergoing what amounted to physical torture. None of our friends had to go to church regularly, but only to special Easter and Christmas services. Their parents felt that Sunday School was sufficient for the time being. Our parents were always remarkably impervious to any argument based on what all the other kids did or didn't have to do, and in this matter they were adamant. Other kids could go climb trees. *We* had to go to church. Period.

Reason tells me that we had our quota of rainy, snowy, foggy, sleety or sub-zero Sundays, but I remember Sunday mornings as being always balmy, bright and dew-drenched, mornings most manifestly made for careless wanderings in the fields and woods or lazy relaxing in the sun. They cried aloud to us to be used properly, and not to be wasted in any stuffy church. However, after a later and more leisurely breakfast than usual, we had to get dressed in clean clothes from the skin out to immaculate, stiffly starched dresses. (People used a lot more starch in those days than they do now.) We had to make sure that we had fresh handkerchiefs, our collection money, and our Bibles and Sunday School quarterlies; and we had to put on hats and gloves. We *never* wore hats and gloves except for warmth in winter, and those accessories alone made us feel miserable and constrained.

Then the church bells began to ring all over town, a really lovely sound drifting through the quiet sunny air, if only we could have listened to it without prejudice. We could easily pick out our own, slightly deeper in tone than that of the Unitarians, which it answered in a friendly manner back and forth across the treetops of the Common. The hour had come. We said goodbye to our respective cats, telling them to be good and wait for us to come home. We knew that they wouldn't. They never did. They were just being polite about starting out on business of their own before we left the yard. We envied them bitterly.

There used to be a special quality to Sunday mornings that vanished with the common possession of automobiles. The few people who owned the unreliable contraptions wouldn't think of going to the uncertain trouble of trying to get them started in order to ride to any destination within walking distance. Sunday was a day of rest for horses as well as humans. The delivery horses of the stores were, of course, off the streets; but those who owned horses for personal use didn't harness them up on Sundays either, unless they lived much too far from the church to make walking conceivable. Everybody walked to church. So the streets were empty of wheeled traffic, and the whole town seemed to be sleeping in the sun, except for the circumspect church-bound pedestrians strung along the shady sidewalks. Nobody ran or shouted or even walked very fast. Everybody looked dressed up and strange as we joined the crowd converging on our own church and climbed the stairway to the auditorium.

There was nothing of the theatrical about the form of worship of New England Congregationalists. No appeal whatsoever was made to the senses or the emotions. Both the service and the place in which it was held were marked by a restraint and austerity almost monkish. The auditorium was a vast white room of utmost architectural simplicity, with tall windows on both sides and the pews curving around slightly to face the pulpit and choir loft. It was a light and airy place in which the only color was supplied by two commemorative stained glass windows near the front that threw lozenges of brilliant red and blue and golden light across the painted pew-backs, and a great arrangement of seasonal flowers or potted plants on the table below the pulpit. The pews were straight and narrow and hard, with racks for the hymn books and little holders for the wineglasses on Communion Sunday attached to their backs.

We'd tiptoe down the aisle to our own pew, subdued by the great space around us, and the solemn faces of those already present, and the soft and sonorous playing of the organ, in established order. The usher went first—although why I don't know, since we all knew and had known for years where our pew was. Then came my father, then Alice and me, and last my mother, to keep an eye on us. She needn't have bothered. We knew what was expected of us. The usher, whom we knew perfectly well in everyday life but who chose now to regard us as complete strangers, would pause with a hand on pew thirty-eight, and our father would step aside to let Alice and me precede him. We were allowed to sit side-by-side as long as we behaved ourselves. If we didn't, at some point in the service our mother would change places with Alice, putting herself between us. When that happened, it boded ill for us after we got home, so we tried to avoid the necessity if possible. After our father had taken his proper place as head of the family at the end of the pew, the usher handed us each a copy of the church calendar, and silently withdrew to the back of the room.

The church calendar was a folded leaflet with a picture of the steeple on the outside front and a list of the church officers and committees on the back. Inside on the left-hand page was the order of worship for the day, and on the right-hand page any announcements of forthcoming meetings of church organizations, such as the King's Daughters or the Men's Bible Class. As a part of his contribution to the church, our father printed the calendars every week, so our family couldn't take the detached view of them that others took. Others may have thought that they descended in a shower from Heaven with every comma correct. We knew better. Almost every Saturday our father was late for dinner, which we had at noon, because the minister had forgotten to bring in his copy or had come in late with a last-minute change. This delayed getting it set and a stone proof pulled, and our father couldn't come home until that was done, since he brought the proof with him for our mother to double check. Then he had to go back in the afternoon, which most men were taking off to work in their gardens, and run the calendars off on the job press. There was sometimes a certain amount of not-too-Christian comment on the thoughtlessness of ministers on Saturdays, when the dinner was drying up in the oven and our father nowhere in sight.

But on Sundays we tried to forget this. Our parents pored over the calendar, not because they didn't know the contents by heart—after all, they'd gone over it with a fine-toothed comb the day before—but to see if they'd missed any typographical errors. If they found that they had, they pointed it out to each other in whispers and exchanged chagrined glances; but this didn't happen very often. Our father was careful about all his proof, but especially careful about the church calendar. In the meantime, Alice and I were scanning our copies and looking up the hymns listed by number for congregational singing in our hymnals. It was something to kill time until the service started; but more than that, we were really interested. We had opinions about hymns. They were the best part of church; almost the only good part.

The first part of the service we could endure, even the long prayer in which the minister called to the attention of the Lord any imperfections in the world at home and abroad that He might have overlooked. We didn't listen, of course. But it came early enough in the order of worship so that we hadn't yet developed aches in our backs, cramps in our legs, or a numbness in our derrieres; and we hadn't yet exhausted the feeble entertainment possibilities of any funny-looking hats in front of us. Once during the prayer we saw a ladybug crawling over the collar of the dress of the woman in the next pew forward. We watched, fascinated, putting up prayers of our own for it to go down her neck. Just as it seemed as though we had the Lord's Ear, the woman behind us leaned forward and asked our mother in a piercing whisper, well laced with horror, that penetrated to the furthermost ends of the church, "Is it a *bedbug?*" (Silly old hen who didn't know a ladybug when she saw one! And why should she think *our* mother was any more familiar with bedbugs than she herself was?) That day our mother took the unprecedented step of separating Alice and me right in the middle of the prayer. In spite of the repercussions that followed later, we always hoped that something like that would happen again.

The taking of the collection wasn't so bad, because maybe an usher would drop his plate and have to scramble for the money. No one ever did, but the possibility was present. The Scripture reading we rather liked (speaking always comparatively), because of the majestic surge of the King James Version, which fell impressively on our language-susceptible ears; and the Responsive Reading was all right, too. The congregation stood during that part, and that gave us a chance to stretch our legs. We could join in the reading, too; although once I became so interested in the text that I went right on reading aloud into the minister's verse, and was so embarrassed that I thought I'd fall down dead. The solos and anthems by the choir were tolerable, since the members made peculiar faces when they reached for notes at the limits of their various ranges, lifting their chins for the high ones and tucking them down into their collars for the low. It made a mild diversion.

But the singing of the hymns we really liked, and not only because we again had a chance to stretch our legs and ease our backs, nor because we could participate. Over and above all that, we really loved some of the hymns for themselves. *Oh, God, Our Help In Ages Past, A Mighty Fortress Is Our God, The Old Rugged Cross, Rock Of Ages*—what could be grander or nobler than those old hymns, what more stirring than *O, Zion, Haste, Thy Mission High Fulfilling,* or more sweetly haunting than *Dear Lord And Father Of Mankind?* They were ancient and familiar and full of beautiful phrases that even if not completely understood, gratified some feeling deep within. What we felt, I'm afraid, had nothing to do with religion; although maybe it did, at that. Maybe sincere and involuntary response to any form of religious expression is in itself the beginning of a religious experience.

After the singing of the next-to-the-last hymn came the really tough part of the service. According to the calendar, we were almost to the end. There were just the closing hymn and the benediction to go—*and* the sermon. Those were the days when a twenty-minute sermon was unknown. A minister who tried that lazy caper would have been considered

derelict in his duty. The congregation expected a solid dis-
course with points plainly labeled from *firstly* up as high as
seventhly or *eighthly,* based on a good orthodox text, adorned
with classical and Biblical allusions, illustrated with examples
from both sacred and profane literature, enlivened perhaps
by lessons from real life, containing food for thought during
the coming week, and all in all instructive, cultural, uplifting, erudite, and doctrinally sound. That's what they got,
too, believe me; and believe me, also, it was all away and
gone over Alice's and my heads.

We sat there in the acute agony that only marrow-deep
boredom can bring to the very young. We squirmed until
our mother laid a restraining hand on the nearest knee. We
slumped onto the middles of our spines, rested our heads on
the hard back of the pew, and stared at the ceiling until a
maternal nudge brought us upright. We scratched ourselves.
We read hymns and the Responsive Readings in the back
of the hymnal to ourselves, and our Bibles and quarterlies.
We counted the number of men in the church and the number of women, and the number of hats with yellow on them,
and the number of coats with braid trimming. We counted
the number of times *and* was used on the calendar, and the
number of words beginning with *h,* and the number of capital letters. We played "Rich man, poor man, beggarman,
thief" on the back buttons of dresses in front of us. We
yawned and we sighed deeply, and our mother looked at us
with pained disapproval. Finally we lapsed into coma and
just sat there with our eyes glazed and our mouths slightly
ajar, so that when the minister went into the last stretch and
came to a triumphant close, he usually took us by surprise.
We'd pull ourselves together, join in the last hymn, and in
somewhat of a daze, as though coming out from under the
effects of a powerful drug, make our way out of the auditorium and down the stairs.

But we weren't yet free to go home. Others who had attended church, adults, moved slowly out into the glorious
sunlight and fresh air, pausing to shake the minister's
hand and comment on the sermon. Our parents were among

them, and while our mother pointed out that she had to go home and slave over a hot stove, cooking us a big Sunday dinner, we felt mistreated. *Nobody* had to go to *both* church and Sunday School, except *us!* The other children of our age were just coming up the board walk, looking crisp and fresh in their best clothes and full of high spirits. We felt bedraggled and wrinkled—as we probably were by that time—and dull and cloddish, as though we'd been up and about since yesterday without washing our faces. However, we went dutifully down the three steps into the big basement room where Sunday School was held, and joined our classes.

The very, very young attended the kindergarten Sunday School in a separate little room at the back, under the tutelage of Miss Emma Maguire. I can remember when I was in Miss Maguire's room. She was sweet. She still is. I met her in the Public Library just the other day and was amazed to see how tiny she is. She comes below my shoulder and weighs probably half what I do. Nevertheless, she looked up at me, patted my hand, and said with no intention of humor, "One of My Little Girls!" I could have hugged her. I'm sure she still thinks of the lot of us as really Her Little Girls, and hopes as anxiously as she did when I had to look 'way, 'way up to see her face that we are *good* little girls. When we were in her Sunday School class, we colored Biblical pictures and marched around the room singing:

> "Hear the pennies dropping.
> Count them as they fall.
> Every one for Jesus.
> He will get them all,"

as we dropped our two pennies—one for the Sunday School, one for Foreign Missions—into a little bank.

The Big Sunday School was something else again. We were expected to show up there with our lessons prepared and our weekly Bible verses memorized: and we did, if we knew what was good for us. I was resentful of every minute I spent there, and certainly had a closed mind if ever there was one. But I'm proof, if any is needed, that contrary to much educational theory, enjoyment and proper motivation are not necessary to learning, and that lessons can be pounded into the most obdurate head. I can to this day identify almost any character in the Old Testament or New and give you the details of his history; I can reel off Psalm after Psalm without hesitation; I frequently find myself sewing up an argument with a quotation from the Bible, which silences more people than you'd imagine; and I find the Proverbs extremely useful in my dealings with the generation before mine. I had an extremely good Scriptural foundation, and now that the dust has settled and the wounds healed, I'll have to admit that I'm glad of it.

It's not only that I find Biblical references useful. Believe me, that's of the least importance, as is the fact that a certain amount of familiarity with the Bible is necessary to anyone who wishes to pose as even half educated. My thankfulness arises from an altogether different source. It arises from the beauty and the power to move of some of the passages. I find inspiration and comfort in them: "I will lift up mine eyes unto the hills, from whence cometh my help" and "The heavens declare the glory of God: and the firmament sheweth His handiwork." The firmament! What a wonderful word for the starry vastness! "Why do the heathen rage, and the people imagine a vain thing?" There's a question for reducing mountains to the molehills they actually are! "Unstable as water, thou shalt not excel" is to me a better way of saying the same thing than "You're nuts; you'll never get anywhere with that." And I know of nothing written anywhere more stately and beautiful than the great chapter on charity, which may be understood as meaning love of one's fellow man: "Though I speak with the tongues of men and of angels, and have not charity—" That's why I am glad I was forced against my will to go to Sunday School.

Church was not for us a matter of Sunday morning observance, and that was that. It was an ever-present factor in the lives of our parents, and therefore in our lives. We knew more about the temporal aspects of its organization, if not the spiritual, than any other children and possibly than many

adults did. We knew, as I have said, what mechanics lay behind the completed church calendar. Our father was a deacon of the church, and as such had to take his turn in
assuming responsibility for Communion Sunday, when the
bread of Christ's body and the wine of His blood were par-
taken by those who, as members in good standing, were
qualified. Alice and I were not church members, since our
parents disapproved—with good sense—of our taking such a
serious step until we were aware of what we were doing. So
we could not participate in the Communion service, when
the plates of little cubes of bread and the tiny fragile glasses
of wine—in this case grape juice—were passed with impressive
solemnity. We participated in our way, however. The bread
had to be cut into proper bite-sizes—which our mother didn't
trust us to do—and wrapped in oil paper—which she did en-
trust to us. Then after the service was over, someone had to
wash the glasses and store them away in the felt-lined boxes
against the next Communion Sunday. Alice and I often did
that, taking great care to polish them until they glittered.
Others might assume that the presence of the bread and the
wine was a miracle. Daughters of Martha, we early learned
that behind most miracles there is ordinary hard work involved, a very good thing to know.

I remember a grave crisis that arose in our household in
connection with Communion Sunday. The day had turned
out to be miserable, with such a blizzard blowing that many
of the faithful were unable to attend church. So there was
quite a lot of bread left over after the service, which our
father brought home, since he was responsible and couldn't
very well leave it at church to attract mice. (You see what I
mean about awareness of the mundane problems associated
with a spiritual endeavor?) The question then came up as to
what disposition to make of the bread; and it was a really
serious question. Putting it into the garbage and feeding it
to the hens would have been out-and-out sacrilege, since this
bread had been blessed. Feeding it to the birds would have
been almost as bad, although Alice and I felt that St. Francis
would have approved. But our church did not recognize

many saints and their opinions. Even if burying it would have been acceptable, it was impossible with a foot of snow on the iron-hard frozen earth. It could have been burned, I suppose. But in the end, our mother made a bread pudding out of it. She thought that the Lord would understand and that He would share her views on waste. I guess she was probably right, although the pudding tasted odd to me and I couldn't enjoy it. I wasn't sure that I ought to be eating it at all. This was a doctrinal quandary in which I feel positive few of our acquaintances of any age ever found themselves.

In addition to being a deacon, our father was also the Collector for the church. This was really a terrible job, involving the keeping of intricate books. You didn't just take over the money in the collection plates each Sunday, count it, and bank it. It was nowhere nearly as simple as that. Each member of the church, at the time of the Every Member Canvas, pledged himself to the payment of whatever sum he thought he could afford weekly during the coming year, and received a little packet of fifty-two envelopes with a number on each, which would be his number for the year. This was recorded beside his name in the Collector's account book, and when that number showed up on an envelope, the sum enclosed was credited to the proper name.

So Sunday afternoons at our house were largely devoted to what was called Doing the Books. Although our father was nominally the Collector, the books were easier to do if two people worked on them, one tearing open the envelopes, taking out the money, and reading the number and the amount involved, while the other made the entry. Our father did the writing, since he was responsible for the appearance of the books, and our mother did the money-handling. Alice and I just kept quiet—talking doesn't make you popular with anyone who is trying to balance someone else's cash—and listened.

We heard some pretty enlightening things, too. We heard our mother's opinion of people who were six weeks behind in their church offerings and yet could afford to go to Boston for a new Easter hat—and it didn't come from any bargain

basement, you could mark my mother's words!—when Miss
Hermann, the milliner in town, was very good at and more
than willing to undertake refurbishing a last year's hat.
You'd think that woman would be ashamed to wear that hat
to church, owing money as she did, but no. Some people
didn't care for anything but Show.

We heard our father's considered decision that he would
not send a reminder to So-and-so, because it would only
make him mad, and then he'd never pay. The man in question was valuable to the church, and there was no sense in
needlessly getting his back up. He'd pay when he got around
to it. He always did. Now with Mrs. Whatever, it was different. She admitted herself that she was scatterbrained, and
she'd be grateful for a reminder; while with the Whobodies—
Well, they'd been having a hard row to hoe, with sickness in
the family, so better leave them alone until they got back
onto their feet. It was a lesson in applied psychology to hear
our parents discussing the collecting of sums owed the
church; a lesson, I might add, that our father never brought
to bear on the collection of amounts owed the *Independent*.

There was a practice common among subscribers to the
church that inflamed our mother, although to Alice and me
it seemed like an obvious course to take and one that we
ourselves would have followed. If an individual had for any
reason been absent from church for several Sundays, he
would usually try to get caught up on his dues on the Sabbath of his return. If he had pledged twenty-five cents a
week and had been gone three weeks, he'd owe a dollar,
counting the current Sunday. This, more often than not, he
would pay by putting a quarter into each of four envelopes
and dropping the lot into the collection plate. That seemed
to Alice and me the logical thing to do. The envelopes had
been provided for use, and he was using them.

According to our mother's reasoning, it was a silly, time-
wasting, bother-causing procedure. The sensible course
would have been to throw away the three outdated envelopes
and put the whole dollar into the current one. She'd sit
there ripping off the ends of envelopes, snatching out the

offending quarters, and announcing with acid disapproval, "*Another* twenty-five cents for Number 276, and him supposed to be such a businessman! Doesn't he ever look at his own books? Doesn't he know how books are run? If this is a sample of the way he runs that business of his, I'm glad *I* don't own stock in it!" We never could understand what it was that made her so mad; but we all have our own personal peeves, and I suppose that happened to be our mother's. After all, she wanted to get through the books and have a little time left of the afternoon for her own pursuits.

Alice and I used to salvage some of the offering envelopes that weren't too mutilated, for our own purposes. They were handy for a number of things, like keeping half-sucked hard candy in, or locks of hair from our various dolls. We weren't the only ones, either. Our mother's button box was full of little envelopes with "Central Square Congregational Church" crossed off and "Extra Button for A's Winter Coat" written underneath; and the tin box that held the garden seeds was bulging with cast-off collection envelopes labeled "Red Zinnia from Miss Pottle. Unusual." or "Mr. Hunt's Summer Squash. Very Early Variety." I don't know how families whose head wasn't Collector managed about small envelopes for oddments, I'm sure.

Church activity was not confined to Sunday by any means. There were weekday meetings of the various organizations like the Sewing Circle or Christian Endeavor Society; and every winter there was a big church sale and supper, when everybody pitched in and helped. I don't suppose these were riotous affairs, but they seemed very gala indeed to Alice and me.

In the first place, they were held in the big downstairs Sunday School room, cleared for the occasion of ordered ranks of chairs, and filled at one end with crepe-paper festooned booths. The other end was given over to the long tables on which the supper would be served. Just this simple transformation of the scene of our Sunday travails into a palace of pleasure, so to speak, was enough to make us slightly giddy in itself. Every group within the church was repre-

sented at the sale, each within its own field and capacities.
The Sewing Circle had a Fancy Work Table, where were sold
all the articles both fancy and not so fancy that the ladies had
been manufacturing since the fair of the year before: pot
holders, mittens, aprons, embroidered guest towels, and
nicely dressed dolls. There was a Candy Table, and a Food
Table, and a Miscellaneous Table, where were sold all the
things that couldn't be classified under any other heading,
like a hand-painted plate, or a good, thrifty little white
begonia, or a pair of beaded moccasins someone had bought
on vacation with this event in mind. Usually there was a
Grab Bag, where you paid your nickel and grabbed a
wrapped package out of a sack. It might be anything in the
world, but chances were that you didn't want it after you
got it, because the grabs were ordinarily white elephants,
donated by attic-cleaning members of the congregation.

The Junior Christian Endeavor, to which Alice and I
perforce belonged, always ran the same booths, consigned to
us as being within our rather limited abilities. We had the
Paper Table and the Lemonade Booth. The Lemonade
Booth explains itself. We took money out of the treasury,
bought lemons and sugar with it, and on the afternoon before the sale met at the home of the minister to concoct lemonade under his wife's supervision. Sometimes it was pink
and sometimes it was yellow—a rather pale yellow, since in
the interests of money-making, we watered the brew down
quite a bit. We always did very well with the Lemonade
Booth, financially. The public came to the fair prepared to
spend money—on things they didn't want, if necessary—and
almost anybody could drink one more glass of weak lemonade.

The Paper Table was a little more complicated. It was
supposed to vend anything made of paper, like stationery or
ornamental calendars or memorandum pads; but since this
rather narrowed our field, we chose to interpret the title as
meaning anything that was in any way connected with paper.
These articles we obtained by soliciting the church roster;
and it occurs to me now that the annual sale must have cost

most members a pretty penny before they ever set foot inside the place. Every organization was around soliciting, and he who wasn't tagged at least a half-dozen times was either very lucky or very agile. In asking for donations, we stressed the fact that our interpretation was loose enough to include things like paperweights, paper cutters, paper clips, framed pictures, or even pencils and paste. As a result, we sometimes infringed on the preserves of other tables, notably the Miscellaneous, a certain amount of bitterness was engendered, and the fact that we were, after all, working for a common cause was overlooked. We did all right, though, with our paper-related wares, more, I guess, because people were impressed with our youthful sincerity than because of the desirability of our merchandise.

There was always an acceleration of trade at about five o'clock, when the men got out of work and came to the church for the supper. Naturally they couldn't just stand around with their hands in their pockets while waiting for the summons to the table. That would have been construed as slightly boorish. They had to buy something from the booths to show that their hearts were in the right place. Men being what they are—and this is not a snide criticism, but rather a tribute—they'd buy anything in the interests of charity, without too close a weighing of value received. We got rid of all our problem items and the last dregs of the lemonade in the fifteen minutes before supper. Then we could close up shop and stuff ourselves with a clear conscience.

Those suppers were something. Throughout the year there were occasionally the traditional baked bean, cold ham, and potato salad suppers; but the supper that followed the sale was an all-out effort. Sometimes we had turkey, sometimes we had chicken pie, and once we had roast lamb. In addition there were always, of course, more varieties of jelly, pickles, and relish than you could shake a stick at, hot rolls, and every kind of cake and pie you'd ever heard of and some that you hadn't. You didn't pay by the plate. You paid a flat rate for the supper, and that meant all that you could eat. Seconds on everything were standard, thirds common, and fourths not unknown. The choosing of your pieces of pie and cake was a nerve-racking business. Even the most sanguine couldn't hope to sample them all. The human stomach does have its limits of expansion. But every woman who had been solicited for a dessert had quite naturally put her best foot as far forward as it would go, sparing neither the butter nor the eggs. There was one dark, rich chocolate cake with a thick, buttery mocha frosting— But why torture myself at this late date?

The hot roast lamb supper I remember particularly, since it was the subject of a long and stubborn altercation. Our mother served on the supper committee that year. In fact, she served most years, when the *Independent* would let her, although it was the policy to rotate the work so that the same women didn't do it all. But our parents felt that since they couldn't make as large a cash contribution as many others did and as they would have liked to have done, they should give all the more freely of their time and energies. The church was really the gainer, as our mother was an unusually conscientious, quick, and reliable worker, and her services worth more than money.

She'd spend the whole day of the supper at the church and attend all the committee meetings faithfully; and because she didn't have anyone to leave us with and we were too small to be left alone, she took us along with her. We understood that we were to be quiet and good and keep out from under foot; and we obeyed instructions. We found that it paid. End pieces of cake came our way, pieces that were slightly crumbly or unevenly iced; and if the first cutting out of a pie looked ragged, we were apt to get that, too. We fared very well, and we also had the pleasantly important sensation of knowing what went on behind the scenes, of being In The Know. *We* knew—although we wouldn't have breathed it outside for anything, having great senses of honor and pride in being good security risks—that Mrs. Blank's cakes never appeared on the supper tables at all, because she used a vegetable shortening in place of real butter, and the committee ladies wouldn't put the Congregational reputation in jeopardy by serving them to the general public; and that Mrs. Hunt's white walnut cake made only a token appearance, since it was so wonderful that most of it was eaten in the kitchen. We knew a lot that we didn't tell.

We knew about the bitter war waged on the issue of the hot roast lamb. At the first meeting of the committee, when the broad basic plan was being drawn up, the question of the main course naturally arose early. It seemed to be a cut and dried matter of deciding between chicken pie and baked ham with raisin sauce, since we'd had turkey last year. Then some brash soul made the revolutionary suggestion that precedent be thrown to the winds, and something Different be served, like, for example, leg of lamb. There was a second of scandalized silence, and then the chairman of the committee, a woman whose word carried weight in church circles, stated quietly that such a thing was out of the question, of course. Unless lamb was piping hot, it was no good. It would be impossible to serve the number of people that the Congregationalist supper always drew lamb that was really hot, after the first few plates. In her opinion, there was nothing less appetizing than a plate of tepid lamb surrounded by congealing greasy gravy. The Congregationalists had always been famous—and rightly so—for their suppers, and she wasn't going to have the high standard lowered by any committee under her chairmanship.

That should have settled that, but it didn't. I think there were other issues at stake than the immediate one of serving a good supper. It was a battle for social leadership that had been in the making for a long time. At any rate, the upstart champion of lamb refused to be squelched. She said that good service shouldn't be too difficult. If they made sure that the plates themselves were sizzling hot before the food was put on them, and had a good, fast carver, even if they had to hire a man to do it, and lined up plenty of waitresses to whisk them to the tables—

By this time such good workers as my mother, who were politically innocent and had no social fish to fry, began to respond to what appeared to them as a challenge. Nobody said anything, but Alice and I could see eyes light with a wild surmise. It might not be impossible, at that, the thought flew around the circle; and if it could be brought off successfully, what a feather in the cap of this committee! Nobody had ever attempted lamb, for the very reasons that the chairman had mentioned. If this committee could put it across, their names would become legendary, and their achievement would certainly give every succeeding group something to shoot at! The idea caught on like a grass fire on a windy day. Before she knew what was happening, the chairman found that she had a runaway committee on her hands, leaving her and a minority of satellites shaking their heads gloomily and disclaiming any responsibility for what was bound to be a debacle.

Confidence wavered occasionally at ensuing committee meetings, and the difficulties involved sometimes bred the beginnings of a bolt back to the safe sanctuary of ham or chicken pie. But these rebellions were abortive, and the renegades were always whipped back into line by the pretender to the throne. The strain told on her, though, and she lost weight and grew cranky. It was as much as your life was worth, our mother confided to our father in the privacy of our home, to open your mouth with a helpful suggestion that could possibly be construed as a criticism. Our mother would certainly be glad when *this* supper was over! So would everyone else, I guess.

The tension in the little, dark, inconvenient church kitchen as supper time drew near was almost unbearable. While the chairman and her cohorts would not stoop to overt sabotage of Operation Roast Lamb, they were not entirely wholehearted in their efforts to further it. They went about with tight lips, doing what they were told to do by those who had taken over command, but doing it automatically and zestlessly. They didn't *really* wish the supper to be a failure, but they'd have been more than human if they hadn't had a sneaking consciousness of the joys of saying "I told you so." They were inclined to pass judgment on a warm plate as being hot enough, when the minimum requirement was that it be almost too hot to handle. In charge of doling out the mashed potato, gravy, green peas and carrots, they moved fast enough not to be open to the charge of dawdling deliberately so that the food would get cold; but they didn't really zip through their duties.

The leader of the Lamb Party stood at the door and inspected each plate as it went out. If she didn't think it was hot enough, she sent it back, and she wasn't any too tactful in the way she did it, either. Tempers all over were so near the explosion point that the air crackled, and Alice and I prudently retired from the scene, putting as much distance as possible between us and the danger area. But even from 'way across the Sunday School room, we could see that eagle eye peering through the crack in the kitchen door at those eating their supper; and we could watch those taut lips moving as each harried waitress—girls from the older Sunday School classes—was interrogated narrowly: "Was it *hot* when you got it to the table?" "Has anybody *said* anything?" "Did anyone refuse seconds?"

The supper was a success. Even women from other churches who had been through the mill themselves for their own faiths complimented the Congregationalists and marveled aloud at how they'd ever done it. It amounted to a seven days' wonder in supper-giving circles; but no attempt was ever made to duplicate it. I guess it just wasn't worth the terrific strain and effort. It had served its purpose, anyhow. A new planet had risen in the sky of church society. The old leader graciously gave credit where credit was due and retired from active affairs to devote more time to her garden and her grandchildren.

The Sunday School picnic was of mixed appeal to Alice and me. Along with Children's Sunday, when each child received a certificate promoting him into the next class, an attendance pin if he merited one, and a potted geranium—my mother still cherishes descendants of some of those geraniums, perpetuated through yearly slipping—the picnic marked the end of the Sunday School year. That was all to the good. But Alice and I shied at organized mob activity, and we'd just as soon have stayed at home.

I'm not quite sure why, because we once went to a Holy Name Society picnic and had a good time. The Holy Name Society was an organization of the Portuguese Catholics in town, and normally we'd have had knowledge of it only through seeing the Holy Name parades with floats and a band once in a while on holy days. But there lived briefly and by mistake, for a short while, a Portuguese family in our neighborhood. Under their odd ways, they were hard-working, respectable people, just arrived from the old country, and Alice and I scraped acquaintance with the woman, who fed us a kind of sweet Portuguese bread that we loved. She carried herself beautifully and scandalized the neighborhood by working barefoot in her garden. She wanted to become a citizen, but she couldn't read English; so Alice and I undertook to teach her.

We did, too; although, since we were only in the grade school and had no notion of pedagogical procedure, I guess our success was attributable more to her determination to learn than to our ability to teach. That hurdle surmounted, she needed some citizen to go to court with her to vouch for her when she applied for her first papers. We couldn't do that, because we were too young. But we sold our mother the idea that it was her duty to go, as encouragement for such a worthy ambition. As a result, the woman felt under obligation to us and invited us to the picnic; and our mother didn't want to hurt her feelings, so she let us go. It was a revelation to us. We'd never seen grown-up people having such a relaxed and hilariously good time in our lives, and particularly not when under the auspices of a church.

But our own Sunday School picnics were different, possibly because of the difference in temperament between rock-bound, self-conscious New Englanders and the laughter-loving and uninhibited Portuguese. They were held on the shore of Lake Nippenicket, known as the Nip, a few miles out of town in the section called Scotland. We got there by taking the Taunton trolley of ill repute, and it was probably the only occasion of the year when you could board that infamous vehicle without misgivings. It was instantly obvious to anyone entering Central Square that this was the day of the Congo picnic. If you happened to be standing at the trolley stop in the milling throng of overexcited children and harassed Sunday School teachers, it was assumed that you were about to entrain for the Nip, and not for the fleshpots of Taunton. For once, the Taunton trolley was respectable.

It was darn noisy, too. By picnic-weather time, the closed winter trolleys had been stored in the car barn in West Bridgewater, and the open summer trolleys were in use. These had no side walls at all and a running board ran the full length both port and starboard, along which the conductor maneuvered to collect the fares. The passengers were accommodated on benches with swiveled backs running the full width of the car. The minute the car came screeching in from Taunton and the backs had been slammed over for the return trip, the Sunday School swarmed aboard, brandishing sweaters, shoe-boxes full of lunch, and water-wings. There was a brisk scuffle for places next to friends or for the choice spots on the end of the seats, and off we took. Hardened as they were to wafting carloads of drunks from Taunton, the conductors still flinched a little on Sunday School picnic days. The uproar was overwhelming, composed of voices raised in angry squabbling, or in reprimand, or in what was meant to pass as song, or in just plain meaningless yelling from sheer high spirits. Cows feeding in buttercup pastures along the route raised their heads in placid amazement, housewives popped out of doors, and non-Congo kids ran briefly alongside, jeering. They got as good as they sent, too, I can tell you. We Congos weren't taking any flip lip on picnic day.

Fortunately it wasn't far to the Nip. The trolley drew to a squealing halt by the side of the lake, and the children poured off under the pine trees. It was a good place to have a picnic. The lake itself was warm and shallow, there was an open pavilion intended for Saturday night dances, but convenient now for sitting in the shade if you felt so inclined, and a large level meadow overlooking the water for field sports. Across the road lived Mrs. Bassett, who rented safe, flat-bottomed boats to the nautical-minded. Alice and I would have loved to spend a day at the Nip on our own, paddling around in the shallow water, ineptly rowing a boat across to the island, exploring the wooded shores, and collecting pollywogs, pond lilies, and other specimens of fauna and flora. The trouble with the picnic was that nobody would leave us to our own innocent devices. They were always rounding us up to participate in organized activities.

These activities embarrassed us. Neither of us wanted to put her feet into a burlap potato sack, have it tied around her waist with a rope, and thus ludicrously hampered, try to run a race. Having the left leg securely bound to someone else's right leg, preparatory to the Three-legged Race, didn't strike either one of us as the ideal way to spend a day at the Nip; not with the lake glinting and shimmering in the sun and the gentle breeze stirring the pine tops with a soft susurrus. We didn't want to enter a potato relay race or a bean bag throwing contest. We wanted to see if we could catch a small snake to take home, or find a triple-banded lucky stone. It made us very uncomfortable to witness the minister, a man of dignity, making what we considered an exhibition of himself in the interests of promoting enthusiasm among others by his own example. Others might comment admiringly upon his good sportsmanship. To our minds, the line between the good sport and the darn fool was very finely drawn, and he was dangerously close to overstepping it. We wanted no part of the grim games, and we tried every subterfuge we could think of—notably a sprained ankle or the necessity of answering Nature's call—to slope off and amuse ourselves in our own antisocial ways. It was always a relief to us when someone announced that it was lunch time.

Lunch was the best part of the picnic. On the band platform in the pavilion were placed two galvanized wash tubs of lemonade with a whole cake of ice floating in each, and you were welcome to drink as much as you wanted, for free. Naturally, this bonanza aroused the competitive instinct in some of our peers, and there was always a contest to see who could drink the most. Records of fifteen or twenty glasses were hung up, to the admiring horror of some of us less talented members of the Sunday School. Then it was usual to swap sandwiches and pieces of cake with friends, so that you didn't have to eat the safe and familiar lunch your mother had packed, but could embark on gastronomical flights into the unknown. Other people's sandwiches always tasted better than your own, although they probably weren't.

After lunch, the affair disintegrated. Everyone was too full to think of more games, and the purpose of the expedition, the consuming of lunch, had been accomplished. It was all right now to go home any time you wanted to, after telling your Sunday School teacher of your intention, so that she could—thankfully, probably—check you off her list. The trolleys passed every hour, so transportation was no problem. But Alice and I usually walked home. It was only four miles, and we'd had enough of our fellow man for that day. The way through farming country was very pleasant, and we had in our pockets the trolley fare nickels that we were saving by walking, to spend at Tinkham's general store—where the sign over the door read *Emporium to the Universe*—at the top of the long hill in Scotland. For a nickel we could get enough penny candy to last us, with care, clear into Central Square.

If anybody had told us that there could be a worse ordeal in store for us in connection with church than the regular Sunday morning sermon, we would have laughed in his face. We wouldn't have seen how there could be, which just shows what sheltered lives we'd led. I don't know what ever possessed our minister of the time to arrange for a course of revival services, because that type of gospel salesmanship was entirely foreign to and outside the province of the Congregational Church. Maybe he felt that a Laodicean attitude was spreading in our church; or maybe it was simply an effect of the evangelist Billy Sunday, who was running rampant at the time. At any rate, he did arrange such a program. Two men whose names I don't remember and whose visit I wish I could forget as completely, were coming to give our church a shot in the arm, in a manner of speaking, by means of services to be held every evening and several afternoons for a week.

Our father was against this move. He didn't say so to Alice and me. Our parents were always very careful about not discussing controversial issues in our hearing. If there was a difference of opinion between them, they thrashed it out privately, came to an agreement, and presented us with a solidly united front. We never had the chance, as some of our friends did, to play one parent against the other for the gaining of our own ends. But as much from what he didn't say as from what he did, we received the distinct impression that our father disapproved of ballyhooing Divine Grace. While the project was still in the discussion stage, I'm sure he as a deacon fought it tooth and nail, if such an expression can be applied to a man as mild-mannered as my father. That didn't do us any good, though. Once the die was cast and the revivalists an impending fact, his loyalty to the church and his respect for majority rule governed his conduct. He and his family would support whatever the church sponsored. That meant that Alice and I had to attend all the afternoon services and a great many of those in the evening.

We were very young and even less worldly and experienced than our years would indicate. We just hadn't been around. In spite of a recognition of the hard facts of economic insecurity and a familiarity with real work that was in advance of our ages, in sophistication we were babies. We believed what we were told and accepted people and events at face value. Nevertheless, there was something about those revivalists that raised our hackles, and it wasn't simply that they were the cause of our being in church where we didn't want to be and where we wouldn't have been, but for them. We didn't know what is was then; but I know now.

It was a spontaneous recoiling from the practiced, professional approach through pure, cold-blooded and expertly handled emotionalism to a matter which we instinctively felt was of the most intimate personal and private concern. We didn't go so far as to think that these men were exploiting religion for the money they could get out of it. We weren't capable of such cynicism then, and I don't know now that it was true. It is entirely possible that they were sincere in their desire to make converts to the Christian way of life, and that they believed that theirs was the best way to do it. Such reasoning was beyond us then. We could only obey our instincts, which told us that this was outrageous, that these men could not possibly be concerned enough about the state of our souls to excuse the display they were making of themselves and us. They didn't know us or anything about us, so it was inconceivable that they should care so much. Therefore the tears they shed—yes, they did, really—over us must be crocodile tears, the quaver in their voices when they paused in their pacing of the aisles beside our pew and begged us to come to Jesus must be false, and their whole act must be phony. Perhaps we were wrong, but that's the way we felt, inarticulately but none the less strongly.

They worked on us for a week, and they didn't hesitate to pull all the stops. While one preached, the other prowled the auditorium watching for a sign of the weakening of Satan's hold on a member of the audience. When this happened, he'd rush to the side of the brand to be snatched from the burning and enter into a low-voiced, intense personal appeal and prayer. Those men knew their business, that I'll give them. They knew the secret and the power of a beautifully pitched, well-handled, flexible voice that could harden like iron against Sin, ring with the sweet hoarseness of a bugle in a summons to the ranks of the Lord, or throb and pulse like a muted cello in the final pleading to forget Self and embrace Christ. They didn't depend on their own abilities alone. They'd brought with them a trained quartet which furnished a musical background of appropriate hymns —not the good old stand-bys that we knew, but a new breed altogether, popularized and colloquial, that we didn't know and didn't like, but that affected us nevertheless. At the end of each meeting the evangelist who had been preaching stepped down from the pulpit to receive the repentant, the other redoubled his efforts among the goats, the choir launched very softly and authoritatively into "Almost Persuaded," and there wasn't a dry eye in the house, including Alice's and mine.

Oh, yes, I was affected all right, and furious and disgusted with myself for every tear I shed. I knew better than this. The whole thing was shameful and wrong. Those men had no right to keep at us and at us until we were reduced to this state. There was something indecent in the spectacle of the quiet, contained people whom I was accustomed to see seated in becoming composure in church on Sunday or going about their daily affairs with inviolable dignity, sobbing and groping their way to the altar. They were *good* people, and nobody had the right to make them feel guilty. I was truly shocked, and I swore that I wouldn't give in, never, never, not if everyone else in the church did, not if the gates of Hell itself yawned before me. I didn't care how ashamed of me my mother was, or how reproachfully the minister looked at me. I wasn't going up there in front of all these people, just because that man said so, to tacitly endorse the colossal lie that I was Saved!

I did, though. And it was a lie. I've never been further from a State of Grace in my life than I was on that last night of the revival. Probably because Alice and I had been present at so many meetings without surrendering our hearts to the Lord, the evangelists decided to concentrate on us. Perhaps we represented a challenge to them. In spite of our tender years, we were outstandingly tough nuts to crack, and perhaps that roused their professional pride. I don't know. Whatever the cause, they teamed up to give us the works. They hovered over us as we sat in tear-drenched stubbornness in the family pew. They exhorted and begged and wept and prayed, and suddenly I'd had enough.

I thought despairingly, "What difference does it make? If it will only shut him up and stop him breathing down my neck—" and I got up and stumbled to the front of the church. The quartet switched smoothly and triumphantly from "Almost Persuaded" to something about the ninety and nine who were safe in the fold while one lost sheep, presumably me, was sought out and rescued from the darkness without.

It was terrible. I knew I was betraying my sister, left alone to tough it out. I knew that what I was doing was a weak denial of everything I held right and honest; but I didn't care. I'd come to the end of my endurance. Let the evangelists think I had found the Light. Let my mother suppose what she wished. God and I knew better, and we were both ashamed of me.

Because the odd part of it was that I did believe in God. His Existence was the verity on which I based my conception of the universe around me. No revival could change that. A world without God? Who then would lay a Hand on the earth in the spring, so that the violets and bluets and anemonies stirred to life and lifted their faces to the sun? Who would hold the stars balanced in their appointed places, and cause the tides to sweep clean the wide-flung beaches of the globe, and summon the four winds from their far caverns? Who would take care of the wild little creatures in the woods, and the fledglings in their nests, and the tiny, busy ants underfoot? Who would watch over *me?*

9

The Thursday Sticks and Stones

WHEN MY FATHER LEFT THE EMPLOY OF THE WESTFIELD *Valley Echo* to become the owner-editor-publisher-printer of the little weekly Bridgewater *Independent,* he knew from experience and observation what he was getting into. He knew all about the slender proceeds from such an undertaking, and all about the disfavor he would meet with from a number of quarters, since nobody can please everybody all the time in any field, and especially not in the field of opinion. He was prepared to catch hell over the telephone or vis-a-vis from all those individuals who were angry because an account of their social activities had not appeared in the paper, and from those who were mad because theirs had. Some people like to see their names in print and some don't, and there isn't any way of determining which is which except by trial and error; especially error.

My father knew all about the delicate path he'd have to tread in order to keep the Advertisers happy, so that the chief fount of revenue wouldn't dry up at the source. He knew about the occasional bribes he'd be offered or threats he'd receive to suppress legitimate news that was discreditable to some individual. He knew that sometimes he would suppress such stories, not as a result of threat or bribe, but because in his own opinion such suppression was for the common weal.

He knew that the decision would be his alone, and that if the
end were the performing of a public service, it would be forever unrecognized and unrewarded; while if his judgment
was wrong and disservice resulted, he would bear the public
burden of the blame.

He had no illusions about what the grand title of Editor
signified. He didn't see himself sitting at a desk, wearing a
white shirt, barking orders and wielding a blue pencil. He
knew he was going to have to work hard and get his hands
dirty in the scores of ramifications of his business. He was
going to write editorials, yes. But he was also going to have
to set them in type, proofread them, run the press while they
were printed, and solicit advertising to pay for the ink and
newsprint and rent and heat and distribution, so that his
brain children would see daylight. Few people buy a local
paper for the editorials.

They buy it to see what's going on around town. Therefore, if he wanted any circulation of his editorials at all, he
was going to have to scrape up enough news of interest to fill
several columns and give the buyer the impression that he'd
got his three cents' worth. Boiler plate, or the prepared cast-
metal filler that came through the mail—items about the
rainfall in Kamchatka or how to prevent starch from sticking
to a hot sadiron—were all very well when used with a light
hand; but if you filled your paper full of boiler plate, the
customers were, quite justifiably, going to feel gypped. Who
cared about the circumstances of the introduction of maize
into England? What the public wanted to know was who got
invited to the Smith girl's wedding, and whether the Gary's
were going to South Carolina this year.

Getting the paper out wasn't all that went with ownership,
either. The *Independent* alone wouldn't support a family of
even our modest needs and thrifty habits for ten minutes.
The income had to be augmented by job printing: programs,
tickets, calling cards, stationery, or anything else anybody
wanted printed. Sometimes the jobs were big and important,
like the paper-bound book that was the Town Report, and
sometimes they were just dollar jobs, like a few fliers (give-

away advertising sheets) on cheap stock. Whatever they were, they had to be done right or a customer was lost to a Brockton or Middleboro printer. The job work was a headache, but if you had enough of it and did it right, it helped pay the dentist and the cobbler. All this my father knew when he left the *Valley Echo,* where he never would have become rich but where he did have a regular pay check each week, and bought the *Independent* from Pliny Jewell, to sink or swim according to the success of his own efforts.

Why did he do it? Because he wanted to be left alone to go his own pace. Because he wanted not only to think his own thoughts, but to express them without censorship; not only to hold his own opinions, but to declare them openly. Because he wanted nobody to tell him what to do or say or think except his own conscience and intelligence. Because he'd rather have less and be more. Because, in brief, he was a Dickinson.

Our father was not a particularly imposing figure. He was a rather small man, with a low voice, a mild manner, and a habit of listening more than he talked. He had blue eyes and fine, blond, curly hair, a fact that struck Alice and me, stuck with our mother's brown eyes and straight hair, as being supremely unfair. But there wasn't much we could do about it except fuss. It's possible that our father's quiet ways were the result of having to live with three talkative females. If driven to it by lack of other audience, we sometimes talked to the cats or to ourselves, and our father must sometimes have found it hard to get a word in edgewise. I don't think it bothered him much. He just let the clatter go in one ear and out the other, while he pursued his own thoughts. He didn't miss much by not listening to us. We never had anything very important to say anyhow; and the same thing was true of our father that I have observed in other quiet and thoughtful people. They seem to have some sort of subconscious monitor that warns them when they'd better come back to earth and take on interest in proceedings. Our father always heard anything worth hearing.

The business premises of the *Independent* weren't **very**

impressive, either. They occupied one enormous room—it was more of a huge loft than a room, really—on the second floor of a ramshackle two-story building on the west side of Central Square. This was rather grandiloquently known as the Independent Block, although I'm not quite sure why. In the first place, it was more of an oversized shanty than what is commonly understood by the term business block; and in the second place, the *Independent* occupied the least conspicuous and desirable part of it. Downstairs on the street were the Chinaman to the right, and E. A. Hermann (Millinery) to the left; and the front of the upstairs was given over to Tom Crocker (Real Estate), father of Miss Rachel Crocker of the Children's Library. From any one of their several windows, they could see what was going on all over the Square.

From the grimy windows of the *Independent*, tucked away at the upper back, we could see only a cinder-covered slot of yard, the big doors of Atkinson's Livery Stable, and—oddly— a small enclosure, lost and forgotten behind a high board fence, where bloomed pear trees and snowball shrubs and currant and gooseberry bushes, with here and there the ragged remains of what once had been box hedges. Once it must have been a very lovely formal garden, and it was still pretty in its wild neglect, so hidden and unexpected behind the untidy rears of the stores. Very few people knew it was there at all; and when we lived on Broad Street and had not much yard space, our father planted a vegetable garden there. Alice and I used to work in it—it was a good one, since the soil was marvelous and rich—and we took a great deal of satisfaction in the fact that this was a really and truly secret garden. It was like a little lost green island, the still air of which was but faintly disturbed by the surflike sound of the unseen traffic in the Square. We loved that fourth-dimensional feeling of being invisible, intangible.

To get into the *Independent* premises, you had a choice of using the back stairs or the front stairs. It wasn't much of a choice. They were both narrow, dark, steep, and dirty. The general public used the front stairs, rising directly off the street and ending on a landing from which a door opened into the Editor's Office. The Office was just a corner of the loft, separated from the rest of the area by an L-shaped counter and a battered gate. The gate was more of a psychological barrier than an actual one, since it was almost never closed; and even if it had been, it wouldn't lock; and even if you had been able to lock it, the most decrepit citizen could easily climb over it. It was supposed, however, to define the boundary between the intellectual aspects of publishing and the manual. If you had business with the editor, you stayed on the Office side of the gate. If you were simply killing time, you could go back of the counter into the shop and visit with the printer, who was the editor in an apron. The furnishings of the Office consisted of a varnished roll-top desk, much the worse for wear, a beat-up swivel chair, and a small table supporting an old Oliver typewriter with the letters standing up like ears at the sides. It didn't work very well, and our father never used it; but it gave a professional touch to the Office corner.

Alice and I used the back stairs more than we did the front. We had to run around to the rear of the building through the alley that separated it from Odd Fellows Block, but the advantage was that the back stairs gave us a chance to spy out the land and observe our father's mood before bracing him for a couple of pennies. The stairs came up under the sink and behind a tall case of type, so we could see and hear without being seen and heard. If our chances didn't seem good, we could just evaporate down the back stairs again and await a more favorable moment for making our touch.

The ninety percent of the loft that was given over to the mechanics of publishing was to us a fascinating place. It was filthy, of course; the warped boards of the worn floor stained with grease and printer's ink and littered with broken type and scraps of paper. Alice and I were paid a nickel apiece for sweeping out once a week, on Saturday morning. We threw a lot of water around to lay the dust and swept up dustpanfuls of debris, but it didn't make much difference in the general appearance. It was still a dirty place; but, as our mother said, it was good clean dirt, by which she meant that it wasn't the same as garbage or night soil. It wasn't full of virulent germs.

This sweeping took us longer than it should, because we were always finding something that we wanted to keep. We were supposed to throw broken type into a bucket so that it could be sold for melting down and recasting, but very often we saved it in our pockets. Why, I don't know. Just the magpie instinct, I guess. Then at the front of the room was a big paper cutter with a knife about four feet long. This was hand operated. When you wanted to trim some stock, you placed it on the cutting table, secured it by screwing down a bar from the top, and brought the knife down by turning a large wheel. Around the paper cutter there was always a treasure of cropped ends—long white strips for making lists or writing Black Hand notes, colored scraps that were ideal for paper dolls' dresses, and oak tag for the covers of the little booklets we were always manufacturing. We were always well supplied with good paper.

There were three presses in all, two job presses, powered by treadles, and The Press. Alice and I could operate the job presses as soon as we were tall enough to see what we were doing. It was simply a matter of keeping your foot going at an even pace, feeding squarely so that the printing would not come out on a bias, spreading the finished product carefully so the wet ink wouldn't smudge, and telling our father when the rolls needed inking. There was really nothing to it. It was a rather pleasant occupation, not too demanding of either brain or brawn and full of a rhythm that was soothing and conducive to long thoughts.

The Press was something else again. We were forbidden to monkey with it at *all*, an unnecessary restriction, since we were too afraid of the thing to touch it with a ten-foot pole. It was a worn-out flat-bed cylinder type, powered by a gasoline motor and weighing about two tons. When it was running, once a week on Publication Day, the din was so terrific that not even by shouting at the top of your lungs could you carry on a conversation within the quarters of the *Independent*. The whole building shook, and it's a wonder to me to this day that the press didn't plunge through the floor onto the heads of Miss Hermann and the Chinaman below. Its clanking, groaning and wheezing could be heard all over the Common and half a block down South Street. It must have predated the Civil War, and anything that could possibly be wrong with a press, short of complete disintegration, was wrong with it, so that I don't think there was ever, repeat, *ever* an issue of the *Independent* run off without at least one breakdown from any one of a number of causes.

The rest of the shop area was taken up by four tall cases of type by the windows, the top cases slanted to accommodate the typesetter on his high stool, the reserve metal and spare fonts stored underneath in shallow drawers; by a flat-topped, potbellied stove in the middle of the room, which furnished the only heat; by a cupboard where supplies were kept, and a cold-water sink in the corner; and by two stones, a large one back of the stove under a powerful droplight for the newspaper, and a small one by a window for job work.

The other day I heard a young man in the printing business trying to explain to a young lady what a stone proof is. He told her that type is set and locked into a form, but that while the form is still on the stone, before it is transferred to the press for actual printing, an impression is made by inking it, putting a piece of paper over it, and running a roll across the paper. This gives a rather rough proof of the work, but clear enough so that it can be checked for typographical errors while the form is still on the stone, to save time and trouble. "It's called a stone proof," he said, "because it's taken on the stone. Of course, it really isn't a stone at all. It's a sort of table made of stainless steel. But 'way back in the early days of printing, the tables actually were made of stone, and we've kept the term, even if it is outdated. I myself never saw a real stone in my life."

Well, I guess that's telling them who's outdated, I thought. " 'Way back in the early days of printing" in the *Independent* shop, the stones *were* stones, six-inch-thick slabs of rock, nicked around the edges and stained with grease and ink, but smooth and solid and comforting to the touch. I can't imagine a print shop the life of which doesn't revolve around the stone, and I don't mean any namby-pamby substitute, either. I was really shocked. No wonder some of the literature of the day is such superficial, cockeyed stuff, if it had its genesis on the material of saucepans. Stainless steel is fine in its place, but it lacks the roots, the soul and character of an honest hunk of rock that was quarried from the living ledges of a mountain. Working over a stone, a real stone, keeps you constantly reminded of the good earth beneath your feet. It keeps you in touch with fundamental things and acts as a curb on any tendency to get too fancy and streamlined.

Alice and I loved the big stone, but we never paid much attention to it until one day it had, for some reason, to be taken out of its frame. We then discovered to our intense and somewhat macabre delight that the reverse side did not present to the world the virgin face of the top. There was a legend carved on it under a stylized weeping willow, flanked by two rather fat-faced cherubs. First came a name and two dates of more than half a century before, and then, in a beautiful running script, chiseled deep and delicate and clear:

> God my redeemer lives
> And often from the skies
> Looks down and whatche

"Wow!" Alice exclaimed. "I'll bet he was mad. All that work, and then spelling watches wrong!" After all, it's difficult, not to say impossible, to correct a typographical error in granite. We giggled, pleased by the vision of that infuriated gravestone cutter throwing down hammer and chisel, tearing his hair out by handfuls, and even maybe swearing out loud, in spite of the sad solemnity of his task. "Anyhow," Alice added thoughtfully, "shouldn't that read God comma my redeemer comma? And cap R Redeemer?" I agreed that it should. We weren't copy-reader's daughters for nothing.

Every time we went by the job stone after that, we tried to

figure out how the verse would have ended. Looks down and watches out/ For the next poor soul who dies? Looks down and watches people/ Who persist in telling lies? Looks down and watches *you*/ In considerable surprise? We were never able to think of an ending that both made sense and maintained the proper reverential tone; and I still can't.

I don't know whether Alice and I were naturally antisocial and secretive little snips, or what ailed us. We may have thought that our more gently reared little friends whose fathers were white collar in fact as well as by designation might be revolted by the grimy and cluttered *Independent* plant. Some of them made quite a Thing of being too dainty and ethereal for this world. We didn't want any histrionic shrinkings from this place that we liked. We liked a lot of things that our associates recoiled from in horror or held up for derision, and we'd learned to divide our lives into compartments, some open to the public, some locked and secret between the two of us. So without ever exchanging a word on the subject, we had a tacit agreement that the *Independent* was such a private compartment. Once in a while, when we had to take a message from our mother to our father, we were accompanied by a friend. On such occasions we used the front stairs, stayed on the Office side of the counter, delivered our message in a butter-wouldn't-melt manner, and left. It wasn't that we were ashamed of the place. We really weren't. It was more as if nobody would understand and we knew we couldn't explain—if that makes sense. We kept our friends strictly away from the *Independent*.

But if our friends stayed away, nobody else in town did. There was a constant flow of visitors, some on business, as many who were not. The six ministers and the Catholic priest were regular weekly droppers-in with their copy for the Church Column. They never left their notes and departed in peace, but stayed to argue with our father about practically everything from Salvation by Grace to who was going to win the World Series. When the Chinaman moved to Broad Street, a florist took over his shop. He came up every morning to this fountainhead of local information to find out if anybody had died overnight, or been hospitalized, so that he could govern his ordering of cut-flowers from Boston accordingly. Advertisers and town officials were in and out all the time, and private individuals with job printing to be done, or items they wanted printed under Local News, or bitter complaints because their names had been spelled wrong last week.

Then there was the Chinaman from downstairs, before he moved away. He didn't have a telephone, so he used our father's. He never made local calls, because he didn't have any friends in town, but he did fairly often call up his tong brothers in Boston. He'd ask our father to put the call in for him, since he had a little trouble making the operator understand his brand of English. Once contact had been established, he'd take over in Chinese. Naturally Alice and I couldn't understand what he was talking about, but we loved to listen to the rippling patter of the unfamiliar words and the strange, singing inflection. It was pretty, like music or water flowing. Sometimes he laughed, and that enchanted us. We hadn't known he could laugh, because no one ever heard him do so ordinarily. It made us feel good to hear him and to see his flat, slant-eyed, yellow face crinkle into a classic mask of mirth.

Old Mr. Cross was a regular visitor, too, although he never had any business to transact. He was a retired Englishman—retired from business but *never* from being an Englishman! —who lived up in Scotland with his son. He was a clean and neat old man with shaggy white hair and an odd English County accent. He came into the Office for two reasons. First, he and my father were friends. Their friendship was based on a common passion for tea, which our father kept steaming at all times on the top of the potbellied stove. What hard drinking-liquor is supposed to be to the traditional newspaperman, tea was to our father. He drank quarts a day, meeting all crises by first downing another cup of the clear, scalding brew. The *Independent* would have folded in twenty-four hours if the teapot had been lost. Mr. Cross liked his tea, too, and matched hooker for hooker as our fa-

ther drank. He said, though, that he was drinking it as a
duty. Englishmen in good standing were honor-bound to
encourage the trade of the colonies by consuming the produce of the tea plantations under British rule.

The other reason Mr. Cross came in was to read the *Man-
chester Guardian,* which—improbable as it may seem—our
father received as an exchange. He had a big exchange list,
and most of the exchanges made sense. I can see why the
owner of a similar publication would want to swap copies,
to see what his confreres were up to in features and composition. I can't imagine, though, what the editors of the august
Guardian could possibly have wanted with the little eight-
page and wholly local *Independent,* although they did once,
to our father's extreme though modest gratification, quote
one of his editorials. What we wanted with the *Guardian* was
easier to understand. Our father wanted to get the British
viewpoint on various international affairs, Alice and I wanted
to add to our list of sidesplitting Anglicisms, and Mr. Cross
wanted to return in spirit to his homeland. He read every
word in it, including the advertisements and the obituaries.
The *Guardian* is a big paper, and it kept him well occupied
over his teacup.

Another regular imbiber of our father's tea was Miss
Hermann, who ran the millinery shop downstairs. She came
up the back stairs two or three times a day, bringing her own
eggshell-thin cup with her, and filled it from the inelegant
old teapot. There aren't any milliners left like Miss Hermann. In those days, a hat was a creation. You didn't go
into a store and buy a factory made and trimmed hat. You
went to the milliner, and she either made you one from
scratch, molded and trimmed one of the basic shapes that
you selected from her stock, or altered and re-trimmed your
old hat. You never met a hat just like yours on the street,
because there wasn't a hat just like yours anywhere in the
world. Some of the things she turned out were pretty
strange and wonderful, although at the time they were considered the last word in chic, with their big wired bows and
beady-eyed birds. The prettiest hat I ever had in my whole

life came from Miss Hermann's, though: a rough, wide-brimmed, natural straw with a wreath of wheat-heads and field flowers—daisies and buttercups and forget-me-nots and poppies. She let me select each one myself from her boxes, and she wove the wreath. It was like picking a bunch of perfect and never-fading flowers in some Elysian field. That was the only hat I've ever owned that I really *loved*.

It's a little hard to explain about the milliner in any small town in those days. For some reason or other, she was presumed by the mere fact of her occupation to be a Fast Woman. I don't know why this should be so, unless it was because most milliners were single women, earning their living by pandering to the more frivolous instincts of their respectable sisters. Then, too, they usually dressed a little more stylishly than anybody else did, as a way of advertising their business. Drummers—as salesmen were known—those notoriously rabid wolves of the trade world, called on them with their samples, and sometimes a customer, coming into the millinery shop while a drummer was there, heard *laughter!* Need I point out what a suspicious circumstance that was? Most women would cross the street rather than be subjected to the once-over by a drummer's lascivious eye; and while it was conceded that the milliner did have to do business with them, she certainly didn't have to act as though she enjoyed it, did she?

What Miss Hermann's private life was, I have no idea, but I would be very much surprised to learn that there was anything questionable about it. I can see, however, why she might have caused a certain amount of head-shaking. She was tall and slim, where other women ran rather to lumpishness, and she had tremendous style. She didn't own many or expensive clothes, but what she did to them and the way she wore them was nobody's business. Men turned around to look after her, and I don't blame them a bit. She was something to look at, with her dashing hats atilt on her pompadour, her starched jabots, and her supple waist. She had elegance; and until the day she died, an old lady who had come into respectability through age and a changing time, she kept it.

She kept something else that Alice and I used to love about her: her talent as a raconteuse and her off-beat sense of humor. She had the cracked voice of a young boy, just before it deepens—flexible, out of control, a little rough, and completely sexless. It sounded strange, coming from that woman-of-the-world, Mona Lisa face. She'd lean against the counter, an incongruous figure in the shambles of a print shop, sipping her tea and telling us the most outrageous tales of her adventures in that cool, boy's voice. She was a good comedienne. She never laughed, no matter how funny she was being, and she didn't mind presenting herself in a ridiculous light.

She was the first bird-lover I ever knew. In those days, people thought either that birds were pretty things, or else that they were a nuisance, building nests in the overhang of the eaves. Nobody dreamed of getting up at four-thirty in the morning to go walking along country roads, *observing* birds. What was there to observe about a bird? Miss Hermann found something, because she got up before sunrise more mornings than not, and swung along the streets leading out of town, smart in hat and gloves and slim walking shoes, to look at and listen to our feathered friends. I don't think that habit helped her reputation much. Early-rising housewives with their hair uncombed and their corsets still on the bedroom chair, seeing her stride lightly past with her fine chin high above her cascading lace jabot and her face serene and happy, found it difficult to believe that all *that* was for the birds. It was, though. I know. Alice and I sometimes went with her, when we were able to drag ourselves out of bed at that ungodly hour. We learned a lot, too. Miss Hermann even showed us an ovenbird's nest, a thing hard to find. She truly did have an absorbed interest in birds. She could become really excited about them. Besides, it was beautiful out beyond the limits of town at sunrise, with the light level and rosy on the dew-drenched meadows, and the world all fresh and new. We could understand why she went, even if no one else would believe.

She'd tell us stories about her own childhood with her sister Rye. We thought Rye was a wonderful name for a sister, and considered rechristening ourselves Barley and Oats. They didn't have the cachet of Rye, though. Lovely Rye, golden Rye, graceful Rye! Her name made us see great fields of grain bending in the sun under the brush of the breeze, while cloud shadows raced over them. It was a terrible blow to us to discover that Rye was just a nickname for Maria. We rather lost interest in her after that.

Miss Hermann carried on her business single-handed for eleven months of the year; but before the onset of Easter-hat-buying, she had help. This help was a little dark-haired woman, Miss Messenger, from way off at the ends of the known earth—Springfield, Vermont, to be exact. What Miss Messenger did during the rest of the year I haven't the faintest notion, or how Miss Hermann formed this alliance with her, nor why she found it worth her while to travel all that distance for a month's work. The fact remains, however, that sometime along in March Miss Hermann would burst into the *Independent* office, an open letter in her hand, her eyes sparkling and her odd voice threaded with pleasure, to announce, "Messenger's coming." She always called her simply Messenger. We'd never heard a woman referred to or addressed by her last name alone, and we thought it worldly beyond telling. But the announcement of Messenger's impending arrival meant more than that. The sleet might be blowing past the windows, the wind might be whining and snuffling coldly through the far from airtight walls of the *Independent* shop, and every light in the place might be blazing at midday to combat the wintry gloom. Suddenly we could smell violets and hear the first frogs' peeping. Spring was almost here. We'd had news of a harbinger more dependable than earliest dandelion or most optimistic robin. Messenger was on her way.

The second harbinger was not long in following the first. Each year—and it seems to me now that it always happened on a dark and dreary night when the spring Line Storm battered torrentially at the still half-frozen earth, when eavespouts were muttering lugubriously, and the street lights showed wavering and blurred through the swaying curtains of the rain—our father would come home, tired and wet, shake the water from his derby, lay down the green baize bag in which he carried his books and accounts daily to and from the office, and say a little heavily, "Well, the Tramp's showed up." We couldn't help knowing that there was something about the Tramp that saddened him, although what it was we didn't know.

I'm not sure yet what it was, since our mother took great care that Alice and I shouldn't develop too close an acquaintance with the Tramp. He was a nasty, filthy old man who had only himself and The Bottle to blame for his circumstances, she told us, and we were to stay right away from him. He was dirty and ragged and unkempt, all right, but in the brief encounters Alice and I had with him, we always found him gentle-spoken, more literate than some of the solid citizens with whom we came in contact, and almost pathetically polite. No one treated us with half as much adult consideration and respect as the Tramp did. So I'm not sure whether our father's sadness stemmed from the regret anyone feels at the waste of a good mind and real ability; or whether it was because he liked the Tramp as an individual and was truly and personally concerned with his welfare; or whether just possibly there was an element of "There, but for the Grace of God—" involved. Newspapermen were bywords for instability and loose living, and our father may have seen in the Tramp what he himself could have become; although I can't imagine that's happening.

When our father made his annual announcement, our mother would pause in her busy getting of supper onto the table, look at him sharply, and say, "And I suppose you gave him money." It was a statement, not a question, and sometimes our father didn't answer at all, because she already knew the answer; and sometimes he said reasonably, "Well, he was hungry. He'll work it out after he gets rested up."

Nothing was said about where he was resting, because we all knew. During his short yearly sojourn with us, the Tramp always slept on the counter of the *Independent* office, bedded down on stacks of newsprint, covered with a spare felt cylinder blanket, and warmed by the fire he kept roaring in the stove. Our mother always prophesied darkly that he'd get drunk and burn the place down; our father always said mildly that he wouldn't; and he never did.

Sometimes our mother bothered to ask if the Tramp had tried to sell our father his latest gadget for controlling the static electricity generated in newsprint as it goes through the press, and sometimes she was too disgusted to bother. She knew very well that he'd not only tried but succeeded, and that the invention, whatever it was this time, wouldn't work. A great problem in press rooms was this electricity, which caused the papers to cling together, to crackle and give the handler light shocks, and generally to create a nuisance. No solution to the problem had been found at that time—and may not have been yet; I haven't been around print shops much lately, so I don't know. Any down-and-out tramp printer like ours, who still retained some vestige of pride, instead of openly begging for a handout would lay claim to having discovered the answer to static electricity, and offer his secret for sale for a small sum. It was a perfectly aboveboard transaction, both parties to it understanding that it was merely a face-saving form of panhandling.

There were a lot of tramp printers around in those days, men with an itching foot and usually an alcoholic tendency, who traveled the country over, often on established beats, working when they needed money and going on when the spirit moved them. They could always find work. No village print shop ever had enough competent help, and these men knew their trade. Besides that, there was a tradition in the newspaper world that made it unthinkable not to give a hand to a tramp printer. Perhaps it was based on superstition, perhaps it was purest sentiment, perhaps it was a fraternal feeling for another pursuing the same unlikely means of livelihood. Whatever the reason, the tramp printers were passed along from small paper to small paper, never accumulating any worldly wealth, but never starving or freezing, either. They were a queer, tortured, feckless breed, men of skill and sometimes of culture, often endowed with superior intelligence and a philosophy, but damaged in some way, having some mainspring broken or facet marred.

Our tramp never stayed with us very long. Perhaps he never stayed anywhere very long, but I have a feeling that the shortness of his stay was directly connected with our mother's ultimatum to our father that that worthless old bum could hang around as long as he remained sober. When he started drinking—OUT. She was doing him a favor, whether or not she intended it or he appreciated it. He always looked better when he left us, after a week off The Bottle, than he had when he arrived. He earned his small pay and then some. He was a versatile printer and mechanic, and he usually managed to iron out a few of the bugs in The Press, temporarily at least. I doubt if God Himself could have cured them all permanently. He came every spring for years and years, looking a little more wrecked and ruined each time, a little blearier of eye and shakier of hand. Then one spring he never showed up, and we assumed, probably correctly, that he was dead; but where he died or under what lost and lonely circumstances we could only imagine.

The climax of the week for the Dickinson family was, of course, Thursday, Publication Day. Everything built up to press time—late afternoon, early evening, or late night, depending on a lot of things. The day started at seven in the morning and ended when the mail sacks of papers were safely bestowed in the vestibule of the Post Office, which could be in the small hours of Friday morning. In any case, the Post Office was always closed and the lucky, lucky employees, who had a definite quitting time, gone about their private affairs. So the vestibule was left unlocked for us, so that the papers could be left for distribution into boxes and delivery sacks by the first clerk to arrive next day. The *Independent* had to be in circulation Friday morning. Not only was our father's professional pride at stake, but there was also the matter of the Advertisers who were running ads for weekend sales, which would be so much wasted ink if we failed in our contract.

The whole family moved to the Office on Publication Day. When we were very young, there wasn't very much Alice and I could do to expedite progress except be quiet and keep out from under foot. We found a number of ways to amuse ourselves in what might have seemed to the uninitiated eye an unpromising and sterile field, the tiny, cramped Office corner to which we were confined in the interests of not bothering those at work. We sat at the desk and drew pictures and wrote stories. We typed our manuscripts on the old Oliver, although between its eccentricities and our lack of skill, they were seldom recognizable as English composition. We made jewelry for ourselves by linking paper clips into chains. We took everything out of the desk drawers, dusted them, and returned the contents neatly. We could do this every Thursday, since in a week's time the drawers would again be hoorah's nests. Someone had left a whole file of old bound copies of a children's magazine called *The Chatterbox* piled up in a corner I don't know why, since they had no bearing whatsoever on the functioning of the *Independent*—and we spent hours and hours reading them. They were full of quaint moral tales about little girls who even to our inexperience seemed innocent to the point of feeble-mindedness. But they were something to read. In fair weather, before it grew dark, we made frequent sallies down into the Square, just to see what was going on.

That took us safely up to supper time. Supper consisted of sandwiches and turnovers, usually. Alice and I made a production of it, pretending that the counter-walled space of the Office was the Alamo and we the valiant defenders, keeping up our strength by partaking of jerked buffalo meat between attacks. Or we crowded into the kneehole of the desk and were cave dwellers eating parched corn. Our parents ate with one hand and continued work with the other, our mother absent-mindedly nibbling a sandwich while she corrected proof, and our father snatching bites as he made up the form on the stone.

In summer, after-supper entertainment was all taken care of. We went to the Thursday night Band Concert on the Common. But our winter evenings were not without *divertissement,* either. Across the eight-foot alley between the Independent Block and Odd Fellows Block with bare windows directly opposed to ours, was a large second-story room, known as Odd Fellows Hall. Various public functions were held there. By some happy dispensation of Providence, Thursday was not only Publication Day; it was also Dancing School Day. In Odd Fellows Hall, from seven to eight on Thursdays, a woman from Brockton instructed our peers in ballroom technique and etiquette. Alice and I had grandstand seats for this spectacle. We'd pull up a couple of stools to the window, press our noses to the dingy pane, and stare across as onto a lighted stage while our friends, dressed in ruffly frocks or blue serge suits, according to sex, and patent leather slippers, gyrated around to the strains of an out-of-tune piano.

If you're beginning to feel sorry for us, poor little outcasts gazing wistfully at the revelry within, you'd better mend your thinking at once. The rot of self-pity was not in us. In fact, the shoe was definitely on the other foot. We felt sorry for the poor goops whose mothers made them participate in this effete and asinine performance. What's more, this wasn't a defensive, one-sided attitude. The Dancing School victims felt exactly the same way about Dancing School as we did, and we didn't improve their morale any by making faces at them, putting our hands to our heads like donkey's ears and wiggling them, and laughing heartily whenever anyone made a mistake. Sometimes we managed to make them so self-conscious that they might as well have had buckets of cement on their feet, for all the airy grace they displayed. I regret to have to report that more than once the teacher, in understandable irritation, stamped over and yanked the curtain down, cutting short our pleasure for that evening. But she always forgot before the next Thursday and so, if we were

smart enough not to carry our goading tactics too far, we
could be sure of an hour well killed on Thursday evenings.
The Little Dickinson Girls, I'm afraid, were not the sweetest
and dearest little girls in the world.

As we grew older—say nine and eleven—there were things
we could do that were actually helpful. We had no formal
induction into the fellowship of working women. The traditional initiation of printer's devils was omitted in our cases.
So long before that it seemed as if we'd been born with the
knowledge, we'd been shown the type lice, a charming trick
which results in the neophyte's getting his face and hair full
of splattered ink. We'd been holding copy for years, ever
since we could read reliably. We loved the legal copy, the
court notices of various natures—settlement of estates, adoption of children, changing of names, or probating of wills—
that by law had to appear in the public print before legal
action could begin. We'd held the legals so often that we
knew the form by heart and would sometimes vary the
monotony of the conventional jumprope rhymes by chanting,
"*Com*-monwealth of *Mass*-achusetts, *Ply*-mouth ss. *Pro*-bate
Court, to *all* persons *In*-terested *in* the estate of *John* J.
Jones—" on to the sonorous conclusion, "—and *show* cause if
any you have *why* the same should *not* be granted." It
sounded impressive.

Nobody ever said to us, "You're old enough now to help."
It was just something that happened naturally, just as it happened naturally that we learned to set type. The tools of the
printing trade were as familiar and accustomed to our hands
as rattles are to babies, and from playing with a composing
stick—the little metal rack that a typesetter uses to hold the
type he's composing—it was an inevitable step to trying to use
it properly. We were fooling around one day, trying to set
type by the trial and error method of picking up each piece,
looking at it, and if it was the right letter using it, but if it
was the wrong one, putting it back, when our father said, "If
you're going to do that, you might just as well learn the case
and do it right."

Learning the case is becoming so familiar with it that you

don't have to think "Now where in heck are the *t*'s?" but reach for them automatically, as one who operates a typewriter unerringly hits the right keys. The case is arranged sensibly with all the letters you use most, like *e* and *s*, in the center front, and the rarer letters, like *z* and *q* in smaller compartments at the top and sides. The small letters are in one case, down near you, and the capitals, which don't occur so often, in a separate case up above. We said truthfully that we'd love to learn the case. So our father took time out to place in each compartment of our cases the appropriate letter in 24 point (or headline) size, to act as guides for us. In not too long a time, we could dispense with these guides and compose a fairly clean stick of type.

We were inordinately proud of our new talent, although typesetting isn't hard to learn. You just prop your copy up in front of you and follow it through hell and high water, working from right to left, instead of the usual reading direction. The result is mirror printing. In fact, an easy method of correcting a stick of type is to hold a mirror before it and read in the mirror. We scorned this sissy refinement. Real printers read directly from the metal, and that was what we were going to do. We did, too. Oh, we were pretty unbearable when we first learned to set type. We annoyed our teachers in school like anything not only by refusing to say "small letter" and "capital letter"—printers say lower and upper case—but also by curling our lips contemptuously at those who used those amateurish terms. When we had our own personal sticks assigned us— Well! A professional composer always insists on using his own stick, considers it better than any other—although it is identical—and gets temperamental if anyone borrows it without permission. We out-temperamented Gutenberg. The only part of typesetting we didn't care for much was distributing: that is, returning the type to the proper compartments in the cases after its purpose has been served. We felt this process to be anticlimactic.

The first things we did to help on Publication Day were addressing the papers and folding them for the mail. We started more to stave off boredom than anything else, one night after the Dancing School teacher had lowered the boom on us. We ended by having regular jobs that we were depended upon to do. The addressing and the folding were two separate procedures, with a longer or shorter interlude between them. The Press had a two-page bed, so that the paper had to be printed in two operations, pages one and eight first and then, when they were ready, pages four and five. The other pages consisted of boiler plate and standing advertisements, so they were already done by Thursday. As soon as the first form was off the press, the addressing could start.

Nowadays most papers, even small ones, have addressographs. We didn't. Our addressing was done by hand, in pencil, from a sheaf of battered and dirty lists in more or less alphabetical order. If someone got mad and stopped his subscription or moved out of town, his name was crossed out. If a new subscriber joined our happy *Independent* family, his name—if it began with H, for example—was added to the sheet of H's, if there was room. If there wasn't, it was tacked onto any sheet providing space, which would probably be the Q sheet, which had just a few Quinns and Quimbys, or the Z sheet, where only Zablowski reigned in his own right, although he had plenty of non-Z company. Someone was always saying, "I *must* take time some day to straighten out this address list and copy it over!" but nobody ever actually did so. We went right on using the same old illegible lists, arriving at correct names and addresses by a sort of instinct based on complete familiarity with the town. The papers were spread flat on the counters, the name was written in the upper right-hand corner, and the sheet was folded back so you could get at the next one. After you'd addressed two hundred papers, your forearm was pitch black from leaning on the green—or fresh and wet—ink. I guess it was then that we learned not to mind dirty jobs, because we discovered that even the most tenacious dirt will wash off, leaving you as good as new, but with the deep satisfaction of having accomplished something.

After the addressing was done came the wait for the second
form to be made up. Our father never—and by never, I
mean *never;* not ever; not even the mildest oaths; not under
the greatest provocation—swore, *except* while he was making
up the second form. By this time I guess even his monu-
mental patience was worn thin and his calm shaken by a
series of irritations. He swore steadily in a dispassionate un-
dertone. Our mother didn't even try to stop him. She knew
it would be useless. She just pretended not to hear. If decades of making-up and locking a form hadn't taught our father to take it in stride, nothing she was apt to say was going
to do so at this late date, and she knew it.

This is not a treatise on printing, so I won't go into all the
confusing intricacies of it. But I will have to explain a few
things, if you'll bear with me, in order to make sense. A form
is made up on the stone. There is a rectangular iron frame,
called a chase, the size of a page of newsprint, and in this the
composed type is arranged, or made up, in columns. This is
a fussy piece of work. Some advertisers have paid extra for
a preferred spot on the page, and that's what they should,
and do, get. The upper right-hand corner is sacred to the
lead, or most important story of the week. Other stories are
allocated according to importance. All these are laid out
first, and that part is fairly easy. But then there are still quite
a number of spaces to fill, of varying sizes, and that's when
the going begins to get tough.

There may be an empty inch-and-a-half in the middle of
a column. The make-up man has to find an item that will
fit it, or can be made to fit it. All around the edge and back
of the stone, waiting, are such items already set, of various
lengths, from a few lines to a full two-inch stick. The
make-up man finds a likely prospect and fits it into the hole,
if he can. If it's too small, he can always stretch it by insert-
ing some slugs—blank strips of metal of less than type-high
thickness—between the lines; but if it's too large, there isn't
anything he can do except put it back where he found it and
look for a better bet. It isn't good make-up to carry over one
line of a six-line item into another column, even if the ad-

jacent column is free. As the page gets fuller, the choice of material gets narrower, and the demands of the spaces more difficult to meet. That's when our father started swearing.

Usually he ended by asking our mother or Alice and me if we knew of any scrap of news that hadn't already been reported that would run to about a third of a stick. If we did, one of us set it, tailored to specifications. But if our minds were blanks, he'd dream up a filler, like "The new drinking fountain at the foot of the Common is for your use, not abuse. This is public property. Treat the rights of others with respect." Or if there was a holiday coming up within the reasonably near future, he could always extend the season's greetings from the editor to his public.

The page full, now came the time to lock the form. This was really ticklish business. Wedges of metal called quoins were inserted between the chase and the composed type and expanded with a quoin key to hold the type absolutely firm and rigid. There couldn't even be one little loose piece, or it would fall out when the form was picked up, others would cascade after, and the whole thing would be pied, or reduced to a senseless heap of jumbled type. I never saw a form pied, but the possibility was a nightmare that haunted all of us. If that happened— Well, mass hara-kiri would be the only course for us. So our father tightened quoins, tested, introduced slugs and broken match sticks into questionable areas, tightened and tested again, and finally decided that it would do. Then we all literally held our breaths while he lifted the heavy form tenderly, carried it around the stove, and gingerly laid it on the bed of the press. Only then did we let out our breaths.

The way The Press worked was, I suppose, ingenious in a fumble-fingered, ham-handed, Rube Goldberg way. The form lay on the flat bed at the bottom. The paper was fed in at the top by the pressman—our father standing on a stool— and was seized and carried down over the type by a rotating cylinder about four feet in diameter. The moment when the paper was in contact with the form was the moment of actual printing, of course. Then a wooden fly that looked something like a picket gate slapped down, the printed page dropped onto it, and it flopped over, depositing the page on an old kitchen table. In the meantime, the bed shuttled to the rear of the press where ink-covered rolls replenished the ink on the type, another page was fed in, and the process was repeated. The whole thing was powered by a long belt running off a gasoline motor sitting crankily in a big galvanized pan ten feet to the westward. The pan was a concession to the Building Inspector's fuss-budgety notions about fire hazards. I don't think the Inspector could ever have happened by when The Press was in operation. He wouldn't have strained at a little gnat like a backfiring motor on a bare, oil-impregnated floor. He'd have condemned the whole establishment out-of-hand.

Synchronization was the key to the situation. If things didn't work together as they should to the split second, any number of things could and ordinarily did go haywire. The print could start halfway down the page and bleed off the bottom. Or the rolls could flood the type with ink, resulting in a fascinating view of the Black Forest at midnight, or inexplicably stop giving ink at all. Or the fly would suddenly go crazy and begin throwing papers all over the room, instead of piling them neatly on the table. Or the clamps that held the paper to the cylinder would coyly refuse to release it at the strategic moment, so that it went round and round, getting blacker and blacker.

If all the gears were meshing nicely, so that papers rolled off with monotonous regularity, The Press still had a few aces in the hole. The cylinder blanket of felt could always tear, necessitating a complete stoppage while a new one was put on; or the belt could break and start flapping wildly while the motor raced and the press groaned to a stop; or the motor itself could simply quit cold. I tell you getting out the paper was a chancy business, and one that developed in all of us extremely sensitive ears. How we could detect one tiny false note in that deafening uproar, I don't know; but we could. It might be the most innocuous-sounding, small clicking. We heard, and turned eyes filled with speculation and apprehension to each other.

When the second printing started coming off the press, we could start folding. No automatic folder for us. We put the inside section on top of the outside section, folded it once down the middle by hand, then across, then across again. It was now ready for the mail sacks, the Post Office, and in due course, the reader. We'd fold and fold, automatically, replenishing our stock of insides from the kitchen table by the press and watching the pile of newsprint above the cylinder waste away under our father's feeding hand. We were on the last lap, now. Pretty soon we could call it a day and go home. Another issue was almost off the press. The week, according to the *Independent* calendar, was almost run out.

I have an uncomfortable feeling that I'm making us sound like the victims of child peonage, like living examples of the sort of thing that resulted in the child labor laws. It wasn't like that at all. In the first place, we knew why we were working. We'd been brought up in an atmosphere of responsibility to and for the *Independent,* and it never occurred to us that this responsibility wasn't ours as well as our parents'. In the second place, we were children, and it is perhaps child nature to play. At first we felt so important to be helping that the work really was play; and then, when it might have become accustomed drudgery, we made it into play. We did all manner of silly, kiddish things that weren't really very funny, but that kept us entertained.

To give just one foolish example: there was a woman whom I will call Miss Mackintosh who didn't get her paper one week. Whoever was addressing the M's just plain skipped her in the jumble of the M page. She came around to the Office on Saturday morning while Alice and I were sweeping, and raised hell with our father. He said he was sorry, gave her a paper, and that should have been that.

But no. The next Thursday, Alice said to me suddenly as we were writing away busily, "You done Old Lady Mackintosh?" As a matter of fact, I had; but I said, "Golly, no! I'd better do her now," and addressed another paper to her. In

260 Innocence Under the Elms

a few minutes, I said to Alice, who was on the R sheet, "Don't forget Biddy Mackintosh!" She clapped a hand to her forehead. "Jeepers, no!" she exclaimed, and wrote another paper for Miss Mackintosh. We kept that up all afternoon, with the result that Miss Mackintosh probably received ten papers that week. All right, so that's childish. We were children, and we were amused.

The grist of news to the mill of a small town weekly is not ordinarily very sensational. A fire resulting in extensive property damage is headline material, and if someone is killed in an accident, that's practically Stop Press. Therefore our father felt justified in tearing his whole front page to pieces on the December day when there was an attempted holdup of the L. Q. White Shoe Factory payroll, down on Hale Street, just below where we lived on Broad. The effort was foiled, nobody got hurt, and the bandits escaped. However, the town was in an uproar. The money *might* have been taken, and someone—the paymaster or the guard or an innocent bystander—*might* have been killed! To the towns-people, they weren't just paymasters and guards and by-standers. They were people we knew well, friends and neighbors. A fine thing, when in broad daylight, right in the middle of our placid village, such a thing could take place. Violence really is a serious and shocking thing to the peaceful and peace-loving, and our father wrote an editorial to that effect, and filled Page One with by-lined accounts by the wit-nesses and available participants.

The holdup was hot news for two or three weeks, but then, since no progress was being made in the apprehension of the culprits, the story died a natural death. However, about four months later the forces of evil struck again in a town not far north of us, and this time the paymaster was killed. The bloodhounds of the Law really went to work now, and the story came to life again. Two or three weeks later arrests were made, and again our father happily ripped out the ac-count of the Visiting Nurse Association's May Breakfast, dug out his seldom-used banner type, and blazoned the tidings to the world. There was at this point no doubt in his or anybody else's mind as to the guilt of the prisoners.

But as time went on and hearing after hearing was held, the *Independent*—which was our father—began to be less certain. There were certain discrepancies in testimony which he thought needed to be explained a little more convincingly, and he wrote editorials saying as much. This attitude was considered a little peculiar in face of the overwhelming popular certainty of guilt, but nobody was very much surprised that our father took it. He was known to have peculiar ideas. He was probably the only respectable person in town to vote against both local and national Prohibition, although he'd rather have died The Death than allow a drop of alcohol to pass his lips. In a time and place where the line separating the sheep from the goats was identical with the impassable chasm between good, reputable Republicans and riffraffish, disreputable Democrats, he was a Democrat and ran a Democratic newspaper, a fact that curtailed appreciably his circulation. He wasn't being merely contrary, either. He was convinced that what a man ate and drank was his own business, and that any attempt at regulation was an infringement of his rights. While he had no desire to become a lush himself, he'd defend with his life, if necessary, another's privilege to do so; and he believed wholeheartedly that the Democrats' political views made more sense than those of the Republicans.

In this case of the holdup men, he honestly thought they were being given a raw deal. His editorials became more and more outspoken against a possible miscarriage of justice, and the long rambling discussions held between him and his cronies dealt almost entirely now with this affair that was monopolizing the attention of the Courts and the public. I remember one such discussion with Elmer Kimball, who came in every day to read the *Independent*'s copy of the Boston *Globe*.

"There is more than reasonable doubt," said our father. "There is considerable doubt whether these two men could

possibly have been anywhere near the scene when that paymaster was killed. According to our whole conception of
justice—"

"They're Anarchists," Elmer retorted, warming his back
through habit at June's cold stove. "They admit they are,
so they deserve to go to the chair anyhow. What difference
does it make *why?* So long as we get shet of them. Electro-
cuting's too good for them is what I say."

"They're not on trial for their politics," our father stated
mildly. "They're on trial for a murder that I for one—and
I've got plenty of company—don't believe they committed.
The time has passed in this world when a man can be exe-
cuted for his political beliefs." Oh, my poor, innocent father!
But then, he was living in an innocent era. "Humanity has
outgrown that. I don't like your politics, either." Elmer was
a staunch Republican, of course. "But that doesn't entitle
me to kill you."

Elmer just looked at him as though he thought he was
crazy.

On another occasion our father had a little verbal hassle
with Paul Revere, direct descendant of the night-riding silver-
smith, and renowned in Bridgewater for his hobby, which
was raising improbably large and perfect Hubbard squashes
with his name tattooed on them.

"But the number of witnesses who have testified to having
seen and talked with them, a long way from the scene of the
crime—" our father said a little tiredly and desperately. The
case had been dragging on for a long time now, with con-
victions and appeals and motions for new trials.

"Witnesses!" snorted Paul Revere. "And exactly who are
these famous witnesses of theirs? Just a bunch of damn wops
like themselves."

Our father said softly, "If you had to provide an alibi for
the morning of April 15, 1920, who would you call upon to
prove you were where you said you were?"

Paul Revere bristled. "I can tell you right now where I
was any April morning of any year. I was out in my squash
patch, and plenty of people will swear to it. My sister Eliza-

beth, for a starter, and Dr. Carr next door, and Gardner Bassett and—"

"In short," said our father, "just a bunch of damn Yankees like yourself."

Paul Revere was too shocked to take even slight umbrage. He missed the point entirely.

The years dragged on, and everybody became bored with the case of the anarchists who had killed the paymaster, except my father. He still maintained that the wrong men had been caught, and he'd still argue about it, if he could find anybody to argue with. Mostly, townspeople no longer cared one way or the other. They had more immediate things to worry about.

Alice and I went into the Office one morning to find our father seated at his desk, doing nothing. This in itself was unusual enough so that we asked what was the matter. He turned a stricken face to us. "We've finally murdered them. I never thought, after keeping them penned up like cattle all these years— But we've finally put them out of their misery."

We looked at him blankly. All this talk about our murdering someone! "Who?" we asked timidly.

"Nicola Sacco and Bartolomeo Vanzetti." He gave them their full names in a kind of solemn requiem. "We shouldn't have done that. We didn't have the right—" His voice died sadly.

I don't remember ever hearing him mention them again, but he never forgot. It hurt him more deeply than it's easy to realize, that the men whom he believed—whether rightly or not I can't say—to be innocent should have been done to death by a system which he endorsed. I wish I could think I was as capable of single-minded devotion to an ideal as my father was. But at least I have an example that I can try to follow.

As to what else he and the *Independent* gave Alice and me, it's hard to say. I know that doctors' sons frequently turn out to be good mechanics, and ditch-diggers' daughters often make wonderful fashion designers or concert pianists. So maybe it's only by coincidence that today Alice is an editor of children's books, and I call myself a writer.

IO

Unicorns' Territory

WHEN ALICE AND I WERE CHILDREN, PEOPLE STAYED PUT MORE than they do now. If we wanted to see a friend of ours, we went to her house. If she wasn't right there in her own yard, she was almost certainly within sound of her mother's voice or other chosen means of summons. Every mother had her own method of tolling home her young. Some called, some beat gongs, some blew whistles. Around our own house there was a circle drawn, imaginary but well-defined in our minds, beyond which we might not go without permission. Its circumference was determined by the furthermost points from the house at which we could hear the sound of the old school bell that had been part of our grandfather Dickinson's equipment when he was earning his way through Yale by teaching in country schools. If our mother wanted us, she rang the bell and we came running. We were like little calves tethered to the stake of home by the tough invisible cord of its authoritative voice. To say that we didn't hear the bell was no excuse at all for not obeying. We weren't supposed to be where we couldn't hear it.

This ruling didn't impose any hardship on us. The bell had a harsh and strident tone that could be heard at a great distance, so we had a wide field in which to carry on our activities and no particular desire to broaden it further. For a long time it seemed to us that the golden circle circumscribed by the sound of the bell was the whole civilized world, and everything beyond its limits was like the blank spaces on ancient maps, where there is nothing but a faint and fearsome legend written, "Unicorns here." As long as we stayed where we belonged, we were in no danger of encountering the unicorns. The bell's clangor would keep them at bay. We went outside the circle only in our mother's company or by special permission, and either armored us against all evil.

I can remember the first time we ever went away from home without our mother. We didn't go very far, and we weren't gone very long, but our sensations were those of Marco Polo, to say the very least. Perhaps this was partly due to the fact that a week of preparation went into this safari, and to Alice and me at the ages of about four and six, a week was an immeasurably long period of time, especially when devoted to a project the nature and purpose of which was extremely vague and mysterious to us. We lived on Spring Hill Avenue at the time, and one day May Tucker and Ina Severance, the Big Girls of the neighborhood, asked our mother if on the following Saturday we could—well, we didn't understand what it was they wanted; but whatever it was, our mother said we could do it. All our friends—the Chadwick children, the Williams children, and Norma Sturtevant—were invited, too, so naturally we were eager to participate.

Nobody bothered to explain to us what the whole thing was about, but we were used to doing what we were told without knowing the reason why; so every afternoon that week, after the older children got home from school, we trouped over to Severances' and cut out circles of pink and white tissue paper, fringed the edges of them carefully, and gave them to one of the Big Girls to make into rosettes and paste onto cardboard crowns. Everybody had to have a crown, Ina said; and Norma, because she had long yellow curls, had to have the prettiest one and carry the Maypole, an old rake handle with a super-rosette on top and long streamers flowing from it.

On Saturday we all gathered in front of the Sturtevants' house—ten or a dozen of us—with our lunches in our hands and our crowns on our heads. I can see Alice now, her brown eyes big and puzzled under the concoction of pink and white paper flowers that kept slipping down over one ear. She wasn't sure that she liked the way things were developing, and I wasn't sure that I liked it, either; but everyone else seemed happy about the whole affair, so we decided that it was probably all right. May and Ina lined us up with Norma, carrying the Maypole, at the head of the column and the rest of us strung out behind, paired according to size. I marched with Olive Williams, and Alice and Esther Chadwick, the two smallest ones, brought up the rear. We turned the corner of the avenue smartly and proceeded along Summer Street around the Normal School campus. Two women stopped on the opposite sidewalk and looked at us. "Aren't they *cute!*" one said to the other, and I decided suddenly that I wanted to go home. I said as much, but May Tucker told me, "No-you-don't-either!"

We walked and we walked and we walked, past the campus and past Mr. Boyden's house and down Plymouth Street, where I'd never been before. The Boydens' dog Jack followed us for a while, but at the railroad tracks he turned around and went back, and we were all alone and exposed in a strange country. "Where are we going?" Alice asked me in a small voice; and because I didn't know and didn't want to admit it, I said airily, "You'll see." But Olive was better informed than I was. "Why, to Hooper's Grove," she said. I'd never heard of Hooper's Grove, but I felt safer just knowing that our destination had a name.

Finally we got there. We'd probably been walking for three-quarters of an hour and covered three-quarters of a mile, but it seemed as though we'd been on the road all day and were far, far from home. My legs were tired and Alice had torn her crown and Norma said she couldn't carry the Maypole a step further, so she left it leaning against a tree by the roadside. We swarmed over a wall, crossed a field, climbed a steep rise, and threw ourselves on the ground in the shade of the tall pines that topped it. This was Hooper's Grove, and for the moment it was enough just to have won our objective.

We must have eaten our lunches, and we probably played games and explored, but I don't remember a thing about that. All I remember is sitting at the edge of the grove and looking down a slope covered with daisies. There were quite a few near me, but at the bottom of the hill they were so thick that the ground looked snow-covered. I decided to go down there and pick a great bunch to take home to my mother. I'd never seen so many daisies in my life as there were as the foot of the hill, and it would take me only a minute to pick bushels. I started down, not bothering with the scattered blooms I passed on the way, because it was going to be so easy to get so many down below. But when I arrived at the bottom, there were no more daisies there than there were anywhere else; and looking back toward the grove, I saw that now it was the top of the field that was unbroken white and gold. I felt like crying because someone was playing tricks on me, but somehow I knew that it wouldn't do any good; and I started picking the daisies at hand, not because I really wanted them any longer, but because it seemed the only thing left to do.

I don't remember the walk home, either, but I remember being very much surprised that some roses my mother had in a bowl on the dining room table were still as fresh and unfaded as when I last saw them, before leaving home; and our kittens, Smut and Whitey, hadn't grown a bit. It seemed to me that we'd been gone long enough for them to have become old, old cats with kittens of their own. For a long while, Alice and I placed events in time as having happened before or after we went to Hooper's Grove.

There were two traditional annual expeditions that our family, along with about every other family in town, took. The first came in the spring, and it was to Taunton to see the herring run. We always went on a Sunday, since that was the day our father didn't have to work, and we took the Taunton trolley, which was all right to do on Sunday, be-

cause everyone knew that the barrooms were closed and so
wouldn't suspect the worst. When word came that the herring were running, the trip was planned for the very next
Sunday afternoon. I knew what herring were because every
spring men used to peddle smoked herring from house to
house, a dozen or so strung through the gills on a stick, as
stiff and black as weathered shingles. They didn't look very
appetizing, but they tasted pretty good, smoky and salty, and
Alice and I used to pick at them as they hung from a hook
in the pantry, stripping off shreds of the cured flesh and eating it like peanuts.

I couldn't wait, the first time we ever went, to see those
herring run. I thought we'd go to a large field, and the herring would be lined up behind a tape, standing upright on
little legs grown especially for the occasion, like the oysters
in the illustrations of "The Walrus and the Carpenter." At
the sound of a gun, they'd start racing like mad down the
field, and it would be a sight to see. I was terribly disap-
pointed to discover that they didn't run at all, but only swam
up a sort of staircase built around a dam in the river.

After a while, though, I became interested in following one
fish from the bottom of the weir to the top, breathing heavily
in sympathy when he stopped to rest in a quiet pocket of
water and talking encouragement to him as he gathered his
forces for the next step. The dark, rushing water exercised a
hypnotic fascination as it poured around the baffles, and I
identified myself so completely with the fish suspended quiv-
ering in the current, their heads upstream and their fins fan-
ning tirelessly, that only my mother's firm clutch on the back
of my dress prevented me from falling in. I could have
stayed and watched the herring run forever, I thought, even
though running was a silly and misleading thing to call what
they were doing.

Then late every summer we went over to East Bridgewater
to visit Alexander's Dahlia Farm. This was an accepted way
of spending a fine Sunday afternoon, and I must say that it
was a diversion innocent beyond believing. You took the
East Bridgewater trolley, rode the three miles over Sprague's

Hill to East Bridgewater, and then walked the little distance
to the dahlia farm. All you did after you got there was look
at the flowers, acres and acres of them in orderly rows that
seemed to stretch to the horizon. They really were beautiful,
great, rich, velvet blooms in the most unbelievable shades
ranging from a red that was almost black to a faint shell-pink,
and through all the oranges and yellows from burnt sienna
to pale cream. But I always had the oppressed feeling that
there were too many of them. They were lovely, yes; but
after a while you couldn't admire them any more. Your mind
closed to their arrogant beauty, and to pick a dusty butter-
and-eggs flower from the side of the road on the way back to
the trolley stop was a relief. It was only a weed, but it too
was wonderful in its way; and nobody expected you to *oh* and
ah over it, thank goodness.

I think everybody visited around less when we were young
than they do nowadays. It was harder to get from place to
place, for one thing; and for another, it was impossible then
simply to lock up your house and walk off, leaving it in
charge of various thermostats and automatic guardians. In
summer there weren't the fires to think about, or the pipes
freezing, but you didn't plant a large garden to abandon it
to the weeds and birds while you took a vacation. And you
couldn't be gone at the height of the strawberry or peach or
string bean season, because what about your canning? Nobody else was going to do it for you, that was sure; and only
the shiftless faced the winter without a preserve cupboard
crammed full of home-canned fruit and vegetables. In the
case of our family, we had an additional responsibility, the
Independent. The paper had to come out every week, and
no two ways about that.

Nevertheless, once every summer we did go to visit our
grandmother and grandfather Stewart at their camp on a lake
in central Massachusetts. We usually set out on a Saturday,
when the *Independent* was safely over for the week, and our
father went with us to see us through the several train and
trolley changes. He returned home to the *Independent* on
Sunday, and we stayed for the whole week until the next Sun-

day, when he came to get us, although our mother always worried about how he was ever going to get the paper out without her help. I'm not sure how he did manage, except that the *Advertiser* staff helped. The *Independent* and the *Advertiser* were rivals until our father bought the *Advertiser* and merged them; but in spite of the bitter competition inevitable between two weekly papers in a town that was barely large enough to support one, our father and the *Advertiser's* editor, Mr. Willis, were on excellent terms. They borrowed fonts of type back and forth, helped each other out when either had a rush of job work too heavy to handle alone, and once when the *Advertiser* press broke down, our father printed that week's edition on his own press, as a professional courtesy. So it was only accepted practice for Mr. Willis, scarcely recovered from the ordeal of getting his own paper out on Tuesday, to turn to and assist our father through his Thursday crisis once a year. Our father would do as much for him when occasion arose.

Although our annual stay with our grandparents lasted for less than ten days, it was the high point of Alice's and my year. We talked about it for the other fifty-one weeks, reliving incidents of visits past or planning projects for the future. It almost seemed sometimes as though Woodville were our true home and the interval spent in Bridgewater only time marked until we could get back there. We loved everything about those days in camp: the water and the woods and the hilly countryside, the boats and the fishing, the relaxing of a rigid schedule so that meals came at odd times and bedtime was frequently forgotten until all hours; and particularly did we love the feeling of being members of a large and carefree family. Our mother was the oldest of eight children, and whenever we were in Woodville, not only were her younger, unmarried brothers and sisters who still lived at home there, too, but most of her married brothers and sisters and their children, our cousins, were visiting as we were.

The cottage was small and not very convenient, and this made for great informality. There was a huge wall-tent out

back where all the men and boys slept on cots crowded so
closely together that you could turn somersaults on them
from one end of the tent to the other without setting foot on
the plank floor. The women and babies slept in a big bedroom containing two enormous double beds, or on cots in
the living room; and the younger girls like us slept in one
section of the screened porch. The other section, around the
corner, was the dining room at meal time and the library,
game room, or annex living room at all other times. It was
impossible to run a tidy and orderly household under the
crowded and primitive conditions, so nobody tried to. The
absolutely essential housework was done, and that was all.
Who cared, anyhow? Nobody was in the house except to eat
and sleep, and what was a vacation for if not to slough off
temporarily the usual routine?

Alice and I hardly knew our mother while we were at Lake
Whitehall in Woodville. In Bridgewater she was our mother,
Mrs. Dickinson, a strict but fair disciplinarian, to be respected and feared upon occasion; a dependable bulwark between us and the world; an efficient household manager with
little time or patience for foolishness; an adult of the same
incredible age and iron imperturbability as all other adults.
At camp she was the oldest Stewart girl, Florence. She did
what her mother told her to do, even as Alice and I, and giggled and whispered with her sisters. She threw water on her
youngest brother Preston, and ran shrieking when he chased
her. She took off her shoes and stockings and dangled her
feet in the lake as she sat on the edge of the wharf and discussed the merits of her second from-the-youngest sister
Maud's beaux with her. Evenings, after we young fry were in
bed, the whole tribe played fan-tan for matches on the oil-
cloth-covered dining table by the light of a kerosene lamp,
and she was just as quick as any of the rest to cry, "Why,
Arthur Stewart, you crooked son-of-a-sea-cook! That was
mine!" If Alice or I fell into the lake, as we did periodically,
she'd just say, "Oh, well— Go change your clothes," instead
of scolding us for carelessness. And once an old man, a friend
of our grandfather's, came to call and said of our cousin

Violet, "She's shaping up real pretty, but she'll never be a patch on Florence and Alice and Carrie. Handsomest bunch of fillies in the county, the Stewart girls were." We'd never pictured our mother as a handsome filly, and it gave us pause for thought.

But not too long a pause. We had too much to attend to, to waste time thinking. We were in seventh Heaven, where everything was perfect. Along a ridge over the waters of the lake a row of cottages stood under the tall pines, rather ramshackle and flimsy structures with thin walls and wide screened porches, something to come into out of the rain. Their lack of elegance didn't bother anybody a bit. They were camps and they didn't pretend to be anything else. They were owned by families from several near-by towns, and these families moved to the lake as soon as school was closed in June and stayed the summer, the breadwinners commuting to their various jobs on the trolley that went by the general store, Caswell's, about three-quarters of a mile away, down off the ridge. This meant that summer after summer we had the same children to play with, children with whom we had a lifelong acquaintance and one important thing at least in common, complete familiarity with and an abiding love for Whitehall and its vicinity. Each year we started right where we'd left off fifty-one weeks before, as though we'd been parted only overnight, picking up interrupted projects, falling into old schedules, continuing familiar programs with the Fairbanks children and the Frayles and our many cousins—Margaret and Violet and Jack and Bill and Stew and Doris and Iris and the rest, and with Winifred, who was really our aunt, being our mother's youngest sister, although she was just my age.

The days weren't long enough for all we had to do. We had only two duties, keeping the drinking water buckets filled and doing our grandmother's errands at Caswell's store; and neither one was onerous. The water for washing clothes or dishes or ourselves came out of rain barrels set under the eave spouts or, if those ran low, out of the lake. But the drinking water had to be brought up the hill from a spring down by the dirt road. We loved an excuse to go down to the spring. We took the empty buckets off the special shelf in the dining porch and started out on a narrow footpath beneath the pines. Three cottages along, it emerged into the sunlight between neglected fields overgrown with sumac and sweet fern and wild roses and purple asters and goldenrod. It pitched steeply down from outcrop of ledge to lower outcropping, through an abandoned orchard where small, misshapened Porter apples and sweet tawny Russets still grew for the picking, and came out on the meandering road. We crossed the road, stepped down two stone steps, and there we were at the spring, bubbling quietly out from beneath the roots of some big elderberry bushes and shaded by lush growths of jewel-weed, loose-strife and the pink joe-pye weed.

The whole trip was wonderful. The hot sun-baked fields were crisscrossed with an invisible mesh of heady, heat-released fragrances, and the warm dust of the road as we crossed caressed our bare feet and puffed deliciously up between our toes. By the spring it was cool, and we always threw ourselves flat to drink directly from it, ignoring the coconut-shell dipper and thrusting our faces deep into the water to watch the little sand devils dance mysteriously on the bottom. The water was icy and tasted of the roots and rocks with which it had been neighboring—like no other water in the world. We'd literally get drunk on that water and reel back up the hill with our buckets, laughing at nothing, talking nonsense, and indulging in wide and extravagant gestures.

The round trip to and from the store was longer and should have taken any reasonably able-bodied and purposeful messenger about half an hour. It took us the entire morning. Our grandmother early learned that if she was really in a hurry for a dozen eggs, she'd better send one of our younger uncles on the errand. One of our troubles was that we always took the short cut along the lake shore and across a little dam instead of the longer way around by the road. Thus we fell afoul of several time-traps. The first was at the foot of the slope in front of the camp, in full view of anyone on the porch. It was a fifty-foot section of two-inch hawser, tied above to a branch of a lofty pine and having at the free end a big knot with a short stick run through it. By climbing with the knotted end to the top of a large boulder under the pine, straddling the stick, clinging rather desperately to the rope, and giving yourself a good hard push, it was possible to swing far out over the waters of the lake in a great, swooping arc. It was the nearest any of us had come to flying, it scared us to death to do it, and we loved it. Sometimes when there were five or six of us embarked on our grandmother's errand, we'd bog down at the rope for fifteen minutes, or until someone at the cottage happened to notice us and shouted us on our way.

The next hundred yards or so was fairly free of temptation, since it simply skirted the shore under the trees and offered nothing more exciting than an occasional frog to catch, or pale and ghostly Indian Pipe to pick. But then came a little cove, defined by a large frost-split ledge thrusting out into the lake. The top sloped up gradually from the shore and then fell in great terraces to the water level, and it had ferns and blueberry bushes feathering from the cracks. It had served us variously as a pirate ship at sea, a robber baron's moated castle, a beleaguered fortress, and a peak in Darien. We could never get past it without turning aside to check on the caches of stage properties we kept stored in the several fissures and to enact another episode of whatever was our current fantasy. This frequently resulted in someone's falling into the water or all of us forgetting what it was that our grandmother wanted at the store. In the latter case there was a long argument as to who should go back and find out, which was always settled finally by the drawing of lots. Everyone promised the loser that we'd walk slowly so that he could catch up with us, although I don't see now how it was possible for us to proceed any more slowly than we were already doing. If it was simply a matter of getting wet, we continued on our way, on the proved theory that by the time we got back to camp the victim would have dried out and no one in authority would be any the wiser.

The next pitfall was the dam, a simple structure with a railed walk along the top and in the middle a two-foot sluice through which the overflow tumbled. To the dulled eye of maturity it would have seemed an unpromising field for entertainment; but we were alert to its possibilities and knew that it was the best place anywhere around for skipping flat stones across the surface of the lake. In addition, it was the playing area for a game that could be played nowhere else. The equipment of each participant consisted of a good-sized chip of wood brought from the environs of our grand-father's chopping block and a long stick, and was stored on the cross beams under the dam between contests. You threw your chip into the lake above the sluice and then tried, with your stick, to prevent its being swept through the gap and down the stream below. The one who succeeded longest won. When your chip went through the dam, you had to scramble down the braces along the face into the meadow be-low and race along the brook to retrieve it. It was a very active and exciting game, fraught with miscellaneous perils, no matter how simple it sounds. It sometimes delayed us for almost an hour.

Once across the dam, we debouched onto the road and for a while the going was pretty dull, nothing more than a pleas-ant walk in the country. But when we came into the tiny village proper, things picked up at once. We'd succeeded in years past in alienating our contemporaries among the native population by a systematic program of name-calling, face-making, and audible criticism of local manners, mores, and modes, so that a state of active hostility existed between the cottage kids and the village kids.

I must explain that this conduct was far from character-istic of the shy and quiet little Dickinson girls, as the people of Bridgewater knew us; and I imagine that our cousins were equally well-behaved and seemly in their own home towns. But the safety that lies in numbers and the awareness of re-laxed discipline on the part of our respective parents went to all our heads, and we surprised even ourselves with our brashness. Alice and I in particular were unaccustomed to having a solid phalanx of family connections behind us, and we found the experience intoxicating. We were deservedly unpopular in the village.

The disaffection spread from the barefoot, slingshot set upward and downward to their parents and dogs. The minute we came abreast of the first house, we prepared ourselves for attack from any quarter. Green apples would come hurtling out of nowhere in our direction. Dogs who had been minding their own business in back yards would rush with raised hackles to snarl and growl at us. Women, probably very pleasant under normal circumstances, would step onto their front porches and stand, arms akimbo, eyes narrowed, and jaws set, ready to holler at us if we set so much as one foot on their lawns. One old biddy who had a low retaining wall around her property—just the right height for sitting on and resting—told us in no uncertain terms that if she caught one of us sitting on her wall, she'd turn the hose on us. Naturally this threat made it a matter of honor with us to sit on her wall every time we went to the village, even if it was the last thing in the world we really wanted to do. Oh, we had a high old time whenever we had to go to Caswell's for our grandmother! Far from wounding our feelings, the general disapprobation set us up for the day. We'd have felt that we were slipping if anyone had been cordial to us.

The trip back to camp usually took less time. We'd sucked the juice from the orange of adventure, and there were matters back on the ridge that demanded our attention. We had a standing arrangement with our grandmother that any time we wanted to pick the blueberries, she'd make blueberry cupcakes. We took her up on this almost every day, poor woman. Then there was a tub full of water on the ground beside the porch that we felt obliged to keep full of pond-lily blossoms. Every day we went along to a shallow cove beyond the last of the cottages, waded into the soft, black mud, and pulled up great bunches of lilies, floating so lightly at the end of their long, rubbery stems. Alice and I never saw pond-lilies at home, and we adored their perfect purity. We couldn't figure out how such ethereal beauty could come from the rather smelly and repulsive ooze of the cove; but we were too young to draw any moral conclusions about it, which is just as well, I guess. Beauty is not a suitable subject for moralization, but only for appreciation of the wholehearted, wonder-brushed quality we were able to give it then.

We had to go fishing, too. The lake abounded in pickerel and perch, but to catch those you had to have a boat. We weren't allowed to take the boats out alone, so we had to confine our fishing activities to the wharf, from which we could catch only an inferior species of carp known locally as kivvers. These were small fish, unfit for human consumption, but so stupid that we could catch any number with our make-shift tackle: alder poles, old twine, and bent pins. We gave importance to our fishing by telling ourselves that we had to catch the kivvers for our Aunt Alice's cat Cooney and our Uncle Preston's cat Jack. Cooney was remarkable only for his beauty, and he was too spoiled to eat our kivvers anyhow. But Jack, an ordinary short-haired tiger of startling size, was truly a cat of distinction. He'd eat all our fish and, if he was still hungry, go catch some more of his own. He didn't mind getting wet at all, and he loved our uncle so much that he'd jump into the lake and swim after any boat that he thought was bearing Preston away from him. If you held your arm horizontally at shoulder height, Jack would jump over it, an exhibition of impressive grace and power. One of the reasons that we liked Preston best of all our uncles and aunts was that he owned Jack.

The other reason was that he had time for us. Although he seemed very grown-up to us, he actually was only a kid himself, in his upper teens. He and his next older brother, our Uncle Arthur, had a motor launch and conducted a rather haphazard boating business, taking out fishermen and transporting campers who owned cottages at the far end of the lake. Arthur, when he was in charge of the boat, couldn't be bothered with a mess of brats; but Preston always let us go with him, if there was room. No matter what we were doing, we'd drop it to go out in the boat with Preston; and about the only punishment that we were ever subjected to

—and that only in cases of such criminal magnitude that they couldn't be ignored—was to be forbidden to go with Preston in the boat. Some of the blackest moments of my entire life were spent standing on the wharf and watching the other kids recede gaily up the lake in the boat, leaving me behind.

I remember particularly a boat trip at night, though why we were out so late I can't remember. Probably some camper from the head of the lake needed transportation. I'd never been out so late at night before anywhere, and certainly not on the water, so that fact alone impressed me. But more than that, I was impressed with the earth itself, which I recognized then for the first time as an independent and pervading fact and force. Heretofore whenever I'd been out after dark, it had been in Bridgewater, where houses lined the streets, sending out cheerful lozenges of light to lie on well-groomed lawns, where street lights marked the way and obscured the stars, where the hand of man was evident all around in his works—the houses, the lights, the paved sidewalks, the evenly spaced trees along them, and the occasional voices that drifted from porch or open window.

That night as we coasted slowly, for safety's sake, up the lake, everything was different. I thought I'd been out in the dark before, but I never had. Here were no street lights, and the moon was down. The countryside lay in a faint shimmer of starlight, and the lighted window of some half-hidden farmhouse up on a hill only emphasized the peculiarly forsaken and uninhabited quality of the night. As we skirted the shore, the trees were reduced to a blurred fretwork of dark, crooked twigs against the sky, stirred fitfully by small searching currents of air that flowed experimentally down from the highlands. An occasional night bird called off in the darkness, a fish jumped and splashed out in the lake, an animal interrupted at its watering place started and crashed away. The whole mood of the hour was secret and busy, both vaguely sinister and darkly gay and careless, as though we had no right there but would be tolerated and allowed to pass unharmed.

We left the shore to cross the lake, and I looked up at the

widest expanse of unbroken sky that I'd ever seen in my life.
The earth was reduced to a shadowy line at the limits of a
dully gleaming prairie of water, and everything else was a
sky blazing with stars. Preston showed me the Big Dipper
and told me how to find the Pole Star by lining up the
corners of the Dipper. I lay on my back on the deck and
looked at it, in that long-past-bedtime state where everything
is both unreal and unusually lucid. After a long time it
seemed to me that the Dipper was changing its position, was
swinging majestically around the anchoring star in a great
arc; and pretty soon, when it tipped so that all the water
would certainly have run out of it, I was sure. Then I knew
that what I had been told in school, and had accepted but
never really believed, was true. The earth did turn on its
axis. Suddenly I could feel it whirling beneath me, steadily
and silently and truly, on and on through the night; and I
knew that nothing that I or anybody else could do would
stop it. People were nothing compared to the ponderous
majesty of the earth they clung to.

I don't think that I'm exaggerating when I say that that
night exerted on me an influence that has lasted to this day.
Never since then have I been able to think of myself or
indeed of all of mankind as anything but tolerated parasites
on a host too powerful and patient to be affected by us in
any lasting way. That isn't, of course, the way I expressed it
at the time. At the time, when we were safely back in camp
and surrounded by voices and lights and mothers telling us
that it was late and hurry up and get undressed and hop into
bed, I suddenly and inexplicably burst into tears. I felt
forsaken and unbearably forlorn because of something I
couldn't and didn't try to explain. My mother said that I
was overtired and overexcited, and I gratefully let it go at
that. But all night long I felt the earth turning beneath me
in my narrow cot on the porch.

Although the interludes at camp were marked by almost
continuous activity, since we had to crowd a lot into a short
time, I do retain from those days a picture that has stood
for me during the subsequent years as the apotheosis of peace

and golden leisure. In front of the camp overlooking the lake there were four large pines growing in a rough square, about twenty-five feet apart. Between them, outlining the sides, were slung four hammocks of the old-fashioned mesh type with a bar and pillow at the head and rings in the supporting ropes so that they could be raised or lowered. The space in the middle of the square was level and carpeted with clean pine needles, a good dry place for sitting on the ground and playing quiet games.

It was believed in those days that a rest after dinner—which we ate in the middle of the day—was not only beneficial but almost mandatory if you wished to enjoy good health and live to an active old age. So as soon as the dishes were done, our mother and our aunts Carrie, Maud and Alice collected their books, magazines, tatting, nail buffers, and Aunt Maud's current suitor's latest confectionery tribute and repaired to the hammocks, where they reclined with their feet up, reading, tatting, polishing (but never painting!) their nails, eating chocolates; and mostly chatting in a lazy, desultory way. We little girls, all quiet and good, sat on the ground in the center ringed round by the gently swaying hammocks, playing jackstraws or making twig dolls and listening to the light, inconsequential talk that drifted back and forth over our heads. Never since have I known an atmosphere of such unhurried calm as those long afternoons under the pines, with the sun sifting down through the needles in a restless pattern, and the little breeze from the lake stirring the neat pompadours of our mother and aunts and rippling the graceful folds of their long, full summer dresses, flowing over the sides of the hammocks. Every one of them is a good-looking woman today, young for her age; and I sometimes wonder if it wouldn't behoove me to spend a little more time lolling in hammocks, eating chocolates, and thumbing my nose at calory charts. I might wear better in the end.

The Sunday that our father came for us was always a time of badly mixed emotions. We didn't want to go home; we'd just barely arrived at camp, for Heaven's sake! But it had been an awfully long time since we'd seen Smut and Whitey. Maybe they wouldn't even know us. We hadn't finished the tunnel we'd been working on for several years up back of the camp, with the idea of popping out at the other end to the amazement of the population of China; but if we didn't go home pretty soon, the Williamses and the Chadwicks would get all the cherries off the old tree in the vacant lot back of Miss Worcester's. "What are you going to do tomorrow?" we'd ask our cousins wistfully; and in the next breath we'd demand of our father, "Has Norma Sturtevant had her picnic yet? Do you think she'll have it this week?" We were attempting the impossible but often essayed trick of living in two worlds at once, and we always ended by being cranky, touchy, and hard-to-get-along-with. It was an extremely trying day for our mother, who would have liked to have left her sisters with the impression that Florence's children were certainly well-behaved beyond the ordinary.

Every year we found rather to our surprise that it was good to be home among familiar things with our fresh store of memories to gloat over nostalgically, good to be living again the ordered existence inside the circle of the school bell's call, good to have our mother back as we knew her, and not as one of the handsome Stewart girls. We reverted to our accustomed routine, an integral part of which was the planning of what we'd do next year when we went to camp.

And then the annual visits that we'd taken for granted for as long as we could remember came to an end. All our uncles and aunts except Winifred, who was too young, left home, and our grandparents gave up the camp. At about the same time our father took over the *Advertiser*, so there was no Mr. Willis to help him out, and it would have been impossible for our mother to get away. I suppose we regretted it, but we accepted it with the easy fatalism of childhood. Thereafter our summer vacations took the form of all-day trips to see Plymouth Rock or the amusement park at Nantasket Beach in the company of our mother, on those days when she didn't have to work.

Then, when I was at that trying and confusing age of

almost-in-her-teens, my grandmother Stewart invited me to come and visit Winifred at the old home place in Hopkinton. She didn't invite Alice, not—she made it very clear—that she didn't like Alice as well as she did me. But three was a bad number, since one was always bound to be odd-man-out; and since I was the nearest to Winifred in age, we two would probably gang up on Alice and make her stay miserable. Therefore, under the circumstances—

I'd never in my life been away from home overnight alone, and I was certainly overcome with my own importance. I listened forbearingly to my mother's instructions about minding my grandmother, helping with the dishes, and brushing my teeth regularly. I was much too cosmopolitan for that sort of briefing, but if it made her feel any better to give it, I'd humor her by presenting the appearance of attention. She concluded her talk by telling me that if I became homesick, my father would come and get me. Homesick! I laughed silently but none the less scornfully at such a childish notion.

Well, I wasn't homesick. I had a fine time with Winifred. But one day something very odd happened to me. My grandmother asked me if I would please run up to the Post Office and mail a letter for her. She wanted to catch the only outgoing mail of the day, Winifred was taking a bath, and I'd have to go alone. Hopkinton is a very small town indeed, the Post Office was near the top of the hill on Main Street, the street where my grandparents lived, and there was absolutely no possibility of my getting lost, run over, abducted, beset by thieves, or subjected to any other form of misadventure short of an Act of God. So I set out with the letter in one hand and a nickel she'd given me for doing the errand in the other.

I mailed the letter first and, that off my mind, stood for a moment on the steps of the Post Office in the sun. A smaller child went by, eating an ice cream cone, and I decided that I'd spend my nickel on a cone and, what was more, go to the little park at the top of the hill to eat it, instead of returning straight home. I bought my cone at the drug store, turned into the park, and sat down on a bench in the shade.

And suddenly as I ran my tongue voluptuously over the frozen custard, it occurred to me that nobody in the whole world knew where I was. My grandmother had a general idea of my whereabouts, but even she couldn't pinpoint me, sitting on a green bench at the top of the hill eating ice cream. As for my mother, she might cudgel her mind as hard as she could without hitting on the exact truth. She might ring the bell until it flew into flinders, and it wouldn't do a bit of good. I wouldn't hear it and obey. I was outside the circle, out in the uncharted spaces where the unicorns roamed. For the first time in my life I was conscious of being alone in a place of my own choosing. Nobody—nobody except *me*—knew where I was; I'd brought myself here, and only I was accountable for what might happen to me here. I was a person all to myself: not one of the Little Dickinson Girls; not Alice Dickinson's sister; not Deacon Stewart's granddaughter. I was Sarah Louise Dickinson, and I alone was answerable forever for what I did or where I went or what I became.

That's all that happened. Anybody walking through the park saw nothing more unusual than a little girl in pigtails and a blue plaid dress licking away stolidly at a strawberry cone. But that was, as nearly as it is possible to determine the exact critical point of such a long process, the moment when I grew up. The moment would be forgotten for long periods, and I'd have lapses into childishness for years and years to come, perhaps for all my life. But never would I lose entirely what I had just found: the knowledge of my personal responsibility, the recognition of my own identity. My childhood was over, and things would never be quite the same again. The spell of the bell was broken and its magic protection gone. From now on, wherever I went, I'd have to be my own guide and guard; and whatever unicorns I might encounter, I'd have to deal with them myself.

CONCLUSION

That's the way things were when I was a child. It's easy to say that things were different and better in one's youth; in fact, so easy that too many people do say it. They were different, yes; but whether they were better or not, I can't say, because I don't know.

Perhaps it is not the world that is different. Perhaps it is we who have changed. To the eyes of a child, perhaps the world is still a place of wonder and beauty and high adventure. The material and shoddy and meretricious things that have taken the place of our golden dreams and great hopes and instinctive faith may not exist at all except as we have brought them into existence, each one for himself. Perhaps when we started to consider and to weigh, we forgot how to feel; when we started to question, we lost a sure knowledge; when we began to seek, we gave up what we possessed. The elements of which the magic of youth was composed still exist in the universe around us; and if the compound is less rich, less glowing than it used to be, perhaps we have no one but ourselves to blame.